Coconuts and crocodiles

This book is memoir. It reflects the author's present recollections of experiences over time. Some events have been compressed, and some dialogue has been recreated.

For pedantic readers who won't let this go, I'm aware that Caimans are not actually crocodiles and just come from the same family.

Author website

www.sergioromagnoli.co.uk

Coconuts

and

crocodiles

By

Sergio Romagnoli

Coconuts and crocodiles

For my dear Max, who taught me that I’m not the kind of dad who would forget a child at a supermarket and of course, my darling Vesi, who taught me that there’[illegible] than the smell of petrol aro[illegible]

Brazil

Day 0 – The Airport

Today is the day. The culmination of months' worth of preparation. Flights there, flights back, hotels, Airbnb reservations, trip bookings, meals, meetings, money and calculations of how much we'd need, excursions, internal flights, cheapest rates for everything, bus journeys, flight timings, rental cars, itineraries, best places to go in the time we have, charts, communications with foreigners translated by the internet, misunderstandings, miscommunications, errors, re-bookings, other bookings, more bookings....

And I did absolutely none of it.

This is the kind of thing Vesi is fantastic at and I am not.

I could write a small book on the build-up to today, including the happy/unhappy coincidence that we moved house 6 days ago, but just writing about it would give me heart palpitations and loose bowels. Therefore, I'll stick to giving a quick rundown of the day up to the airport.

We were up at 07:00 and had a shower but no breakfast as we had to get out and go places. Vesi went to see some tosser... ahem... recruitment consultant... and I had some last-minute errands. Then I met up with Vesi at our *old* house to pick up some final items and we were off.

I say *old* house because we are finally moving into a new house after 12 months of searches, offers, rejections, fall-throughs, vendor solicitor issues, wasted money, wasted time and numerous other misadventures. If you've ever bought a house you'll probably know what I mean. The levels of stress are similar to those felt by a British tourist in Tunisia bartering for a set of egg cups that cost 10p.

Several months earlier, in a galaxy not unlike our own, in a solar system similar to ours, on a planet very much like the one we live on, in a country where most of the people understand the local language, in a city where the local accent is not unlike that of a farmer… an unsuspecting couple named Sergio and Vesela (Vesi) were booking a holiday.

But this holiday would commence so many months after the booking date that, surely, they would have finalised a purchase, moved house and had a couple of months respite to earn a little more money so that their cash flow wouldn't be hit too hard, right?

Well, it can be said that Sod was truly out in full force this month, laying down his law without mercy.

As I said, after more than 12 months of searching, we finally managed to finalise the purchase of a house, but the moving-in date happened to fall 5 days ago. Yes, we have had 5 days to move all our belongings to the new house and ensure that it was left out of sight as we are moving to an area undergoing 'gentrification'. This means it's a dodgy area that is meant to be slowly improving, so houses are becoming too expensive for people synonymous with the area to purchase. We also had to pack, argue with the old landlady about how much notice we had agreed on, run some last-minute errands and leave.

Now, why didn't we prepare for this earlier? I hear you ask. Well, completion of the house happened rather suddenly. At this point, we were expecting to complete the process after our return from Brazil, so it was almost a shock to us when they said, "Ok. All done... come and collect your keys and your complimentary mug and move in asap."

So, new house and a holiday to Brazil within 5 days of each other? No, we're not rich... in fact, I'm generally in competition with tramps to see who can get to other people's rejects first. Just a couple of days ago, someone had dumped 4 chairs outside their shop. I was told about this and after a quick examination, I managed to get 3 of them into our office. I didn't manage the last one because someone else made off with it. I could just see the headline, 'bum has chair taken from him...... by homeless guy'.

The reason we had to rush all this was because I didn't (and bloody rightly so) want to pay for a rented bedroom in a house for the 3 weeks we were away and, on top of that, the first mortgage payment too – as I said, we're not rich.

So, after the errands, meeting up with Vesi and carrying the last few bits from our room to our new house, we were off. Next stop, Brazil... well, actually, no, the next stop was the Murco petrol station, but the stop after that... no, that would be my brother's house. OK. One of the next 20 stops was Brazil.

Just a couple of hours before we had to check in, we pelted down the motorway as fast as our little wheels would carry us and with only a small breaking of the speed limit. God, I hope I don't get another speeding ticket. I just paid one off this morning. £100 for doing 46mph in a 40mph zone. And this was just after having emptied my bank balance to some solicitors to pay off the deposit of the house so not a good time to be caught.

I'd love to know how there are always enough wankers in Mercs and BMWs on the road to make it seem like none of them ever get speeding tickets. You could say that paying the £100 is nothing and is a price worth paying to go 90mph, but surely, along with the monetary fine, they should be receiving points on their licenses, shouldn't they? Then why are they all still pissing well out there?

Anyway, we stopped at Priscila and Alessio's house – my brother and my sister-in-law – who started this whole thing off. She got it into Vesi's head that we should go to Brazil as we have been invited to the wedding of someone we've never heard of but who happens to be Priscila's close friend. Alessio and Priscila will be joining us on the last week of the holiday. We'll be staying in Priscila's dad's caravan, and considering she's had very little to do with him since he and her mum split up, I'm not expecting much.

He lives in a small town called Bonito and I don't know anything about it other than the fact that it's near the Pantanal – Wetlands in the south of the country. Now, I've not done any research but I imagine it to be a mosquito-infested jungle, so god knows what kind of caravan we'll be sleeping in. 1 punctured tyre, listing to one side, dirty walls, large enough to comfortably sleep 2, but very cosy with 4 and situated in the middle of a swamp. I just hope it's got windows that keep mosquitoes out and a toilet so I don't have to step outside and piss against what I think is a tree log only to find out it's a horny crocodile.

To be honest, I think this trip will be pretty good, but I'm not looking forward to it as much as Vesi. I mean, I love the idea of the jungle, and Rio and the wetlands of the Pantanal, but realistically, Rio is spread over the media as lovely – but dangerous. You have to be dead careful there. One false move and you'll find yourself at the end of the barrel of a gun having to hand over your prized possessions in exchange for seeing another day.

The idea of the Amazon is a lovely, romantic place where you can live in a treehouse, most of the animals are your friends, and you have a clean, exotic woman called Jane. The real Amazon is a place where everything wants to either kill you, eat you, or lay eggs inside you and have them eat you from the inside – and Jane, who is actually called Jean, has bad breath and hairy armpits. Everything hates you in the Amazon. You go swimming and if you don't get eaten by piranhas or crocodiles, you're being fed on by leeches or having things crawl up your urethra (pee-hole to the layperson) and stick themselves inside you. Oh god, who would *want* to go to the Amazon rainforest? 45 degrees C, mosquitoes the size of cats, unknown bugs that give tropical diseases, poisonous plants that infect your skin and monkeys with rabies or other disgusting diseases. Besides, watching Jean bite the heads of lizards would kill the romance a tad. I only like the *idea* of the rainforest. I'm not so curious to find out about the real thing.

Vesi, of course, jumped at the opportunity to go. "When will we get the chance to go again? It's now or never," and all the rest of the talk that women do to guilt us men into doing their bidding. I guess I'm glad she did. I would never have gone otherwise. I'd never have felt financially ready, so I think I'm pleased.

We stopped at Alessio and Priscila's house for a bit of lunch and then it was off to Gatwick airport.

I was impressed when we got there. So many airports are run by corporate vampires these days and they charge you to drop people off as well as pick them up. I may not have been to that many airports in Europe; a few in Italy, one in Spain, one in Bulgaria and a couple I've not driven to from what I can remember, but out of all of these, the UK has, by far, the most expensive airports and it wouldn't surprise me if they were among the most expensive in Europe and possibly beyond. Some of them have a 'pay to drop off' policy but, fortunately, Gatwick hasn't introduced that yet. Hopefully, the infrastructure isn't capable of handling it.

On entering Gatwick and seeing the hundreds of people rushing around, a load of memories came rushing back. If I've said it once, I've said it a hundred times; airports are the hubs for the lowest forms of life outside of politics and boardrooms. The scramble to check in or drop off bags and the undoubted scene where the person in front of you has either tried passing off a 70kg suitcase as 20kg, insists that the passport photo of the 7-year-old girl is actually him or is outraged when they tell him he can't carry live chickens in his hand luggage.

Frankly, airport people exist purely to piss you off, so it's hardly a shock when customs workers treat everyone like terrorists. Although, having said that, it's bloody annoying.

Our (criminal) politicians (practically all of them) decide to bomb some poor country which coincidentally happens to be full of brown people and then try to tell us that "terrorists" are trying to bomb planes. And because once there may or may not have been a plot to bomb a passenger plane using a liquid explosive, since that date – real or not – people can no longer take bottles of more than 100ml of liquid through security. There is a distinct irony though that you can take multiple bottles of up to 100ml and an empty container. Has nobody twigged?

It could all just be a marketing ploy to make people buy the more expensive water that's available just 5 meters after the metal detectors.

I was listening to the conversation between some customs schmo and some girl. The customs schmo had just confiscated the remainder of a 500ml bottle of water from her. Paraphrased, the conversation went something like this:

Customs schmo: "Sorry, you can't take that on board."

Girl: "Oh ok, here you go."

Customs schmo: "Do you want to finish drinking it?"

Girl: "No, it's ok."

What's the problem with that? I hear you ask. Well, we were told that these "terrorists" had plotted to blow up aeroplanes using a liquid. Now, liquids that are so volatile that they can explode – or would explode when mixed with another liquid – would not be drinkable. Chances are that a liquid like that would be highly toxic or, at the very least, would make you really sick pretty quickly. So, how about drinking some of the flipping liquid being carried to prove that it can be drunk easily and safely?

So, the customs schmo said, "Do you want to finish drinking it?" Whereas, he could have said, "If you drink some, that will prove that it's not some dodgy, volatile liquid."

Anyway, where was I?

Airport people… yes.

We got through customs and security, queued up (the humorous farce that Ryanair and easyJet have made it), I performed my little ritual and boarded the Air Europa plane.

I have a little ritual before boarding any flight. It's pointless, but it's just something I like to do. Before walking onto the aeroplane, at the door, I like to rest my hand on the outside of the fuselage and keep it there for a couple of seconds. All it is, is physical contact with the outside of the aeroplane. Pointless maybe but sacred to me, and ever since I started doing it when I was at college – when I decided to do aeronautical engineering as a degree subject – I have never forgotten it. And you know what? We've never crashed. I'd like to think that it has always been thanks to me.

Yes, ok, I'm kidding about the 'we've never crashed' bit, I'm not one of those OCD-ridden ritualistic weirdos who has to do something or something bad will happen; it's just something I like to do.

The bane of my life on aeroplanes, more than the seat pitch, is the little button that allows the seat to recline about 3 inches. Almost pointless to the person reclining the seat, but devastating to the person sat behind if he/she is tall… like me.

After weapons, PLC companies and 99% of civil lawsuits, these reclining seats have to be the worst invention in history. Ryanair have had this removed and that is absolutely great, but not Air Europa. And when you have some morbidly obese dwarf bitch in front of you, you just know she's going to *do the dirty.* And sure enough, as soon as the seatbelt light went out... Slam! Back went the seat followed closely by her fat and ugly husband.

The only redeeming part is that I made her journey to Madrid more painstaking with constant knees to her back for more or less the whole flight, until the end when she pulled her seat back. So, there I was, gleefully ignoring her when she turned around to give me evils. "Well if my knee in your back is pissing you off, don't recline your fucking seat." I didn't actually say it though. It's one of those things you tell yourself that you regret not saying – but only after you've left the airport at your destination and are half way home.

About 10 years ago, I had some short American do that on a flight to Colorado in the USA. 10 hours, 4 of which were spent kneeing her in the back and the rest spent walking up and down the aisles and hanging out at the back, talking to the gay stewards and 50-year-old stewardesses – BA... equal opportunities. I suppose that's a good thing because it means I didn't spend the whole time drooling over the stewardesses and their lovely legs. So, before getting off the plane at the end, she said in her dozy voice, "Yow needed moure ligroom didn' ya?" I smiled sweetly whilst thinking that I could have jabbed her in the eyes with an ice pick.

So, we got off the plane in Madrid and sat in a waiting room/departure lounge. The flight to São Paulo was delayed by an hour. Technical reasons... which could mean anything from, 'there's a sticky button in the cockpit' to 'the wing needs to be glued back on'.

At least I managed to have a poo. Small one, not even enough to make a rabbit proud but at least it was out of my body. I also took occupancy of the disabled toilet so it gave me the chance to have a wash too because you don't half get some strange looks in public toilets when you wash your arse in one of the sinks. I was in front of a mirror though, so it was a bit disconcerting. Had it been in the UK, there would probably have been a CCTV camera behind it with some pervert from MI5 watching.

We flew in an Airbus A330. Now, that may not sound impressive, but to someone like me who is an aeroplane fanatic, it's a big deal. The check-in allocated seats were 37F & 37G. Meaningless? I THINK NOT. I hate being in the middle of 3 seats. Window seats – fine, aisle seats – fine, but middle? NOT FINE. It's already a pain on a 2-hour flight, but this would be a 10-hour and 20-minute flight. That's almost half a day, during the night, squashed between Vesi and what is likely to be some fat, sweaty, hairy, bearded woman with bad breath who either snores or talks incessantly, and to top it off, probably behind some short-arsed twat who puts his seat back before take-off.

And it's night time, so everyone will be asleep. I'm crap at sleeping on planes. I always seem to snooze and wake up with a neck pain comparable to a criminal who has just been hanged.

I don't like to put my seat back on flights. I hate it when people do it in front of me, so I try to avoid it. Call me a sucker if you want, but I prefer to think of myself as slightly over empathetic.

So, I was telling Vesi, "Seating plan... it'll be twin-aisle – undoubtedly – so if the seating goes up to G, it can only be arranged 3,1,3 or 2,3,2 (3 on one side, 1 in the middle, 3 on the other side) or if that check-in woman lied to us and we weren't by the window, then it could actually go up to H and the seating arrangement could be 3,2,3... and I've got the bastard middle seat."

So, I somehow managed to stress myself out even before getting on the plane.

The queuing process before boarding, as always, was a total circus. Out of roughly 300+ people who were to board, about 200 started queuing about an hour before the flight, which was then delayed by over an hour. I've always found this intensely moronic behaviour for the very simple reasons that (a) everyone had a seat, and (b) everyone's seat was allocated – so queuing up from an hour before was completely pointless. But in that situation, can you tell people this? NO. This happens on every flight I go on. Sometimes, just to get a seat in the waiting area at the gate when the plane is delayed, I *casually* walk up to the front and look at my watch to make it look like I'm queuing up and within a minute about 30 people have appeared behind me salivating with FOMO (fear of missing out) attitudes and leaving seats empty. I then piss off out of the queue and sit in one of the empty seats myself for the last hour or so before getting on the same flight. It's possibly the remains of behaviour that evolved after the birth of Ryanair and easyJet where seats aren't (or at least, weren't) allocated, so boarding the plane was like going into an arena of the Colosseum when they were throwing the Christians to the lions. I remember this one time a few years ago getting off the bus to see the first couple of people running for the aeroplane as though their lives depended on it. I remember thinking, look, if you want to be first on the plane, don't wear high heels you dozy bint. Then 1) you might get there *oh* so much quicker and 2) you won't look someone trying to walk a tightrope with a chilli pepper in their arse.

When the time came, the aeroplane was filled by rows, so even though Vesi and I didn't join the queue, we were among the first 50 people to board – to the obvious frustration of those who'd been standing or sitting in the queue on the cold marble floor for 2 hours. And in those circumstances, it's hard not to look smug when walking past them.

Aeroplane seating arrangement, 2,3,2. Vesi and I had 2 seats to ourselves. Perfect. No fatties, no smellies, no lepers or gross hairy women with sweaty upper lips... god, how I love people.

However, on take-off, the minging slag in the seat in front of Vesi did the dirty, even though you're not meant to recline until the seatbelt sign has been turned off. But she didn't care... either that or she didn't know. But to be honest, the flight attendants didn't realise either, even though it's their job to. I just hoped the pilots weren't as bad; *"ooh, what does this button do?"*

As such, we did the best of British. We tutted and frowned at her. To no effect, of course, because (a) the plane was noisy so she couldn't hear us, (b) we were behind her so she couldn't see us and (c) she was foreign so she couldn't understand a bloody word. Occasionally, politicians have the right ethos... kill and maim.

The flight started to fill. It looked like we'd have loads of space as lots of the seats in the central section were still empty. Clearly, some of those sitting there thought that too and the guy in the seats to our left took his shoes off, put his blanket on, lifted the armrests to the other seats and stretched out, practicing his position in readiness for a long and comfortable flight. But people kept boarding, and pretty soon, the look of contentment on this guy's face changed to the look of false politeness and obvious frustration as he realised that he too had been left with just 1 seat. In fact, by the time we landed, his face was ashen and he looked like he'd been deprived of several nights sleep.

The seats about 4 rows behind me were empty though and several people were eyeing them up. It was a spaghetti western moment... the tumbleweed that rolls down the aisles, eyes flitting from side to side, lips and fingers twitching, a swift take-off and as soon as the seatbelt lights went out, a 'casual looking' mad dash for the seats whilst pretending they weren't actually going for them. I made it to one of the rows along with a couple of others, and those who didn't casually skirted away trying to make it look like they were never aiming for the seats in the first place, but everyone knew.

Unfortunately, Vesi and I had to fly in separate rows but it also meant that each of us had 2 seats, so that was good enough for a few hours.

We each had a little television on the seat in front with a selection of films/programs to watch. Otherwise, there were a number of CDs/music tracks to listen to. The entertainment was actually relatively – well – entertaining, even though a lot of the channels didn't work. However, I'd have gladly given it all up for an extra 20 cm of legroom. We also had the option to watch a screen giving information about the flight and we could effectively watch the miles tick down, but really, that would have been like watching the sand fall through a 10-hour egg timer; intriguing for the first few minutes but gets very dull very quickly.

The female flight attendants (in these days of free speech, you get shot for saying stewardess – spot the irony) were quite sexy but were all a bit naff. During times of turbulence, the captain would put on the seatbelt signs and they'd be ignored by both the passengers and the flight attendants. Then after the turbulence had stopped, the captain would forget to turn the sign off for about 2 hours and nobody even bothered telling him. Frankly, I bet the pilots were wearing parachutes and were ready to bail at the first sign of trouble… trouble that they'd probably cause – *"ooh, what does this button do?"*

Fortunately, the aeroplane had been built by Airbus and we landed safely at 05:35. The flight crew even managed to bugger that up and told us it was 04:35.

We had arrived in Brazil.

São Paulo - Foz Do Iguaçu

Day 1 - São Paulo - Foz Do Iguaçu

Not only were we in Brazil but we were in São Paulo, one of the largest and busiest cities in the world and we can't understand Portuguese any more than we can understand Glaswegian. We collected our bags and were out by 06:40, but our first port of call was actually Foz do Iguaçu and we had a flight booked for Foz at 13:15. We had to spend the best part of a day waiting around at an airport. Airports – my favourite places. After all, if they turn polite Brits into rabid savages, god knows what it's like in a country where people have passion and wear their hearts on their sleeves.

It felt like a complete waste staying at the airport to watch insane people running about like headless insane people; panicking about catching the flight, the right flight, having their passports, wondering if they can have 12 carry-on cases, etc. Vesi suggested going to town, getting a coffee, looking around a bit and then coming back.

Now, I'm actually more risk-averse than Vesi is, so I wasn't over the moon about that idea. I've often been more of a safe than sorry person and have missed out on loads of adventures because of that[1], so I decided to go with it. I think that's from my mother's side of the family. My mother is so worried about everything that 80% of her conversation is telling people to be careful… and the other 20% is saying, "I told you so." But even

[1] OMG – Vicki at university being one. Ok, she was probably riddled with disease but OMFG did she have amazing legs. She would have been worth a touch of gonorrhoea or genital warts

that's pretty diluted compared to my aunt, who is so incredibly cautious that she hasn't crossed the road outside her house in several years – and that road is a dead end.

That thought gave me courage. Vesi knows what she's doing most of the time, so I was pretty sure things would be ok. If it was up to me, I'd probably end up taking the wrong bus. Vesi instinctively knows which bus to take. It's like her sixth sense. Instead of "I see dead people," it's more like, "We must take the number 6."

We spoke to the guy at the information desk who spoke English. We told him our plan and he looked at us the same way you'd look at a ginger pubic hair in a shop bought sandwich. Why would we want to go all the way to town to get a coffee only to come back again? To be honest, I was in partial agreement with him. Do we really want to travel for 1 hour on public transport to get a coffee in a strange town? Vesi gave a resounding nod, so I guess we were on. There was a blue shuttle bus that went straight to town and took about 45 minutes.

We locked up the bags in a short-term locker – 25 reals for 24 hours – and went to get the bus. Tickets were 36.50 reals per person, each way… in total, 146.00 reals. 40 quid for 2 coffees? Jesus – If I wanted to pay £40 for 2 coffees, I'd have gone to Starbucks[2] in the UK. £40? Seriously? But this is Brazil. Brazil

---

[2] I am not endorsing Starbucks in any shape or form. I never go there. Given the company's ethical stance and corporate actions in the past, I only stop there if I need to take a shit – and even then, I don't flush.

should be *less* expensive than the UK, not *more* expensive. Ok, so it is a holiday and we fully expect to pay extra for things because, on holiday, you're prepared to pay more for things than you normally would, but this was taking the piss.

It was a bit of a gaffe on our part. We really should have checked the cost of a bus ticket *before* paying for the bags to be locked up.

As luck would have it though, someone did mention the metro (underground), so we hunted around for it. It turns out we had to take a local bus to the metro, which would drop us off slap bang in the centre. At 4 reals per bus ticket and 3 reals per metro ticket, the total price was 28 reals (roughly £8), which is much more acceptable.

We were super nervous about taking the public transport, but finding the bus was easy; even with the language barrier. Most of our 'conversations' were expressed using the international language of violent gesticulations.

The buses were a frottager's paradise. Frankly, it wouldn't surprise me if everyone here got some sort of perverse pleasure out of rubbing up against someone else. I wouldn't have minded so much but they were practically all men.

A 40-minute bus journey and a 15-minute metro ride later, we reached the stop in the centre that we were told to get off at – "Republica" – and took our first step into the urban jungle that is São Paulo. We exited the metro station and stepped onto actual Brazilian concrete. I looked at Vesi and uttered the very first words that began our Brazilian adventure... "this place smells of piss." Admittedly, not quite the words that would be uttered by the presenter of a holiday program, but that was the reality of the situation.

It was about 8 in the morning, 13 degrees and cloudy. In all honesty, looking around, it was pretty dirty. This could so easily have been London but the sun was trying to shine through the clouds so we were clearly somewhere foreign.

We walked around aimlessly for about 10 minutes trying not to look like tourists, but with our clothes, skin colour and general demeanour, we looked like Aretha Franklin and Ray Charles at the annual general meeting of the KKK.

I remember thinking, 'my god. For being one of the largest and busiest cities in the world, there's no bugger about.' And it was true, very few people and very few cars. It was more like a mountain village on a Sunday.

To be honest, São Paulo – this part at least – was pretty grimy. However, realistically, all large cities have that grimy feel to them in part, so this was no exception. Also, I noticed that there was a lot of American influence there. But I suppose that's to be expected. On the world stage, Brazil is actually quite close to the USA. Think of it this way... If there is a steaming cowpat in the middle of a field, the smell will spread a few feet.

Aside from the graffiti, dirt and general smell of piss, São Paulo was actually quite a nice city – as far as cities go. I say *as far as cities go* because although cities can have different characteristics and focal points, they are pretty much always grey, and as a result, I personally don't find them especially attractive. They have their charm, don't get me wrong, but in the same way that some people find pleasure in being in the hustle and bustle of a city, I tend to find more pleasure in the countryside where, instead of the sound of cars and the chatter of people, there is the sound of birds and rustling leaves; and instead of the pungent smell of exhaust fumes, the most pungent smell in the countryside is usually that of dung – maybe not to everyone's taste but at least it doesn't give you cancer.

We stopped for some breakfast at a little corner bar. By this point, it had warmed up to about 19 degrees. There were loads of these bars dotted about and they all had fruits hanging from the ceiling or in large bowls behind the counter – bananas, mangoes, big yellow round things and lots of others, but unlike the UK, these places were all independent. The UK and its government seem to fight against these types of places and much prefers the idea of chain stores. So, the UK equivalent of these little bars would be a fancy version of Greggs the baker. UK's shops are nothing if not homogeneous.

We had some bready blobs called pão de queijo (cheese bread) and a mixed fruit smoothie, or 'Vitamina' as they call it, which is a blend of various fruits and sometimes a berry called açaí. The pão de queijos were fresh from the oven so were still nice and warm. Crusty on the outside and on opening them up, the cheese in the bread (which is made with tapioca flour) gave them a sort of gooey texture, but a really pleasant one. They were really lovely and moreish. The Vitamina smoothie was also utterly fantastic. I don't know what makes them different to smoothies in the UK, but these little corner bars – that might not survive in the UK because the Brits seem to be obsessed with recognisable brands – sell some seriously delicious smoothies.

From that, we immediately went to another one to get some more. This time, we tried some Calabresas. They were bready-like pastries that tasted a bit like pizza. Also very nice. I'd have loved to hang around for a couple of days to try out all the different things they had on offer but, realistically, these places are common in Brazil so I was sure we would eat lots of these.

Total price of 2 smoothies: 7.50 reals, roughly £2.10. UK price for a similar (usually less tasty) smoothie: £3.50 EACH – Bargain.

Açaí smoothies are a really big thing in Brazil and these are different to 'Vitaminas'. They are like dark purple slush puppies with fruits added if you want, although the main fruit is the açaí berry. These are normally more expensive than the 'Vitamina' smoothies. Açaí is pronounced A-SAAEEE... not AKEY as I've heard some Americans pronounce it. But I guess each to their own. I remember the brand, Sergio Tacchini. Tacchini is actually pronounced TAKKINI, whereas I spent my entire youth being compared to a Sergio Tasheenee. I guess it's just how people read it. Feng Shui, on the other hand, is bandied around as Feng Shwei… where the hell did they get the 'WEI' from? Some dyslexic advertiser maybe?

Açaí is a berry that grows on a particular type of palm tree. The berries look like large blackcurrants – about the size of grapes – and are meant to be a superfood. The name açaí comes from the Tupian word ïwaca'i (no, it's not an Icelandic word), meaning 'cries/expels water' as in the *fruit that expels water*.

And before you ask what Tupian is (or more likely, you read it a couple of times and thought 'is that TOOPIAN or TUPPIAN?' (BTW it's TOOPIAN)), it is pertaining to the Tupí people who were an indigenous people who (it is believed) first settled in the Amazon rainforest about 2,900 years ago and slowly spread south through Brazil.

This could be where people's idea of cannibal tribes from the jungle comes from. They were divided into separate tribes of a few hundred people that kept waging war on each other (I dunno… maybe to establish control of the TV's remote – like in most households), and they used to capture their enemies and eat the stronger ones because they believed they would absorb their strength. Conversely, they wouldn't eat the weaker ones for fear of absorbing their weakness.

It is also said that they used to eat dead relatives as a way to honour them. I don't know about you, but I think that gives new meaning to when kids say, 'mummy… I don't like granny'.

Also, I'm not sure if that's how I'd like to go. There's something somewhat disturbing about the idea that after I'm gone, my family will be scoffing my buttocks along with a packet of instant mash. Although, I can't think of a hugely better alternative... eaten by maggots? Incinerated by flames? Buried with my arse sticking out of the ground so Vesi has somewhere to park her bike?

Then, yadda yadda, the Portuguese came and killed a load of them and took over, etc. Usual human killing human thing.

Personally, I found that bit of history to be *berry* interesting... (sorry)... apart from the people killing people bit.

We walked around the area, and by 09:30, the temperature was up into the 20s. We visited the Theatro Municipal, (some theatre) and then to the 'Catedral da Se' which was lovely, but in the end, it's still a cathedral and you don't have to travel nearly 6,000 miles to see a beautiful cathedral.

The cathedral was built in 1589 when the small village of São Paulo needed a central church. It has undergone several demolitions and rebuilds since then, of course.

The area in front was a pedestrian zone and like before, most of it smelled of pee. I put that down to there being a lot of homeless people living in and around the area. I found the homeless people here quite different to those in the UK. No buskers, no one saying they needed money to get into a hostel and we weren't accosted by anyone saying how they needed just another £1 to get a train to the other side of the country where their friend lived and how they'd send the money back if you gave them your address. No, these homeless people were generally sitting or lying down on the ground. Enough to make your heart weep, but not enough to make you give them any pocket change – I don't know... maybe I've been hardened off too much by the bullshit given by chain-smoking beggars in the UK wearing Prada trainers, or Romanian gypsies selling the Big Issue magazine who are actually saving up for a second home.

By the time we decided to make our way back to the airport, we were feeling pretty confident walking around São Paulo, so we hopped on the metro and bus without the apprehension we felt earlier in the day.

On the bus on the way back, we were sat directly in front of a married gay couple. I love how, in Brazil, people are confident enough to be themselves. It's not totally uncommon in the UK either but this felt even more overt. The shorter guy was talking to the taller guy all the way back... I'd love to have understood what he was saying. He never shut up. He always had something to say. But for the whole journey, I couldn't help thinking, which one of them plays the woman? Do they take it in turns? The guy on the right was shorter, seemed clingier and looked dirtier. The taller guy seemed a bit – well, snootier isn't the right word because it has negative connotations, but imagine the word snootier without the negative connotation. Also, when the taller guy moved, he was very effeminate. It was really hard to tell.

In the end, I thought I'd just wait until they got off the bus and see which one walks like a croquet hoop. He'll be the woman. In the end, that didn't work either. Hmmm.

Check-in and flight to Foz do Iguaçu; the fucker in front put his seat back for the 1.5-hour flight. Personally, I think it should be legal to kill those people... Or at least throttle the airline bosses for having reclining seats on their aeroplanes.

On a positive note, they didn't do all the unnecessary "you can't bring water onto this flight. It'll blow up". But then again, I don't think Brazil have dropped any bombs on countries full of brown people in the middle-east to invade them and steal their resources or just for empirical reasons, so it stands to reason that Brazilians are not the hated targets of the people whose lives have been destroyed by the west's bombers – which is more than can be said for the UK & USA.

After landing, in baggage reclaim, we waited... and waited... and waited... and waited... and waited... and then, finally... the belt stopped. "Oh shit." Neither Vesi's nor my bag had come out. A million things rushed through my mind, including, "This will throw off our schedule", "it'll be really expensive to replace some of the things", "I'm so pleased I've got 2 pairs of pants in my hand luggage", "can I survive for 3 weeks on 2 pairs of pants? At home, I manage on just one pair, so maybe..." and a whole bunch of other things. Plus, we were a bit bemused. Both cases... Isn't that exceptionally strange?

We went to the lost baggage desk and as soon as the guy saw us, he whipped the cases out from behind his desk. HUGE – Great big PHEW. We'd been waiting by the wrong belt. Crisis averted and we could carry on with our holiday as intended.

The bus trip into town was an experience and a half.

We were at the stop for a few minutes and a bus arrived. It looked quite full and there were about 20 people in front of us and some behind too, so we thought, ok, we'll catch the next one. A few people boarded, then some more, then more, and more... people just kept boarding. Everyone in front of us boarded and the people behind us kept walking forwards to usher us on. In the end, everyone managed to get on. It was fuller than a UK bus during rush hour – and lots of people had suitcases. I'd never been on such a full bus in my life. We were so squashed that I lost the feeling in my right leg and the veins in my neck started throbbing.

On the way to the centre of Foz, we made a number of stops and at each of the first 6-7, we, *somehow*, picked up more people – and this was on a bus that was already so full, if someone pricked the roof with a pin, it would pop like a pimple spraying around 120 people out onto the road. But no, at every stop, people were climbing on. Yes, occasionally people got off, but more people boarded. Frankly, I was worried that my pockets would be picked, things would be stolen and I'd be getting off at the other end in just my socks and clutching a handle that used to be attached to my suitcase.

But no, we reached the terminal in the same shape (well, maybe a bit flatter) we left in; a bit sweatier, but all good and nothing stolen. The 2 amazing things here were that:

(a) The immense crush was completely normal to everyone... and why shouldn't it be? We're the outsiders in Brazil, not them.
(b) Nobody smelled bad. It was crazy. It was mid-afternoon, about 27 degrees and we'd just been on a bus where I'd had about 25 people less than 30 cm away from me; surely there must be at least one person out of these 100+ who has BO, but – at least around me – nothing. They smelled less than Europeans.

Now, the image I had of Brazil was one from the western media. I'd had a lifetime of being led to believe that all the women were beautiful – ok, not necessarily ALL, but a larger portion than from other nationalities – and the men were average or a bit on the ugly side. Also, they were all thin and tanned and if they wanted to go anywhere, instead of walking, they samba'd there – except in Rio De Janeiro where everyone was out to mug you or pull a gun on you, but oh how I've been misled. The girls were *not* mostly attractive, not everyone was slim and there wasn't so much as a hip shimmy in sight. So, Vesi and I did our own tired little conga to the Airbnb we were staying at where we were greeted by a dog.

This dog was followed by a man who spoke very good English. Really good guy, he showed us where all the things around Foz were, what to do, where to eat, where to catch the bus from if we wanted to go places. He was really decent ... but we still hid our cash behind one of the pictures in the room. Why didn't we keep it on our person? Well, neither of us felt safe walking around anywhere with an excess of £3,000 in our money belts. This arrangement was done through Airbnb. We've (well, Vesi) managed to find a load of places for a fraction of the price of a proper hotel.

This guy directed us to the hotel around the corner from the Airbnb and told us the girl at reception would tell us what to do and could arrange the trip to the Argentinian side of the waterfalls for us, and he gave us her name, which I forgot the instant he said it. Fortunately, Vesi didn't. Hmmm, I really must learn to be more like her... and yes, Foz *is* that close to Argentina... I could almost smell the steaks... but that turned out to be the place around the corner that did the churrascaria (Brazilian barbecue). I'll talk about that later.

We went to this other hotel – which was a hostel – to talk to this girl. She was brilliant. She arranged our trip to the waterfalls on the Argentinian side, told us where to change money at the best rate (the commercial centre), told us what to change and how much to change into Argentinian pesos – all this whilst answering a thousand and one questions from some Brazilian kids who were staying at the hostel and questions from us... She was really good.

We went to the commercial centre. It didn't have a Brazilian feel to it at all. I don't know what a Brazilian feel is, but before this, I always pictured shops to be on a long road... all independent shops with their owners, but there were not very many of those. Where we ended up was a soulless mall – like the ones in the UK/USA... a large building with shops inside... no sense of character at all, but then again, that style of mall is just another shit imported idea. Mindless zombies walking around buying crap in the hope that the excrement they saw on the advert will somehow improve their lives slightly. "ooh, that's nice, a toaster coaster. A coaster for toasters. That would raise the toaster off the surface by 3 mm and extend the life of the work surface by all of 0.3 seconds... I'll buy 2." Unfortunately, that kind of mindless consumerism has infected Brazil – remember the cowpat?

Anyway, we were there to change money. The exchange rates were fantastic. We changed $1,000 into reals and a further $50 into pesos for entry to see the Iguaçu waterfalls (that's the only currency they take on the door). The guy at the exchange place gave us a bit of a suspicious look as if to say either, "hmmm, you two are into money laundering, eh?" or "just wait till I call my friends, they'll relieve you of this money. Mwahahaaa" [villain smooths moustache with finger & thumb] – and he probably meant the original version of money laundering, not the definition you get these days in the UK which is everything from accidentally taking home a pen from work to ripping someone's heart out with your bare hands, taking a bite out of it and showing it to them before they die. Oh, sorry... unless you're a large company, then money laundering is actually allowed as an unwritten rule and any 'punishment' they receive, whether it be a little fine or a truckload of handouts, is not for the money laundering itself, but for being caught and having it put in the public eye.

So, in the end, we walked out with more than 3,600 reals and around 500 or so pesos, and with it still being our first night, I was pretty nervous carrying around that much money but we made it to the restaurant without being killed, mugged or raped. Yes, I was a little paranoid – maybe a little too much with hindsight. I even suggested to Vesi that she put on another layer of clothing or that we swapped T-shirts to fool the guy at the exchange rate place. In the end, I settled for just turning my glasses upside down for a bit which made me, to others, look stupid and made others, to me, look wonky.

When we got back, we went to eat. For our first night, we went to a Churrascaria, aka Rodizio. There were two very close to each other. This was the more expensive one. This was a truly epic dinner. I would sooner forget the names of my future children than forget a dinner like this.

A churrascaria is a buffet. All you can eat salad bar with lots of different vegetables and salad mixes and such... BUT... it's all you can eat meat too, and that is the epic part. The waiters do the rounds holding one big long skewer in one hand and a knife in the other (like serial killers in waistcoats). From there, they offer some to you and if you say yes, they cut slices off onto your plate. Usually one slice but more if you want. And this is how it goes for the whole meal. They keep coming round with different meats and cuts and carry on until you say stop to all of the waiters who come. The meats include chicken, pork, lamb, beef – with different cuts and also things like chicken hearts or pork sausages with cheese… and beef at various stages of cookedness (just made that word up, but you get it).

The meat is just rubbed in salt too, nothing else, no crap like barbecue sauce or sweet and sour gloop, just salt – so you get thirsty. One waiter did come to us to offer what looked like grated parmesan from a little bowl. It looked tempting but I didn't fancy cheese on my meat. That 'cheese', we found out later, was actually raw grated garlic. I think we dodged a bullet there. I didn't fancy raw garlic on my meat either. We are ambassadors from Europe here. We can't walk around Foz with an exclusion zone around us that even bacteria would be afraid of entering. Also, we were just around the corner from our Airbnb so were unlikely to be mugged on the way back. Thanks, but no thanks.

Towards the end, when you really start flagging, they come around with barbecued pineapple coated in cinnamon on a skewer too and slice it off…a mouthful of hot, sweet and juicy pineapple with the extra dimension of cinnamon… just bursts in your mouth when you bite it. I swear, you think you've died and gone to heaven.

We left 1.5 hours later, 200 reals lighter (about £58) and about 4 kg heavier. Back at the Airbnb, we were dying for some water after all the salt… but what a dinner.

Early night for our first night in Brazil, but before, there was the anti-mosquito spray ritual followed by the hunt for any mosquitoes in the room which involved whacking any black dots on the white walls with a towel just in case. Mosquitoes are the only animals I have no pity for… oh, apart from politicians, but I class politicians as a subspecies of animal. If mosquitoes went extinct, some animals that eat them might suffer a little, but if politicians went extinct, world peace could be achieved and world hunger could end – but that's a different story.

Here I am now finishing this. Tomorrow, we're going to Argentina… crikey, I never thought I'd say those words in my life.

Day 2 – Foz Do Iguaçu – Argentinian side

Up, awake and alert by 07:30. This was our first actual day in Brazil – technically our second because we arrived yesterday and did get to go around a bit, but it was the first time we woke up in a bed in Brazil, rather than awoke from a half-sleep on the aeroplane with an armrest in my back just 2 feet away from some weirdos staring at my morning erection.

Breakfast consisted of grape juice – and that's the delicious purple grape juice that can be found in the UK too but it is really expensive (the grapes themselves can't yet be found in the UK) – papaya and melon slices, bread with jam and a lovely guava flavoured drinking yoghurt. There was also some coffee that tasted how I imagine battery acid swilled around in the mouth of a dung beetle would taste like.

It was waterfall day today and we were just going to Argentina for that. I still find that incredibly cool... "hey, we're just nipping off to Argentina, can we get you anything whilst we're there?"

So cool.

We went to the hostel to wait for the minibus to come along and pick up a group of us to take to the waterfalls. The minibus came – well, a 5-seater – and the group consisted of Vesi, me... and that's it. My notorious sense of self-preservation kicked in and I eyed up the driver with a look of suspicion. Hmmm... I thought... is he really going to take us where we want or is he going to take us somewhere in the middle of nowhere, rob us and leg it? Yes, my mum has taught me well.

In the minivan, we got talking to the driver... well, I did because I'm the only one who pretends to speak a bit of Spanish, but having studied a bit already, I realise that Spanish is actually quite different from Italian (which I do speak). In fact, it's like a whole different language. And some words are actually the same but have a completely different meaning which is the most difficult thing to get used to in Spanish... apart from the lisp. E.g. 'burro' in Italian means butter and in Spanish it means donkey. In the past, I have made some people very confused and annoyed by asking them for donkey on toast whilst drenching them in spit. Either way, the driver was one of those people around here who could speak both Spanish and Portuguese. I managed to chat to him a bit and even though he looked like a dirty drug lord, he was actually a good guy and, fair enough, we paid for the trip, but he normally takes groups to the waterfalls, not just 2 people, so we were quite grateful for that too.

The journey to the Iguaçu falls included a most surreal experience. Now, I'm not talking about one of those experiences where you wake up in the morning and your head is at the foot end of the bed, no, I mean an experience with the same 'surreal' factor as the "I'm just popping over to Argentina" moment. Something I never thought I'd experience – little things and all that, I guess. Oh, I've built it up too much now, you're going to think it's pathetic. Ok, ignore what I said. As we were driving, we reached a fork in the road where there was a road sign. In one direction, some Brazilian town, and in the other, it said Argentina. Now, in my life I've had some pretty weird experiences; I've been offered a threesome with women in a gay club in Manchester, I've nearly died under a parachute and I met someone who used to be a vampire (who ironically had drunk so much alcohol in his life he only had 6 teeth left at the back of his mouth), but I never thought in my life I'd ever see a road sign that points to Argentina. There it was, in the same way you see a sign on the motorway pointing to Bristol or London, they were saying, "Hey... Argentina is this way." Ok, so I may have failed in imparting how amazing this was to me; maybe you had to be there, but as you can tell, I was blown away.

We crossed the border out of Brazil, 'you are now leaving Brazil' (also cool), but where we were was not quite Argentina yet. It was a bit of a no man's land. The kind of place where if you gave birth there, you could literally say... (in a grim, mysterious voice) "In no coun'ry were 'ee born".

Actually, entering Argentina was quite straightforward but we did have to give our passports to the driver who took them to the customs bods. Still, pretty soon after that, we were in Argentina. Wow, we were in Argentina. And just a few minutes before, we were in Brazil.

The first thing I noticed in Argentina was that the roads were generally smoother than in Brazil and, overall, were in better condition. I have no idea why, I thought that economically, Argentina was completely messed up, so I was surprised to see such smooth roads. I don't know, maybe it's just a show between Brazil's border and the waterfalls to make people think that Argentina is perfectly ok. Maybe the other roads in Argentina are just dirt tracks... I doubt it, but I don't know.

The road that took us most of the way was rather like a Roman road. Very straight and very long and with the season being very much off-peak, there were very few cars. There were signs on the sides like the ones in the UK warning of animals crossing, except the animals there were not only deer or sheep. The animals crossing there were deer, coatis and tapirs. Really... tapirs. I've only ever seen one of those in the zoo and I've never even seen a coati except on television.

I find it amazing looking down a dead straight road for miles and not seeing a single car. It happened to Vesi and me once when we were driving through Greece. We reached a point where, similarly, the road was dead straight for as far as we could see and there were absolutely no cars at all. We stopped the car in the centre of the road and got out to take photos.

On arrival to the national park of Iguaçu, our driving man dumped us at the gates and said he'd meet us back there at 5pm. The entry fee was 200 pesos each to get in, which is roughly £14. Frankly, I see that as a major bargain. It's cheaper to enter a national park with some of the most spectacular waterfalls in the world and walks that go through beautiful nature than it is to walk around the remains of the rocks of Stone Henge – which, if I'm absolutely honest, is more of a let-down than the effects of the millennium bug.

There we were, expecting chaos… "planes will fall out of the sky" – somehow… I don't know, maybe the wings will vanish or something… "microwaves will take 3 years to do your 3-minute chips", "computers will explode because they think they haven't been invented yet" and what happened? Nothing. Not even my digital Casio watch got it wrong. And I've seen a program where they said that it was the massive amount of work behind the scenes that saved everything, but in the same way as me saying that yesterday, by meditating, I changed the trajectory of a massive asteroid that would have collided with the earth in 30 years' time… we will never know – so, I err on the side of caution and say that program was total bollocks.

So, I totally understand if people go to the attractions the UK has to offer and feel ripped off, but when we saw how large this park was for the entrance fee, we were totally overwhelmed.

The entrance fee could *only* be paid in Argentinian pesos, but inside, for some reason, payments for various attractions that weren't included and other tours could be made in pesos, reals, or even dollars and they didn't rip you off with the exchange rates either. They clearly weren't taking advantage of people using other currencies.

The first thing we did there was the "Eco tour". We took a little train up to the top of the waterfalls – one of those open, slow-moving trains like you get at various attractions – and boarded a large inflatable dinghy. There were around 8 of us in there plus the oarsman. The eco tour was just a calm ride along the

Iguaçu river to see the wildlife around the area. This was one of those trips that you just didn't want to end – particularly over the lip of the waterfall. The boat floated along the slow-moving river and even passed by the front of parts of the waterfalls themselves. As we were floating peacefully along the top, just tens of metres away, the water was dropping down with extreme ferocity. We were never in any danger of being dragged over the edge or anything like that but it's partially unnerving to float by the most violent part which is called 'la Garganta del Diablo' – the throat of the devil where a mist of spray can be seen rising up high into the sky. It's really quite spectacular, it almost looks like rising smoke from a fire below.

As far as nature was concerned, there were lots of butterflies of all different sizes and colours. We also saw wild toucans flying about as this is their natural habitat. I always found toucans astounding. Their disproportionately large beaks must unbalance them, but there they were, flying, and I think I finally understand how. (#1) their wings are actually quite far forward, so that counterbalances the weight of their beaks and (#2) they flap their wings like someone has just set fire to their arse.

We even saw a small alligator, which was just hanging around on the bank, and the guy pointed out a snake somewhere but we didn't quite see it.

By the end of the eco tour, I had a big smile on my face as we walked back down the hill the train had come up. Our next adventure, funnily enough, was called 'Gran Aventura' – no prizes for guessing what that was... and no, it's not grandma's adventure. *Grandma's* adventure would involve one less potato for lunch and an extra square of laxative chocolate... No, Gran Aventura means Big/Great Adventure.

I found this slightly less impressive as it felt counter-intuitive. About 25 of us were loaded onto this convertible – i.e. without a roof – tank-like vehicle. We were meant to be going out to spot some monkeys and other tree-dwelling animals like sloths, but frankly, I can't imagine many would hang around at the sight and sound of about 25 people taking flash photos in a massive tank-like vehicle that sounds like an unsilenced machine gun. We had seen some monkeys on the walk between where the last trip dropped us off and to where this one departed so that, at least, had been something. Somehow, even the sloths managed to leg it from us. To top it off, it rained ever so slightly, but it was still nice and warm.

The guide at the front with a *microphone* (another loud gadget to scare the crap out of any wildlife within a 50-metre radius), on the other hand, was quite interesting. She talked to us about monkeys and other wildlife and also mentioned where the word 'piranha' comes from. It comes from an old indigenous language – Tupi-Guaraní – and means one of a couple of things: *Pirá* means 'fish' in the old Tupi language (of the indigenous Tupinans of South America) and the other part too could be one of a few things. *Sanha/Sainha* meaning 'tooth' or *ánha,* meaning 'cut' in old Tupi or *ánha* from the Tupi-Guaraní language meaning 'bad', or 'devil'. (Confused?

Bloody hell, I am.) Given that the word is piranha and not pirsanha, I'd say it pretty much stands to reason that it means bad, or devil fish. And the tour guide lady in fact said, "eet meen devil fish".

So, although the talk had been interesting and we got to see lots of butterflies and birds, we didn't get to see any monkeys or sloths. Shame... I love sloths. They are such dudes, even the girl sloths.

Next was the boat trip – and this was no ordinary boat trip, this was a trip past and approaching some of the waterfalls and *through* some others. As we walked down to where the boats were, a butterfly landed on my glasses and didn't budge. Butterflies are amazing creatures; they are born as caterpillars and spend the first part of their lives eating and getting fat. All they think about is FOOD-FOOD-FOOD-FOOD. Then they cocoon themselves up and change into a butterfly... they pull their way out of their cocoon and the first thing they say is... HORNYYYY, HORNYYYY, HORNYYYY, HORNYYYY, then they fly around for the remainder of their lives looking for food and for something to have sex with so they can lay some eggs. I suppose I should be flattered, a bit like when a dog has sex with my leg. However, to my slight disappointment, the butterfly wasn't trying to have sex with me, it was just eating the salt from my glasses. Pretty grim actually, it must have come from the remnants of the years of sweat that had built up on the rims. Oh well, I suppose one man's sweaty forehead is a butterfly's meal for a couple of days. I swiftly became a photo model for random people who wanted to take pictures of the butterfly. It stayed on my glasses for a good 15 minutes before it had had enough and flew off.

I wasn't particularly looking forward to this boat trip. I'm not a fan of getting wet, especially with my clothes on, and on this trip, we were guaranteed a soaking. I was not happy, but I put on a brave face, which meant I made it clear I hate getting wet and moaned like a big pansy. In the end, we went anyway. We were all given waterproof bags to put our personal belongings in, we climbed into a 20-seater boat and were off.

A 10-minute ride up the river through the gorge and we got our first proper look at the waterfalls. What a spectacular sight. It's pretty unbelievable how many individual waterfalls stretch along the long ridge of this gorge on the lead up to 'la Garganta del Diablo'. For a small stretch, the water was coming from both the left and the right-hand side. We were entering the splash zones of the waterfalls...I hate getting wet... and passing directly underneath the less ferocious ones... I still hate getting wet... and the guy at the front of the boat was filming us all... getting wet... then we passed under some other falls... I hate getting wet... and then passed through some others backwards... I hate getting wet. We slowed down in front of 'la Garganta del Diablo'. The sight of it was absolutely awesome, frightening, huge, intimidating but beautiful. The intensity of the spray and the absolute ferocity was terrifying. This fall is in a 700-metre-long U shape with the water falling off its entire length. The 2 opposite sides of the U are 150 metres apart and it is 82 metres in height. It's impossible to see the water as it falls to the river below due to the intensity of the spray from the thousands of gallons of water per second crashing against the thousands of gallons from the opposite side that are crashing against the thousands of gallons falling in from the curved edge, making for an almost cataclysmic collision at the bottom with legendary spray up. And that is why they call this – the devil's throat.

Funnily enough, I went to a cave in Bulgaria called the devil's throat, the story of which is quite eerie and fascinating as there is a system of underground caverns that are, as yet, not fully understood. It seems this Devil character has been around quite a bit – especially his throat. Maybe for the purposes of not doubling up on the devil's various body parts with other attractions around the world, they should have called this cave the devil's colon or maybe they should have named the waterfall the devil's bladder... but if they had, maybe visitors would have been few and far between.

So, on went our boat journey, and at the most opportune moment – that is directly underneath one of the (smaller) waterfalls whilst getting drenched – I asked Vesi if she wanted to marry me. Clearly, I didn't get down on one knee because we were in a boat with seats in front and there was no space... it was impossible... and totally wet... but I asked her. Now, I find that proposal about a thousand times better than the dozy romantic down on one knee somewhere romantic-looking type of proposal. The crappiest thing I think would have been to wait until we were in Rio at the large statue of Christ the Redeemer, gotten down onto one knee in front of a bunch of other monkey tourists and proposed like that and received a round of applause by a bunch of people I was not looking to entertain and whom I would never see again. That is the kind of proposal that makes my stomach turn… oh, by the way, she said yes.

So, when we were completely and totally saturated… I hate getting wet… we headed back to dry land and disembarked. Overall, the experience was incredible, even though, and you may not know this but – I hate getting wet.

Fortunately, it was really nice and warm so we did not get cold. It wasn't particularly windy either so there wasn't any major rush to get changed.

We found some toilets for Vesi and me to change in, and thank god for the disabled toilet cubicles. These are absolute lifesavers when it comes to getting changed in public places. It means I don't have to hide behind some bush or tree, and I feel ok going into them because there isn't usually a queue of disabled people waiting outside when I finish. I tend to use them quite a bit as they are usually quite spacious. The one thing I *don't* like about disabled toilets though, and this applies to the UK mainly, is that there is often a pretty huge mirror in there, so when you sit on the proverbial throne, you find yourself staring at yourself… your *whole* self and it's actually a pretty grim sight. On top of that, knowing what the UK is like in its objective to spy on everything and everyone all the time – like in the book 1984 – as before it wouldn't surprise me if there was either CCTV behind the mirror or some GCHQ loser. (GCHQ – replete with some of the UK's biggest traitors (i.e.

spying on the public in a Stasi-like *guilty until proven innocent* kind of way) along with some arms of the organisation that do some good work (i.e. supposedly trying their best to prevent cyber-attacks from other countries)).

Following that adventure, we bought some food and sat down to eat, and you know how in the UK when you sit in a park to eat some food, you get pigeons appearing and staring at you with those expressionless eyes that still tell you they want to eat whatever you drop… well, here, they had the same thing but with Coatis. Lovely little things but they've got sharp teeth and we are in a country that has rabies, which there is no actual cure for. You have to get to a hospital before any symptoms show or – put simply – you're dead… so, however remote the chances of catching it are, I was pretty alert the whole time I was there.

After all this, we still hadn't walked around the trails and actually looked at the waterfalls from dry land, so we did just that. We followed various paths and trails that led to different viewpoints. I can only imagine what this place must be like during the high season and I dread the thought. At the corners of every viewpoint, there were always queues of people taking photos and having photos taken and it was a waiting game to elbow our way in, as politely as possible, take some photos and ask someone to take a photo of us with the waterfalls behind. I kind of felt sorry for some people – and I know I shouldn't but you just can't help it sometimes – who were there by themselves taking selfies. YES, I know a lot of people travel alone and it's often the best way because (a) you meet people on the way and (b) it's the best way of seeing what you like to see without it being diluted by someone else's desires... but still, there's something about someone smiling for a selfie with a DSLR camera that makes you want to go over and give them a big hug and say, "Aww don't worry, hang around with us" – to which their response would naturally be "piss off, I'm on my own on purpose".

I swear, Vesi took so many photos that if we printed them all off, we'd end up with a perfect flicker book of the holiday – but it would take around 6 weeks to flick through it because Vesi likes to take at least 2 photos of everything.

The views of the waterfalls were absolutely spectacular, possibly more spectacular than when we were on the boat because we were looking from higher up and we had better panoramic views. Rainbows upon rainbows – double rainbows – rainbows that seemed to spring up from nowhere, the colours were amazing.

As we learned, the falls comprise of 275 individual drops along the Iguaçu river, dividing it into the upper and lower Iguaçu river. They are literally on the border between Brazil (in the state of Paraná) and the Argentine province of Misiones. The name comes from the Tupi or Guarani language and means "Big or Great Water" which, I would say is quite apt because they are humungous. The highest peak is, as I mentioned before, 82 metres high (269 feet) and they stretch along a 2.7 km-wide (1.7 miles) ridge – that's taller than Niagara and twice as wide. It is reported that when Eleanor Roosevelt (ex-first lady of the USA) first saw the falls, she exclaimed "Poor Niagara", which are around 50 metres high.

There are 2 similar legends that I've read regarding these waterfalls. One is that a deity planned to marry a beautiful aboriginal girl named Naipí against her wish. She escaped with her mortal lover, Tarobá, in a canoe. In a rage, the deity sliced the river, creating the waterfalls and condemning the lovers to fall down them for eternity.

The other is that as Naipí walked along the Iguaçu river, the god, M'Boi (the serpent god), saw her reflection and fell in love with her. He demanded she be sacrificed to him. She and her lover, Tarobá, escaped with a canoe but M'Boi noticed them and started to chase them. Tarobá managed to keep ahead, and in his fury, M'Boi split the earth in front of the canoe. The boat fell down this crack (the waterfalls) and Tarobá survived by jumping out of the boat while Naipí was transformed into a rock. Seeing this, Tarobá rushed toward her and was turned into a palm tree on the precipice.

Now, I can't say I've ever seen evidence of a person turning into a rock... Or a tree for that matter, so I believe that story to be untrue. And to be honest, I didn't actually see a palm tree. There probably was one but I wasn't paying attention. I'm pretty sure I saw some rocks though. I'm guessing one of them was Naipí. I'm confident that there are creationists and anyone from the state of Kansas who *do* believe it though. The actual story is much less fantastical as the falls were caused by an enormous volcanic eruption that left a huge crack in the earth about 132 million years ago. I've read that this eruption was possibly the largest in the history of the last several hundred million years – however, not enough people have been around long enough to confirm it.

Vesi and I walked around for a good couple of hours along various trails and ended up having our photo taken at the top of one of the larger waterfalls. The butterflies were so much braver than the ones at home. I picked some up on my way... simply by putting my hand near them and then gently nudging them onto my finger. Being your usual sweaty and greasy bloke, the butterflies loved hanging around on my hand and feeding off the salt left behind. At one point, I had one on my hand for about 40 minutes – and it's not like it can be said that "oh, so many people come past that butterflies must be used to people by now." Well, given their lifespan is measured in hours or maybe days with few species lasting longer, I don't think they get much time to get used to people before they finally turn their proverbial toes up.

At 5pm, we met our driving dude, and not long after, we were back in Brazil. He told us that in Foz, people often go to Paraguay to do some of their shopping because, to Brazilians, things in Paraguay are cheap. Unfortunately, our schedule didn't allow us time to go and see what this was about. Our driving dude told us we'd be overcharged. Naturally, I thought, and rightly so too but in the end – with a bit of haggling – we could have bought some good gifts, fruits, souvenirs and paid less than we would have done at a jumble sale for old ladies.

Vesi and I had a discussion in the car about whether to tip him and how much to leave. We had thought of 10 reals originally, but then because we were the only people on the trip, we both thought we should leave him 20, which we did. The look on his face told us everything... we'd gone over the top. Still, he was happy and we hadn't left him all that much anyway. In the end, everyone felt good and that's what it was about. We didn't feel any pressure into tipping either, which is great – unlike going to the USA where you're forced to tip, even if some tosser holds the door open for you.

Food in the evening... we went somewhere that the travel guide Vesi brought with her recommended. The place was called 'Tropicana'. Inside, it was just a popular looking café/restaurant. It was self-service night... on veg... so we loaded up and sat down. The waiter guy brought us a plate of about 6 thin steaks and we had another tasty steak-filled evening – not quite like last night but very satisfying all the same, even though, at one point in the evening, we saw a fly come in and land on one of the vegetable plates on the self-service table. Ahh, whatever doesn't kill you makes you stronger... unless it's a stroke.

And if we were to be convinced that not all Brazilian women are slim and beautiful, this was the place that convinced us.

The total cost of food, 2 x 660ml beers and 2 x Caipirinhas = 53 reals – roughly £15. Bargain... and the fly was no extra charge.

Tomorrow, we will see the falls from the Brazilian side.

Day 3 – Foz Do Iguaçu – Brazilian side

Not a good night's sleep. After having walked around the room before going to bed and flicking any black dots I saw on the wall with a towel, I barely slept. I kept tossing and turning and even tried sleeping on the couch in the lounge area outside our bedroom, which still didn't help. I did finally manage to get some sleep in the bed but woke up with a shocking headache.

"Oh no..." I groaned, "I've got malaria."

"No, you haven't," Vesi replied, "this isn't a malaria zone."

"Oh no..." I groaned, "I've got dengue fever."

"Not this quickly you haven't"

And it went on for ages until I'd listed every possible reason for my headache I could think of, right down to tennis elbow and athlete's foot.

As it turns out, I'm just a pussy lightweight and it was a hangover. This was confirmed by my 3 alco-shits. They normally help clear my hangover but I think my body knew I was going to go out so it evacuated my bowels very early on and got me to take 2 paracetamols instead (listen to your body is the lesson there). I had virtually no breakfast and what breakfast I did have came up again in the toilet 10 minutes later, therefore, I felt quite rough when we went out.

We got on a bus and rode it right up to the last stop at the northern tip of Foz to see the other main attraction of the region... Itaipu dam.

Itaipu dam is a hydroelectric dam at the southern tip of the Itaipu lake which is fed into from the north by the Paraná river. The water from the dam then continues as the Paraná river and then forks off about 15 miles downstream into the Paraná and the Iguaçu rivers. The Paraná river then continues down through Argentina, whereas the Iguaçu river goes over the waterfalls and continues south towards Uruguay.

We took a bus tour that went up and along the length of the dam, stopping occasionally to let us take photos – photos? Of a dam? Seriously? Surely that goes hand in hand with train spotting, or worse... roundabout spotting (yes, there really is such a thing. I have a book about it – morbid curiosity purposes rather than genuine interest).

A girl came on board and did the whole tour in both Portuguese and English. She was actually really good and it gave Vesi and me the opportunity to pick up some Portuguese.

The bus actually took us out of Brazil and into Paraguay. Wow, what a life Vesi and I lead... Brazil, Argentina and now Paraguay in 2 days; we are proper citizens of the world. However, it does sound better than it actually is. We only entered the part of Paraguay that had the dam and it was more of a no man's land. No passport checks or anything. Technically, we were in

Paraguay but in name only. It felt a bit like crossing the border into Wales.

The name Itaipu comes – surprise, surprise – from the Guaraní language and means "Singing Stone" which was the name given to a rock that was on the site in the fast-flowing Paraná river. It is the second largest hydroelectric dam in the world – the largest being the Three Gorges Dam in China that was completed in 2012. Itaipu's construction began in 1975 and electricity generation started in 1984. With 18 enormous turbines, the last couple were completed and switched on in 1991. Since then, it has been expanded and that expansion was completed in 2003.

Like the waterfalls, this dam spans 2 countries, but this time, it is Brazil and their old enemy, Paraguay, and it produces so much electricity that it is able to supply Paraguay with 78% of its electricity needs and 17% of Brazil's (according to official figures). That's pretty astounding. it produces about as much as 10 nuclear power plants.

Yes, it all sounds wonderful but there are, of course, some negative sides to the building of this dam – like the relocation of more than 8,000 families so that they could flood the area just before the dam, the destruction of rare fruit trees, orchids and other vegetation. Also, believe it or not, it's not 100% green. Greenhouse gasses are produced from the reservoir. How? Well, when the area is flooded, the vegetation that was in the flooding area dies and rots underwater without oxygen (anaerobically) and this produces methane that is a major greenhouse gas – more so than carbon dioxide. This release of methane is more pronounced in the tropics, but Foz is right down south below the tropic of Capricorn. It doesn't mean that methane isn't produced, it's just reduced – I don't understand why it's more pronounced at the tropics but that's what I read. Besides, I'm on holiday, I'm not undertaking a field study.

Future dams, however, can be built with this in mind to reduce/eliminate the threat of greenhouse gasses. The energy production itself is very green. In fact, overall, the use of hydroelectric dams now feeds around 80% - 90% of Brazil's electricity needs, which is great for the coming generations, but on the downside, the process has been rather destructive to the areas around the dams. Do the ends justify the means? – Discuss among yourselves.

In comparison, there has been a proposal in the UK to build the Severn tidal barrage to meet up to 5% of Britain's energy needs at an estimated cost of £30 billion. The government have said it wouldn't be good for the economy or the environment. SO, instead of green energy production, they have decided to stick to HS2 (a train set) which will tear the shit out of a slice of the country and will cost anywhere between £38 billion and more than £60 billion – which is clearly much better for the environment, and with costs predicted to be more than double the original estimate, clearly much better for the economy too. Yes, unfortunately, the UK government has about as much intention of doing good to the country as the bombers did to Hiroshima and Nagasaki in August 1945.

Brazil's energy future at the moment is looking relatively good in comparison to the UK, where the conservatives have all but annihilated large swathes of the renewable energy industry and are focusing on giving their money to fossil fuel companies. The energy needs of our children (and hence, our economy) are looking very bleak.

Sounds crazy? Well, it's happening in the UK.

Ok, so there was a little history and general information about this hydroelectric dam, but seeing it is a whole other experience. The entire length of the dam is almost 8 km (7,919 metres) and there are 20 turbines in total. It is an absolutely awe-inspiring sight. You'd think a dam would be boring, however, it's anything but.

Out of the 20 turbines, 18 can be kept running all the time while 2 are stopped for maintenance. Why can't they run all 20 at once? Well, it's in the contract between Brazil and Paraguay and that's that – and don't forget, that little piece of paper says what goes.

At the end of the tour, we all got off and shook hands with the guide. On closer inspection, I realised that she was actually a he. Oh, how I did laugh and thank my lucky stars that I realised. It would have been so wrong to have him as some kind of fantasy during sex (on a personal note, I reckon he was working to save enough money to go to Thailand and work there).

We could have done a tour of the insides of the dam but it would have taken a few hours and we still had a busy day ahead of us.

It was about 12pm – lunch time – and we boarded an empty bus and headed off to the waterfalls that lay on the Brazilian side. These were at the opposite tip of Foz. Within 5 stops, in true Brazilian fashion, we were crushed up against the windows with a gap no thicker than a credit card through which to breathe with people around us acting as though this was completely normal. Having 40 people within 15 cm of my face IS FAR FROM NORMAL.

But these were mostly kids and, again, nobody had BO. What is *wrong* with these people? There was one drunkard on there talking very loudly at everybody and nobody and even though *he* stank of alcohol and that grim musty breath that only alcoholics have, he didn't have BO either. You have to wonder at this point... were these people born without sweat glands?

It took about an hour on the bus before we were at the other end of Foz and the waterfalls. This time, the view was from the other side of the river and, ok, it looks like the Argentines do hog most of the better views, but this side has a metal bridge that goes right out and almost faces the devil's throat – from a safe distance, of course. But there is an enormous amount of spray back and it's a 15-minute walk along the path where there's always a crowd queuing to stand in the best photo position. And even then, it's hard to get a shot that doesn't include some hairy chinned woman with a half squinty-eyed expression, clutching her camera and looking as though she's waiting in the queue to be the next person to stand in the best photo position.

I have to be honest, the photos are lovely, but when you're there, it feels very forced and rushed because you have about 15 seconds to get a couple of decent shots in before feeling like you have to get out of the way... and then when you do get an accidental photo-bomber in it with a squinty expression, it detracts from the magic of the moment where you're trying to make it look like it's just you in front of this waterfall. But still, these are the kinds of things people feel it necessary to put on Facebook for some unknown reason.

Several flicker books of photos later, we made our way to a higher platform right next to the upper lip of the waterfall around the devil's throat, where we posed for some more photos even going so far as to have one professionally taken and printed on a calendar... for the prior year (well at least they are trying – albeit not very hard)

As we were walking away to catch the bus to the bird park/enclosure (yes, there was a bird enclosure too... I told you we did a lot on this day), some little oriental woman (I don't want to commit myself and guess where she was from, but statistically speaking, she was probably Chinese) – probably mid-40s, maybe early 50s – stopped Vesi and me and took a photo of us with her camera, thanked us and then walked away. It was quite a bizarre moment... almost celebrity-like, except Vesi and I are more well-known than some of the Z class c'lebs and more loved than most of the filth that ends up on some crap reality TV show [e.g. 'Big brother – the Jews and Muslims series' or 'caged with a hungry lion']. We weren't sure why she did that... no explanation, nothing. Maybe she was just a bit lonely, or maybe she wanted to take a contract out on our lives for some reason, or maybe she just wanted to show people back home that she'd made some friends.

"You see... these photos were my newfound friends, called err Chico and Chica...

This is them hugging...

This is them hugging again...

And again...

This is them looking at me a bit annoyed...

This is them looking furious...

This is them walking away...

Now running...

This is Chico trying to punch me through the camera...

And this is the actual restraining order they got against me...

We're just going to remain pen pals."

Anyway, we left on a bus and got off at the bird park/enclosure – Parque des Aves. This was just a bird zoo but the birds in there were astounding.

Inside one of the domes, the birds were flying about freely – which was amazing. There were orange beaked toucans, green beaked toucans and numerous birds that I can't identify. As we walked along the path that trails around the dome, there were a couple of green beaked toucans chilling on the handrails. Poor bird must have been so used being manhandled that it didn't flinch when we stroked it on the breast. After a couple of seconds of being prodded and poked, it jumped off the handrail, pooed on the path in front of us and decided to eat my shoes. And this is where I questioned its intelligence. If I tried to eat a piece of rubber once and didn't really like the taste, I'd probably give up. It took the toucan a good few minutes to realise that. In the end, it keeled over, coughed a few times, flapped its wings, gave itself the Heimlich, coughed something up, shook its head and walked away to look for something else to eat.

We walked around and sat down on a log. Some bird about the size of a turkey spied my camera dangling from the string and it did a funky little walk (you know how birds have a funny walk) over to me where it proceeded to try to eat it. All I can say to that is... 10 out of 10 for perseverance. After a while though, it got the message that the camera was not edible, turned around, pooed on Vesi's shoe and walked off. I guess the bird had the last laugh there.

We met the coolest toucan in one of the cages, it was a black beaked toucan… we couldn't go in there and it couldn't get out but when we stopped outside, it spied us through one of its eyes, jumped down from the branch it was on and side hopped over to us. I poked my finger through the cage and, naturally, the toucan tried to eat it. After several failed attempts, it simply stopped trying but didn't hop away. It stayed put. It was almost as though it was enjoying the company and us talking to it… now, of course, it didn't understand a bleeding word we were saying. We were speaking English, not Portuguese. We were putting our fingers through the cage, stroking the feathers on its breasts, then its beak and it almost seemed positively content with that – well, as content as a bird can look with its lifeless black beady eyes, no eyebrows, and a face that shows absolutely no expression whatsoever.

We then went through a parrot enclosure. They were so noisy it was incredible. One would start squawking, then another, then they all joined in… no words though. I did try to get one to give the first 2 lines of Hamlet's 'To be or not to be' speech, but even after a bit of persistence and chasing it around the enclosure, I realised it wasn't one of those talking parrots… It just kept looking at me with a look that said, 'and you think that toucan was dumb because it tried to eat your shoe? You should look at yourself now, you twat – chasing a bird around an enclosure, reciting Shakespeare.' Then it pooed and hopped away. Pooing was very much the theme in this bird park.

There was also a butterfly house with some really big butterflies. I don't care what anyone says about how ugly they look close up... they're still beautiful to me.

We left the bird park around 5:30/6pm and as we sat waiting at the bus stop, we watched the sun on its descent. Spectacular though it was, I was more concerned with what happens *after* the sun disappears below the horizon. When that happens, the mosquitoes come out. Watching the beautiful sun going down slowly reminded me of the film 'Pitch Black' with Vin Diesel, where this group of people are on some strange planet and when the sun sets, big ugly flying creatures come out in their thousands and eat people. There is a scene where they are gathered to watch the sun go down, and as it does, thousands of these alien creatures come flying out from holes in the ground and attack the group. Well, this was similar-ish, except instead of being on another planet, we were at a bus stop. Ok, maybe less glamorous than being on another planet, but still. Waiting for the bus reminded me a lot of that film and that scene... If the bus didn't arrive in time, we'd be bait for the millions – no billions – no wait – trillions (but not as much as America's debt) of mosquitoes that fly around after dark... and ok... instead of having our brains mashed out or our heads chewed off, we'd just get a bit itchy for a while, but it was still a cause for concern. What if I get bitten behind my ear? It's really annoying there. Or on the forehead? Well, that's just unsightly.

We sat and waited... and waited... and waited some more whilst watching the sun get lower and lower... and then we waited some more while the sun continued to get lower... still no bus... and then the sun started to hit some thin clouds over the horizon and we knew it was only a matter of time before the sun hit the horizon itself... no bus... lower... no bus... then it got dangerously low, so I took action... (like Vin Diesel but in a less dangerous way) I took out the mosquito repellent from my bag and we covered ourselves in it.

Yes, ok, sorry if that was a bit of a pathetic end, but what kind of a story would this be without a touch of suspense? Sorry if I ruined it, but since mosquitoes seem to love me – and Vesi – it would be bloody stupid to go out without mosquito repellent here... it would be like a chicken walking into a fox's den without a machine gun.

And for a particularly spectacular anti-climax, the bus arrived before the sun went down and we returned back to our Airbnb before it was fully dark.

Dinner in the evening was maximum debauchery except without the sex, drugs or alcohol – so really, it was just a food fest. We went to eat at this gaucho churrascaria. This was another one like 2 nights ago where they keep coming with meat, meat and more meat on skewers and you can have as much as you like until you say stop.

Vesi made the cardinal mistake of putting too much from the salad bar on her plate, including veg with chicken mixed in. No... this is not the place to fill up on bread and vegetables. Unfortunately, the more I told her, the more she piled on... But like me, she still stuffed her face with beef, pork, chicken and lamb until she could barely walk. And you'd imagine it to be embarrassing. Brazilians eat until they've had enough, but we Europeans eat until we're on the verge of being sick... then we eat some more until we feel dizzy... then we stop several helpings after that. Even the waiters were laughing at us never saying no to the meats that came around. Then we had the delicious cinnamon coated barbecued pineapple... oh god. This place was easily as good as the place we went to 2 nights ago, maybe even more so because it felt more down to earth and less snobby. No waiter in a waistcoat prostrating and offering us spoonfuls of raw garlic. And whereas the place 2 nights before cost us 200 reals, this time, we paid 89 reals.

After managing to waddle back to our room, we went on a mosquito-killing rampage looking to squash every single black dot on the wall (and if any oversensitive people or tabloid journalists are reading this... that's not me being racist... or anti-Semitic given it's one of the UK's perpetual hot topics when they try to smear people) and pretty much anything darker than the wall that moved – or looked like it could move. Even my own shadow got a pretty good pounding, I can tell you.

Tomorrow, it's Rio de Janeiro but I don't think I'll eat a thing when I'm there.

Rio De Janeiro

Day 4 – Rio De Janeiro

Several mosquito bites later, I woke up. It was 7am... little bastards. Where do these bloody mosquitoes hide?

Breakfast was really good. Grape Juice, toast, melons, papaya and yoghurt – which, on day 1, I thought I was drinking yoghurt... it turned out I just hadn't shaken it.

We left and went to the bus station. In front of it, we noticed there was a zoo which was free to enter, so we did (with our luggage). There were some birds, monkeys, crocodiles, etc. but after what we've been to see already, it was all pretty ordinary. Really, the day you see a crocodile or peacock and think it's pretty ordinary, you know you've seen some spectacular things. Besides, it was a bit of a sad little zoo. The animals didn't look particularly happy there and the monkeys didn't even try to throw poo at us, which was most upsetting.

We said our goodbye's to Foz and took the bus to the airport.

On the flight, from the window, a long stretch of the Iguaçu River leading right up to the waterfalls could be seen. It was supremely spectacular... far better than when you look at it on Google maps. As we lifted up into the sky, I turned to take hold of Vesi's hand, looked at her and said, "thank you."

I intend to write a little 'what I've learnt'/'my observations' bit every time we leave somewhere explaining – well – what I learnt about the place – and maybe whether it was different to how I expected and anything particular I observed.

What I learnt in Foz:

#1

São Paulo (before Foz) – We weren't there for very long and it may be obvious, but it simply feels like any large city. It's not like going anywhere different such as New York, Venice, or Florence. There are some obvious cultural differences like the food shops, but apart from that, if you were dropped in blindfolded by an alien race, you wouldn't instantly think... Hey, we're in São Paulo.

#2

Brazilian women... Don't believe the hype. Don't believe the lies. They aren't all fantastic and beautiful. There are some shocking specimens here just like everywhere else. In fact, in Foz may I say, there are a surprising number of *American*-sized specimens... Maybe they're eating loads of sugary foods.

#3

A lot of the men here are a bit on the large side too. Guess they're buying into the whole processed foods thing that has been brought down from a nearby neighbour from the north, but you know what? Nobody around here seems to care much. A lot of people here have that – 'yes, I'm fat, so what?' look about them.

#4

Health and safety. Non-existent. The limits to this are: please fasten your seatbelts and it's not recommended that you place your wedding tackle in the lion's mouth before slapping him in the face.

#5

Something I haven't mentioned yet... the toilets here are cleaner than almost everywhere I've ever been to in the UK (including our house). Coupled with that, the people here – even on buses – did not have BO (unlike me after a day under the hot sun).

#6

There are lots of different types of looks here... the Hispanic look and the Native American look –more commonly known as Indian, i.e. the indigenous people of the land before white man came and BROUGHT PEACE AND DEMOCRACY.

#7

Even though Foz has its hectic parts (to be honest, mainly on the buses), the whole town feels quite relaxed and not at all as dangerous as might be inferred from the media. They make out Brazil is this lovely place but poverty is extreme and half the people are out to mug you. This is clearly completely dependent on where you go.

#8

From what snippets I've seen, TV is just as bad as the UK and Italy (they love their soaps here).

#9

The bus system here, although crowded, puts the UK system to shame. The buses are significantly cheaper, and all joking aside, even though they do squeeze more people on, it's not actually by much. It's more like getting onto a super crowded tube in London.

#10

There are more bins than in the UK... especially at the airports. But there are not many countries that are pissed off with Brazil, so there is no need to worry too much about terrorism.

Rio De Janeiro

The doors of the aircraft opened and the waft of warm air floated in through the cabin. Right the way through to the arrivals lounge of Galeão airport, I could not stop singing Mas Que Nada to myself – the song made famous by ME... well, not me... by Sergio Mendes. It's a song that has what I would class as a genuine Brazilian feel – not to impugn the validity and Brazilian feel of another famous song – oh, what was it called again? – Ah, YES, of course... 'Brazil'.

In amongst the feelings of tension (brought on by the media), I was incredibly curious to see what Rio was like. I've seen it on TV; bright lights, Sugarloaf Mountain, Christ the Redeemer, Copacabana Beach, Ipanema, and hot, tanned, big-breasted, naked chicks running naked through the beautiful white sands in rapturous and naked – and not to forget – nude ecstasy – yes... we've all had that fantasy, especially me.

However, given the experience in Foz, my galactic expectation of these hot women was slightly bruised, and instead of multiple hot naked girls running through my head in my fantasy, there was now only one – and even she needed a slight nose job.

We asked the guy at the information desk how best to get to the centre and how dangerous Rio was. Basically, can we get there using public transport without being mugged, knifed, killed or raped?

The premium bus was 13.50 reals per person, or if we took the public bus and then the metro, we'd pay 6 reals in total to get to where we were going. "Both are safe" – but don't hang around the Vincenzo de Carvallo tube station when it gets dark as it's a bit of a rough neighbourhood.

It was at this point my instincts kicked into thinking straight. It was 2pm and we had until 6pm before it would get dark, so that left us with 3.5-4 hours to get to where we were going in a city we didn't know and speaking a language to which we could only *listen* fluently. "Let's take the direct bus," I said, meaning the 13.50 reals one. No chance. Vesi was leading and so we went the cheaper way.

It was at this point I took my hat off to my beautiful girlfriend. As with the walking around in Foz, she was in absolute control all the time. Had I taken charge, yes, ok, we'd have arrived at our destination – Botafogo – but it would have taken longer and it might have been dark by the time we got to where we were going. But with Vesi at the helm, I have to say in all admiration, it was almost as though she knew instinctively which way to go (sixth sense, eh? I see dead people moment, eh?).

I jumped on the bus that Vesi said we should board in readiness with my cat-like reflexes in case someone tried to mug us, although striking a defensive pose when I landed just made me look a bit stupid. Anyway, it was unlikely to happen on a bus near the airport, so off we went. The bus was one of those bendy in the middle buses and it was really clean.

Although I doubted anything would go wrong, I kept a hawk eye on our bags, just in case, and it was lucky I did.

No... nothing happened, but it made the 1-hour journey pass more quickly.

The bus had a lane all to itself, literally. We encountered no traffic jams and cruised all the way, stopping only occasionally. The UK and its terrible road system could really learn a lot from this, but they won't – unless it makes a profit. Screw the people, money comes first, especially short-term profit – and that's one of the many reasons the UK has unmanageable debt.

The journey was quite an eye-opener. The airport – Galeão – is situated in the North of Rio on a little island, and we were staying in south Rio, so we had a bit of a journey ahead of us. As the bus travelled along its lane, the city revealed itself to us and, in all honesty, it was not a pleasant sight. There was more graffiti than there is in Italy – and that's saying something. In Italy, even the beautiful Rialto Bridge in Venice had incomprehensible scrawls covering it when I visited. Here in Rio, it looks like the same twat had done the same thing, except that here, somehow, the twat was so determined to vandalise buildings that he managed to defy gravity and float up to the unreachable height of 4-5 floors above the ground, away from any windows and doors. I swear, whichever plonker did that could do something so much better with his superpowers.

As we passed through the city, I kept thinking to myself that we'd made a mistake coming here. It was really quite grimy and nothing like the picture painted by the television. But then again, TV always paints things in the very best or worst light, so I thought maybe there were some nicer parts to Rio. Hidden maybe... but nice.

I was convinced we'd – well, Vesi – would find them.

We eventually reached the stop where we had to change for the metro, Vincenzo de Carvallo. It was about 3pm so we still had a couple of hours till sunset – a couple of hours until the evils from Pandora's box come out and mug the hell out of us.

The metro was genuinely impressive. The trains all had air conditioning and were about 50% wider than the London underground, and the carriages were all joined up like a bendy bus so you could walk uninterrupted from one end of the train to the other. Still, credit to the London underground, it is much older – I'm not dissing it.

A number of stops later, we reached Botafogo and exited the metro. I was getting my super Kung Fu, Ninjutsu reflexes ready, which included grabbing Vesi and running away if necessary.

Botafogo was actually quite nice. It wasn't graffiti'd from top to bottom. It looked quite clean and the people seemed, dare I say... normal. I think deep down, I was quite impressed – does that make me a snob? I don't know. I live in a white trash area of Bristol which happens to be mostly a council estate and there are a lot of couples in this area with 5 kids of all different colours and no one seems to work in the household, so based on that, I don't think I can really call myself a snob.

We walked to our Airbnb place, which was about a mile away, dragging our suitcases behind us which was a little tough. The pavements were narrow, broken and full of obstacles like bins, lamp posts and artificially planted trees that were made worse by having a lot of people on them so there were lots of blockages and people pushing and shoving. As we were walking, in the distance we could see one of Rio's main icons, Corcovado Mountain with Christ the Redeemer and his stretched-out arms on the top. It was quite far away but it was a fantastic image, so much better than the dilapidated buildings in northern Rio, and for the second time, I started singing Mas Que Nada by Sergio Mendes again. This was the Rio I had imagined.

After only 20-25 minutes, we made it to a lovely little hotel-type place run by a woman called Giuliana. We were greeted by her niece, Tiah, who came out and hugged us both warmly as a hello. Naturally, I made sure I hadn't just been pickpocketed – Hey, this is Rio, not the Vatican where I'd be more worried about being fondled by a cardinal. But she'd not stolen anything and the hug was genuine, so I started to relax – but I still kept my wits about me in case I needed to whip out some Ninjutsu runaway moves with Vesi.

We had a nice double room with an en-suite shower located inside an apartment with a kitchen and lounge area. There were 3 rooms in this little apartment and the hotel-type place had at least a couple of other apartments. We weren't going to get breakfast so we needed to pick up some food from one of the little markets we passed on the way.

We considered going to the beach areas. Rio, after all, is the home to the world's most famous beaches. Ipanema beach, which was made famous by a beautiful girl who inspired the song by Antônio Carlos Jobim with lyrics by Vinicius de Moraes and Copacabana beach, which was made famous by a man with a funny nose called Barry.

The song, 'Girl from Ipanema' was written in 1962. While Antônio Carlos Jobim and Vinicius de Moraes sat in the Veloso bar next to Ipanema beach having a few beers, a lovely 18-year-old girl with long black hair and green eyes walked by, either going to the beach or returning from school. Her name was Heloisa Eneida Menezes Pais Pinto (Helo for short, luckily) and she was the inspiration for that song. She never actually made any money out of it, even though she technically became as famous as the football player, Pelé.

Later, she opened a boutique, naming it Garota de Ipanema (Girl from Ipanema), and the sons of the writers of the song tried suing her for using the name. (People suing people for sod all – which is basically people getting money out of others for virtually nothing ... quite a burgeoning business as the western world fills with corporate lawyers and the economies have started turning to shit). Public support was in her favour (luckily) and in the end, the court ruled in her favour too (good... the sons should have had corporal punishment bestowed upon them too to punish them for the flaming cheek).

We were fortunate enough to meet and get a lift from one of the owners of the Airbnb. He couldn't have been any older than 25. He had opened this Airbnb with Giuliana (business partner) but had a job in the hospital either cleaning or doing admin. His parents had paid for the Airbnb, and with the plush Lexus-like car he had, he was clearly one of the lucky ones in Rio.

He was a genuinely decent guy, which worried me slightly. Hmmm, why is he being so nice? My suspicions were raised. Then I realised it might not be good for repeat business if a hotel host gets his guests mugged – so I relaxed a little. He drove us down past the beach where the city was truly alive with bars, restaurants, shops, etc. and showed us various points of interest, including Copacabana and Ipanema beaches. He pointed out a pacified favela on one of the mountainsides too. I was pretty nervous about the favelas but he said that all the favelas in the south had been pacified. In the north, they were not so lucky and they were dangerous places.

The favela on the mountainside looks like a really tightly packed town with houses of varying colours. From a distance, it looks like a bit of a party town with its many colours and people living so close to one another, but when you get closer, the varying colours are basically a mix of dirt, rust, grime, patchwork and different brick colours. It almost looks like one of those red cars with one green door, one brown door, a blue bonnet, grey boot and furry dice in the window in an attempt to make it look less shit. And the favelas have become quite touristy too, with people wanting to go and see what they are like. We would have been ok to go and walk through them if we wanted to, however, I wasn't sure if I'd feel quite right doing that, even though the favelas are now a tourist attraction, it felt somewhat voyeuristic. It was a bit like some kind of zoo – and that may sound snobby, but really... favelas are shanty or slum towns, so why do people want to go and see how life is in the slums? Is it out of morbid curiosity? Is it so that they can go there and consider themselves lucky that they don't live there? People say, "well, it's interesting." What's interesting? The morgue in a hospital is interesting but I don't have much of a desire to go there just to have a look. Also, depending on the favela, you're less likely to get mugged in a morgue, especially by the residents. As such, we didn't end up paying the favelas a visit.

We also drove past the Panda Hotel. This 'hotel' is actually more of a motel and '*motels*' in Brazil mean one thing... secret sex. They are places where you can rent rooms out by the hour. And for those of you who think "oof... what dirty pervs" or "oof... how sick" ...shame on you. The motel idea is absolutely wonderful because it's a hell of a lot cleaner than shagging in a nightclub toilet – or on top of some bins outside a Co-op. Also, as we discovered from our host, housing in Rio is prohibitively expensive and most people live at home until they are married before trying to find a place with their partner. Even then, they may end up living with one of the sets of parents for a period before accumulating enough money to move out.

Our host (I wish I'd written his name down or bothered remembering – apologies for that. I only noted it in my head as 'bloke' and that was definitely not his name) said that he'd been to motels before with his girlfriend and it wasn't just for illicit or promiscuity reasons that people went to them. It was literally a place to be alone for a while in a humble (or not, as the case may be) place of their own, even if only for a couple of hours... and to have sex, of course.

These motels, though, are also used for affairs and reasons of pure promiscuity, and at the entrance of the Panda motel when people drive in, the car's number plates are immediately covered up to conceal the identity of the owner. Clearly, the Panda motel does not discriminate. I must admit, I'd be dead curious to see what one of those places is like – but it's not within our budget so I must be content with having sex in one of our own hotel rooms.

We were dropped off in an area with loads of bars and restaurants just outside a small Vitamina and fruit juice place. The host recommended trying the açaí with banana. The Vitaminas, juices and açaís were still cheap compared to the UK but more expensive than in Foz and São Paulo (around 7.50-8.50). I honestly think you'd have to be a connoisseur to claim that the banana açaí and the passion fruit (or maracuja) açaí taste any different. The açaí with sugar itself is quite overpowering, but mix that with the numbing sensation of the crushed ice, and frankly, by the 4th sip my mouth was so numb that I could have been drinking cold mud and I wouldn't have known any different.

One thing that was noticeably different to Foz though, was the look of the people. The mix was quite eclectic but, in general, the people were better looking. The women were more attractive and the men were more toned. People seemed to look after themselves better here. Even in the heat of the evening, there were lots of people jogging on the allotted paths that were located at the sides of the roads.

Realistically, we weren't going to spend lots of money on food here given our budget, so we walked around instead and it actually felt quite safe. The TV had lied to me once again. I think I'm going to have serious words with the telly when I get back to the UK. We walked around part of the lake in southern Rio called Lagoa and it was quite remarkable to see so many people exercising – it was now around 9pm and about 29-30 degrees centigrade. I was pretty hot already, just with walking, so hats off to them. The lake is linked to the ocean via a small canal and although it has some fish living in it, many have died because of the pollution and the ever-increasing algae that is robbing the lake of its oxygen. It covers the surface, preventing oxygen from reaching the water… perhaps the algae don't produce enough oxygen to counter the negative effect it's having – I don't know.

The lake itself was pretty amazing though. It was surrounded by buildings and it reflected the sparkling lights, so it almost looked like a mirror. It even reflected the many lights of the favela in the distance, making it all look quite beautiful. On the flip side, it had an array of smells – ranging from stagnant lake, to nothing, to wet dog, to fish then back to wet dog before settling on a mix of stagnant lake and wet dog.

On our way back to your room, we walked part of the way back and boarded the metro for the rest of the journey. The metro – just to say it again – is pretty great here. Once we reached Botafogo, we stopped in a supermarket. Now, when I say supermarket, I don't mean something like Tesco or Asda. These supermarkets are microscopic in comparison – basically, 2 tills are enough in these places. We were mostly after fruit and things we could take for lunch. As citizens of the world – well, Vesi being a citizen of the world and I being her tag-along sidekick – we couldn't afford to have breakfast, lunch and dinner out. We had to economise and this meant buying food from supermarkets and making it ourselves.

We walked around the supermarket as though it were a museum. Lovely papayas... which I really like, lovely looking guavas, avocadoes literally 4 times the size of the ones found in the UK, and clearly cheaper because they grow in this country. There was also a funky looking yellow fruit about the size of a grapefruit with hard, smooth, glossy skin. It looked really funny but when I buried my nose in it, it smelt of passion fruit. This? A passion fruit? No way... passion fruits look like barbecued testicles (which is why I always have to ask Vesi to cut them in half at home). It was massive, so we bought a couple to try.

The food was cheaper (clearly), but then, looking at some of the prepacked foods, the price suddenly shot up. A jar of jam... 15 reals – roughly £4. Holy crap, you can make it for a fraction of that price, especially with the fruit being inexpensive. Cheese – variable but all prohibitively expensive. Butter – 8.99 reals, which is just under £3. Holy crap again. And follow this logic – here, the meat (mainly beef) is not really expensive at around £10 per kg. Butter comes from the cream that is found resting on top when a cow is milked... and they clearly have lots of cows here (as they are a massive exporter of beef), so by that logic, why the hell is butter so expensive? Do they not have any milking cows?

So, we picked up bread, several fruits and some sandwich meat (smoked pork) and went back to our room.

Today, I didn't go into too much detail about the nightlife for 2 reasons. (1) We did not experience it fully and (2) what we did experience is like that of any city and so there was nothing particularly new.

Tomorrow will be our first full day in Rio. I look forward to it.

Day 5 – Rio de Janeiro

At 06:45 in the morning, I was up and ready for another day. Superhero? No. Noisy traffic below. I looked out the window and there was already a blockage of cars on the road. We capitalised on this, and by that, I mean I woke up and made sandwiches for lunch while Vesi slept. She managed to sleep right up to the point where I went into the room, opened the blinds, coughed several times and poked her in the bum.

After a breakfast of papaya, passion fruit and a huge segment of avocado, we headed outside. On stepping outside, the sky was a beautiful blue, the sun was shining and it was lovely and warm. It was one of those days where it felt good to be alive – not that other days don't, but it's just that, some days, it's more pronounced than others... like waking up on a grey rainy Saturday when your house is a mess, the kitchen is dirty and the bathroom plugholes are blocked by years of un-shampooed pubic hairs. On those days, you don't get out of bed, breathe in deeply and say, 'it feels good to be alive.' But today, day 5 of our holiday, was one of those days.

This is the weather you need if you want to have an outdoor lifestyle – to wake up in the morning on many days of the year and be able to walk outside and not be blown over by the wind, drenched by the rain or have you knackers frozen off by the cold. The difference is amazing. Coming down the stairs to find the guy who cleans the rooms sitting outside at 8am doing his thing (whatever that is) is a very rare sight in the UK. It is something reserved for those few days of Summer when the sun is out and the wind is low. But still, there is a definite difference – I'd say a fairly tangible difference between how it feels in Rio and how being outside on a warm day feels in the UK. By the people's behaviour in Brazil, it feels totally normal. In the UK, it's a privilege. I mean, 3 days of good weather in the UK and it looks like there has been an invasion by the lobster people (yes, ok, cooked lobster – don't get pedantic on me).

This morning was the trip to the rather large botanical gardens in Rio, so with bags on our back, sun cream on our noses, maps, Vesi with a look of cool determination and me with the look of a lost child pretending not to look lost, we walked out and to the bus stop. While I was doing the important duty of checking the bus timetable and which number to take, Vesi dragged me onto one of the buses. I'm sure she cheated, she didn't even look at the bus timetable or the time the bus was supposed to come.

The buses in Rio are the same as the ones in Foz. I know that it's the same country, but Brazil is pretty much the size of Europe so they could be forgiven for not having the same buses in the north as they do in the south, or in big cities compared to smaller cities. I think I expected Foz to have older style buses compared to Rio, but they still employed 2 people per bus; one to drive and one to sell tickets.

To be honest, it actually makes sense. In the UK, the buses are run privately by a company with shareholders, so they run things at minimum cost... some might think that's more efficient, but it's not. It's just cheaper for the company. They often have single decker buses when a double-decker is needed, and that's not efficiency, it's just bad service. If there is a queue of 2 people, the buses appear then disappear within 30 seconds, and if there is a queue of 15 people, they have to wait around 5 minutes. I know that, occasionally, they wait at a stop for a certain number of minutes, but that doesn't happen all the time or when the bus is late. With a second person on board, the bus can run more to schedule because the driver doesn't have to sit there taking payments. It also gives jobs to more people. The buses in Rio are not private which is probably why there are more than in the UK and they are actually quite more reliable, but then again, in the UK, the incentive is not service, it's profit. They'd staple people to the sides if they could. In fact, I shouldn't say that too loudly, the UK chancellor, Osborne, who is a genuine corporate whore and would sooner displace people from their homes than refuse something to a large company, might hear and I might be giving his empty head some ideas.

So, we went to the botanical gardens – Jardim Botanico. On entering, some guy was standing there and when he saw us, he said, "chikich". Oh great, I thought... here we go, some random bloke is going to try to mug us in broad daylight. I tried to ignore him and walked on when Vesi stopped me and said, "he's the guy collecting tickets".

"Ohhh, so that's what he said... cool. I've learnt a new word in Portuguese. *Chikich*". It wasn't until later that day that Vesi explained that the guy had actually said it in English. In Brazil, the letter T, depending on its position in the word, can have a

CH sound. So chikich *is* ticket… I just wasn't astute enough to understand.

The gardens themselves were astounding – huge – and astounding. It was like a little green paradise in the middle of a city poisoned by exhaust fumes.

It had a lake in the middle with a little wooden bridge over it and various species of cool looking trees, including one type of Amazonian tree where the roots split out about a metre and a half from the ground and reach out, making it look like an old man's stretched neck – it's not easy to describe. This is called a *buttress* root system. I recommend looking at photos of these online, they are impressive. They grow like that because the soil in the Amazon is very poor and the nutrients are close to the surface, so the roots don't actually go that deep. They also have to be wide so they can support the tree.

There were also cinnamon trees, and I – as any other self-respecting person would do – had to have a tiny taste. It must have looked pretty weird to people who walked past to see some guy with his lips clamped around the trunk like some sort of a tree vampire. Alas, it didn't taste very strong; in fact, it tasted of tree bark. Maybe I clamped my lips around the wrong tree and was just sucking on ordinary bark… I tried a few other tree types just in case.

There were also some really strange trees that shed their bark – like snakes shed their skin. They were in various stages of shedding… some were just starting to peel, some had large swathes of bark falling off and some were mostly bare. The bark was paper thin and brown but was sturdy to the touch like some stiff laminated plastic, and the trunk underneath was very pale beige – almost white – and incredibly smooth. I really hope the people who walked past me at the cinnamon tree were different to the people who walked past and saw me rubbing my cheek up and down the smooth trunk of one of these trees. But hey, I paid to enter, so I was going to experience these plants with ALL my senses. What was next on the list? Ah yes – the fanny plant... ok, just kidding.

There were some trees with enormous watermelon-sized fruit on them (although they weren't actually watermelons); this would be totally disallowed in the UK as the health and safety demon wouldn't allow it. They hung from the trees above from little stems attached to the trunk and were positioned next to the paths where people walked, so if one dropped and hit someone, it could do some serious damage. To top it off, the skin of the fruit was tough and was covered in very shallow pyramid-like structures – like spikes. Vesi said, "those look like a type of fruit you can get in Thailand that really stinks". In fact, a picture can say a thousand words – I have since discovered that it looks a bit like the fruit called *Durian*. Look Durian fruit up to see what they look like and then tell me it wouldn't kill you if it dropped on your head from 4 metres up. Whatever these ones were though, they were not edible.

There was a large greenhouse – well, I call it a greenhouse but, realistically, it was just a building. I doubt they really need greenhouses since it's never cold. It was full of orchids and Vesi *loves* orchids. I like them too but not quite as much. To me, they often look like someone has placed a small explosive charge in a normal flower and set it off. They also remind me of the T1000 robot from the film Terminator 2 where, at the end, just before falling off a ledge into the molten steel, he/it is shot by Arnie with some kind of explosive charge. Then, when it goes off, he's/it's all bent out of shape and looks really random. Sorry about the spoiler if you haven't seen the film. Simply put, some orchids just look like really fucked up mutant flowers.

Orchids are quite amazing flowers though, it has to be said. There are some species of orchid that produce the wonderfully fragrant vanilla pod. It's an absolute miracle these ever survived the process of evolution… a bit like the panda bear where the female is only sexually fertile for 2-3 days a year and even then, that's when the male says to her… 'sorry, love, not tonight I'm watching the Grand Prix' (and then nips off himself for a quick wank. Ok, I made that last bit up but you can imagine her having a headache for almost the entirety of the year, rejecting every one of his advances, and just as he's built up a little fantasy bubble involving grizzly bears, polar bears and maybe the odd koala, she says, "hey, sailor, let's get it on," by which point, he's thinking, "piss off, love, I've got my own thing going on here.") BTW – this is not a reflection of Vesi's and my life in case you got the wrong impression.

The vanilla orchid flower waits until it is fully grown, then one morning, the leaves open… like some bimbo spreading her legs… and then closes later that afternoon. And that's it. If it isn't pollinated in those few short hours, it won't be, the flower dies and it has to wait for another year – and I bet you thought the panda was fussy. This is why they are very often done by people these days. (NO, not the pandas... Christ, you'd need some proper pervert for that task) I mean the orchids. Some poor sod has to sit there pressing 2 flowers together so they get fertilised.

I have no idea how they survived evolution for so long before commercial vanilla farming – and that means some brown-skinned guy sticking 2 orchids together in the hope that they would 'have sex' and spawn a vanilla bean, which is then mercilessly plucked by another brown-skinned guy to treat, dry, prepare and flog to the highest bidder.

On top of that, about 1/3 of the 30,000 species of orchids are – well, I suppose the technical name for them is – bastards. They lure pollinators into their little den with the promise of nectar, force the pollinating insect through some miniature obstacle course where it brushes past the pollen, and then out the other side with absolutely nothing – sod all – zilch – not a drop of nectar. Not even a gloating sign saying, "fooled you, sucker". Basically, it remorselessly screws the insect over. How the hell did they survive evolution? I'll tell you... it's because pollinating insects are stupid. They fall for the same trick over and over again. And it's not even a difficult one to spot. One little bee says to his mate:

"Oi, George."

"What's up, Geoff?"

"Don't do the assault course on those flowers that look really fucked up like the robot in Terminator 2 that gets blown up at the end. I got suckered in... phew, never again."

"Eh? I've not seen Terminator 2. Ooh... look at that fucked up looking flower. How pretty"

And so forth...

Well, you get the picture. Small conversations like that and both vanilla and bastard orchids would not exist these days.

In the gardens, there was also a medical research centre where they try various combinations of plant and vegetable matter in an attempt to cure diseases.

And through the rows of palms and bark-shedding trees, we got to see a black beaked toucan flying around as free as a... well... bird, which is completely different to seeing them in cages or even in a large enclosure where they are able to fly around but not so freely. Standing next to a tree where a wild toucan has decided to sit is something not many people in Europe can say they've experienced. It is... for want of a better word... cool.

All in all, the gardens were pretty spectacular. But by the time we were ready to leave, it was very hot. We had to sit down in a little café for a quick coffee before disappearing off.

We got the bus to the central part of Rio du Sul (South Rio) and that was an experience in itself. Forget Alton Towers… it's expensive and even by riding Oblivion, you don't get half the white-knuckle thrill you do on some of the buses in Rio. Cornering on one of these can only be likened to cornering in a Formula 1 car.

We got off the bus outside Copacabana Beach, which is one of Rio's most famous beaches. Everyone knows the song by Barry Manilow… At the Copa… Copacabana. The hottest spot north of Havana – and so on; well, we were there and it was remarkably unremarkable. Ok, that's a bit harsh. It's a very pleasant beach but it's just one of those situations where you build something up in your mind and then when it actually comes true, it doesn't have the same impact as you hoped. The best examples I can give to represent this are the Star Wars and Matrix films. Massive films, and when people heard that they had made the sequel – or prequels in Star Wars' case, they got so excited, but when they went to watch these films, they didn't meet the expectations. Well, of course they didn't… it's almost impossible to meet the expectation of a fantasy. With Copacabana, it's a famous beach and everyone knows the name… wow… I wonder what it must be like. It must be special… different… better somehow… but how?

As it turned out, it was just another beach. Of course, it had nice white sand, but that's about it.

We didn't go on the beach itself. We went to a small bar just off it for a drink where I ordered a coconut. I've had a green coconut before in the UK (not a usual thing though, it was a festival day) but the experience was exceptionally different. It's far less pleasurable drinking from a green coconut whilst walking on an asphalt road when it's cloudy, 17 degrees, just rained 5 minutes ago and I'm looking out for traffic and gangsters because I'm in a busy yet dodgy area, than it is sitting opposite a lovely looking beach in the toasting sun where the main thought running through my mind is, "How cool is this? I am in the hottest spot north of Havana – even though we're south of Cuba". It's just a totally different experience.

The coconuts are nothing like the brown, dry coconuts available from the supermarkets in the UK where you need a pneumatic drill and seventeen sticks of dynamite just to crack the shell. Those coconuts are great, don't get me wrong… the white flesh, the dense milk… but they are nothing like the ones you can buy out in Brazil.

The coconuts in Brazil (as in many other places – including the one I mentioned I tried in the UK) are large and green and instead of having to use explosives, they can be opened with a large knife – or machete. In fact, the opening ritual is pretty funky looking. They pick up a coconut, whack the machete down on it a few times at various angles that looks random, and the top just pops off… along with the occasional finger no doubt. When the top does finally pop off, the coconut is absolutely full of water. I worked it out… it could probably hold about a pint of water depending on the size of the coconut, maybe just under. Then sitting down and looking at the coconut full of water is quite a tribute to nature.

Coconut in hand, I think I came to understand what true happiness and serenity really feels like... and for me, it is drinking cold coconut water in a really lovely place. Why's that? You might ask. Well, truth is, I'm genuinely obsessed with water. It covers about 70% of the earth which sounds impressive, but out of that, about 96.5% is salt water and 3.5% is freshwater which is made up of rivers, lakes, reservoirs and frozen water – and considering that frozen glacier water is not hugely accessible, imagine how little of that 3.5% can actually be used by us. Then consider the fact that for us to be able to drink it, the freshwater needs treating, so just imagine how little water there is for this ever-expanding population to drink and, of course – with less need for treatment – for irrigation, washing and all the other things we use water for. Water is so incredibly important and people still waste it as though it were infinite. It breaks my heart that we are so incapable of looking after this planet, but that's a different story. My point is, water is vital which is why I'm obsessed by it.

So, to me, the water inside a coconut is like that perfect little gem of life. It just tastes so clean and when it's cold, it's so fresh, with just the slightest, almost indistinguishable hint of coconut. And it's such a fantastic, natural product. In my opinion, it is just one of those very few perfect things in the world. It is its own mini water treatment unit, without the chemicals and expenditure of energy artificially generated by us.

After I'd finished the water, the inside was shell-like. I've seen them where the white flesh has started to form, and with its jelly-like consistency, it's still soft enough to scoop out with a spoon, but the flesh hadn't started forming on the ones I drank from yet.

Unfortunately, Vesi doesn't do coconut water (I guess she has to look elsewhere for the meaning of true happiness) so she had a peach iced tea. We also had lunch before taking a bus to Pão de Açúcar – Sugarloaf Mountain. Brazilians must be taking the piss here somehow. The word Pão, which means bread, is also a rude way for them to say willy. The difference being a slight change in pronunciation and I believe in the spelling there is no squiggle over the letter *'a'* to make it pao instead of pão. So, when we asked which bus we needed to take to visit Sugar-knob Mountain, the locals laughed and – hopefully – pretended not to understand. And if it's true they didn't understand, what a bunch of donkeys. We're foreign, you fuckwits! We don't get funny when you come to the UK and ask for a *piss* of cake – because you all bloody do it.

Anyway, we got there in the end.

Before going to the top, we went to a nearby beach called Praia Vermelha – the red beach. This is a tiny little beach where the sand is said to have a red tinge to it. On the way, we picked up a couple of free pamphlets about the area and the beach and had a chat with the guys at the stall. They were really friendly.

"Welcome to Brazil and Praia Vermelha."

"Thanks. Can't wait to see it. Is it really red then or is it just a name?"

"No, it's really red."

"Wow."

We walked to the edge just before the beach to soak in the view. It was completely flipping normal. Not a hint of red in sight. Not even a tinge from a discarded tampon.

I jumped down and rummaged through the sand like a dog, but nothing. Not even a red sweet wrapper. There was sand... normal sand... rather coarse sand but it was still just sand. We'd been lied to by everyone. Either that or the original colour-blind twat that thought it was red managed to convince everyone else until they believed it... like in the emperor's new clothes. I was that little boy who shouted, "the emperor's naked," except, in this case, it was, "the beach is bloody normal." Except, instead of the realisation that until now the entire world had been duped, I just had someone look up to me and say, "ju aar een mai son".

The only reason I can think to suggest it was given that name in the first place is that because the sand is coarse, the colour is a darker shade of... well, sand, and so in certain lights, (particularly – ahem – red ones) and especially if you're a bit colour blind, it might look a little red. But don't be fooled by any photos you see on the internet. The sand is not red – it's just a slightly darker shade of sand – which is usually beige. But then again, who would want to visit Praia Beige?

And this is why I don't dare get too excited about things very often. I'm a sensitive soul and hate shock disappointments, and having expectations is a sure way of never having those expectations met. I call it the 'Matrix' effect. I've just coined it now whilst writing – cool, eh?

We walked along the sand and it really was coarse. So much so, in fact, that it was actually quite difficult to walk on. Every time my foot went down, it felt like it sank down much more than on most other beaches. Now, I'm not quite the fat bastard you might think from that description, but it was quite difficult to walk on – compared to finer sand that is. It is still a lovely beach with a couple of walking paths on either side. It's nested within a little cove and does actually feel quite cosy, although some people with claustrophobia might want to stay away.

We did eventually go up Sugarloaf Mountain. It was quite late in the day and we were hoping to go up there to catch the sunset.

Sugarloaf Mountain is a mound jutting out of the sea and is so called because it looks a bit like a mound of unrefined sugar with its curved smooth top. Just next to it is the smaller, separate peak called Morro de Urca which is a smaller mound jutting out of the sea, but this doesn't have the same pronounced shape as Sugarloaf Mountain

It takes 2 cable car trips to reach the top. The first one stops at Morro da Urca which is 220 metres high. The view was pretty spectacular. We could see the whole south side of Rio, downtown Rio, the beaches, the airport a few miles away and Sugarloaf Mountain itself. Then there is a visitor's centre, some toilets and a couple of places where you can pick up some souvenirs. There is also a hiking trail to come up to this peak, but being your average plebby tourists, we didn't do that... we came by cable car.

The cable car trip itself was stunning. I love cable cars. It almost feels like flying... except for the cables, the fact that you're inside a box with windows going in one direction only and there are 30 people around you taking photographs and speaking Chinese. But apart from that, it's quite a bit like flying. The views were superb. I find I always take lots of photos on cable cars but the pictures never seem to even begin to do the views justice.

I think that's one of the beauties of visiting places rather than just seeing photos of them. A photo can make a place look fantastic and attractive, but actually being there means you can feel it with senses other than just your eyes. The feel of the warm air, the sounds (depending on where you are) and the *feel* of a place. I'm not talking about touch... I'm talking about something within... the feeling on the back of your neck when you see something wonderful but unexpected... the feeling in your chest when you can't take everything in at once and wishing you could freeze time. It's like that moment in a perfect sunset where the sun is just above the horizon and it has painted the landscape orange – you look around and wish somehow you could absorb the view into your body.

That's what I find to be the difference between being somewhere and seeing the same image on a photograph.

We took the second cable car up to Sugarloaf Mountain. The cable car rides took less than 5 minutes each. These cable cars were envisioned by an engineer called Augusto Ferreira Ramos in 1908. He was given funding by some of Rio's high society figures, then he started building and the cable car was opened in October 1912. There have been modifications since it was built, including increasing the capacity of the cable cars so that now they each hold up to 65 people.

The view from the peak of Sugarloaf Mountain was similar to the view from Morro da Urca. It *is* higher at 396 metres, so the panoramas are slightly better, but they are only improvements of what we saw from the peak of Morro da Urca. Now, I know that sounds a bit flat, but they really were fantastic views. We stood on one side to watch aeroplanes take off and land, then we moved to another side that looks out to sea, then to another side where there was a fantastic view of the south side of Rio and immediately to the left of that was a side view of the statue of Christ the Redeemer.

As you might imagine, we weren't the only bright sparks who thought about watching the sunset from Sugarloaf. Other people had the same idea.

Watching a sunset is meant to be a lovely, peaceful moment, but that's somehow tarnished when you are one of 700 people trying to cram onto one side of a viewing platform to watch it go down. The magic, somehow, disappears when 200 people in front of you lift their hands up in the air to take photographs, and because they have hundreds of people in front of them too, they wave their hands about to get an unobstructed view. So, from the outside, I can only imagine that this group of however many hundreds of people looks like a flock of ostriches bobbing their heads back and forth, left and right. And don't think for a second that I am looking down on these people with an air of superiority. In that moment, I was one of them. I took a number of crap photos.

Isn't it amazing? No matter how many crap photos you take, you always take some more, only to keep them all, make a decision of which one is the least crap of the lot and barely glance at it again. And while you're doing this, you're missing the sunset itself because you're too busy taking crap photos, knowing that they will be crap but still hoping that they won't be... which they inevitably are.

The sun went down behind Corcovado – which is the mountain that Christ the Redeemer stands on. It doesn't go down behind the statue itself, which would look amazing. It goes down just to the left, which still looks amazing admittedly but slightly less perfect than it would if it went down behind the statue itself.

I can't say that watching the sunset was the experience that I had hoped for... again, maybe I had expectations which weren't met (matrix effect), but more than anything, I think that watching a sunset crushed between 30 people is less wonderful than watching it alone or with a partner or a small group of friends.

Still, everything was lit up with an orange hue which was beautiful. The sky, the sparkles on the sea, the reflection on the glass of the buildings and even people's faces looked a bit more orange. Even Praia Vermelha looked slightly red. And as the sun slowly disappeared behind Corcovado, the lights on the south side of Rio started switching on. There is something amazing about the lights of a city being switched on at dusk.

After the sun had gone down, a lot of people left but the viewing platform we were on remained busy and we kept watch over the side, looking at the lights along the shoreline and in the city itself. Then, as the darkness drew in and the sun faded completely, all that remained were the varying colours of the lights of Rio beaming up and around.

To our left, on the top of a very dark Corcovado mountain, Christ the Redeemer was lit up too; a small figure of light in the middle of the sky surrounded by complete darkness. It did look quite spectacular. I tried to take photos of it but it was too far away to get a decent image with my little camera, so those photos will end up filed under 'crap photos of something cool'.

The other side of the viewing platform looks right out to sea and it might be a beautiful open panorama during the day, but at night, staring out into the darkness is quite chilling. It's like when you're on a boat at night and you look out to sea while standing on deck. There is just an eerie darkness going on to infinity.

We bought a couple of drinks which were about the same price as you'd get in the UK, so they were not cheap, and sat down for about an hour or so to watch the twinkling lights of the city.

It was a bit like my trip to New York in 2001 with Alessio and Priscila (before I knew Vesi). I was lucky enough to go up to the top of the World Trade Centre before it was demolished later that year. From the top, we could see the whole of Manhattan Island. We went up on a sunny March day in the afternoon, so we got to see the view during the day, and then, as the sun went down, we watched the city lights coming on slowly as the sunset turned the whole city orange. After the sun disappeared, we saw the city in the dark with all the various coloured lights from the cars, signs and buildings. It was all breathtaking.

We were among the last people to leave Sugarloaf Mountain. We had been up there for about 2 hours. We left and took the 3 km walk back to Botafogo, stopping for an açaí with banana and then at a supermarket to buy some fruit, bread and dry meats. Again, thank god Vesi was there, she knew exactly where to go. Alone, I'd have been lost within 5 minutes.

We skipped dinner altogether. When we got back to our room just after 9pm, we were shattered so we made some sandwiches and sat in the kitchenette eating them, looking like a couple of stoned zombies after a 3-day party. We went to bed.

Tomorrow, we're going on a free walking tour.

Day 6 – Rio De Janeiro

Breakfast consisted of papaya, bread rolls, avocado, cheese and dry smoked pork. Superb. Another glorious day outside; the perfect day to go out and look around Rio. So, we did.

Our original plan was to go to the Christ the Redeemer statue, but at some point after we arrived, Vesi suggested going on a free walking tour of Rio instead, so we did that instead. Don't forget, this whole thing was planned by Vesi and she knows what's going on. She has looked at the lonely planet guide and checked out all the best places to go – so she's the one in the know here.

We travelled to the centre of Rio. Wow! What a difference. The south side of Rio where we are staying is lovely, modern and beautiful and you actually feel like you are somewhere exotic, especially when you walk around the beach areas, but the centre... Jesus... you might as well be in Birmingham on a sunny day. We got off at the metro station *Carioca* and walked out straight into a pedestrian zone. If I were to describe it in a few words, I'd say dirty, grimy, grey, smoggy, busy, oppressive, and there was a generally uneasy feeling about it... so, exactly like Birmingham on a sunny day.

There were 3 police cars and about 10 policemen standing around the area. It felt a bit like New York. Then there were some weird shouts, a couple of screams and some police sirens, and even now, I still have no real idea what happened. We heard a few words being muttered about someone having stolen something, but it was in Portuguese so they could have been saying that it was a particularly warm day that day for all we know. However, with the look of mild alarm on people's faces, we think that something dodgy happened.

We went to a certain part of the pedestrian zone where there were people congregated who all looked a bit lost but were pretending they weren't. They must have been there for the walking tour. Vesi and I joined the ranks and put on our pretending not to look lost faces too. That is the face where you try to look like you belong while secretly keeping an eye out for anyone who could be the guide and surreptitiously taking photos of various bits and bobs that might seem interesting, hoping you don't get conned into walking away with someone who later turns out to be a mugger.

A girl appeared. Quite tall, not super slim but with a friendly face, 'Ahaa... she must be the one,' I thought, 'sent here to pretend she's our guide and take us somewhere where a bunch of blokes will beat us up and nick our wallets'. You might have guessed by now, I don't trust people very easily... too many times have I been given the wrong directions to suddenly trust a random person in a red T-shirt who says she's our guide. 'We'll see how this plays out. If things get a bit weird, I'll grab Vesi and leg it', I thought.

She started telling us about Rio as a city. Ok... she had my attention, but I didn't let my guard down.

In Brazil, there are 2 seasons: Summer and Hell. Summer is actually Winter, which is our Summer in the UK, i.e. early September. Hell is Summer, which is actually our Winter and is terribly hot. Clear? ...What do you mean no?

OK... Brazil is a hot country and it's warm in Winter too. In fact, so warm that it's almost always hotter than Summer in the UK. She said they call Winter, Summer because it's nice and pleasant outside. It's hot but you can do things. But they call their actual Summer, Hell because temperatures can rise into some pretty horrendous levels... i.e. the mid-40s.

In all honesty, I doubt they actually call their Winter Summer. It's probably just something they tell pasty vampire white UK tourists to highlight how it's never cold there, and while we are burning natural gas or huddling around a fire to try to stay warm, they are mostly naked and lying on a beach fanning themselves to try to cool down.

The locals in Rio are known as Cariocas (one Carioca, two Cariocas) which comes from the indigenous Tupi language – pronounced Karaioka – and it means "white man's house". When the white Portuguese arrived, the name was adopted for them. I am surprised it doesn't actually mean "pasty vampire wankers who came here to steal our land and kill people," because that would have been more apt.

The Portuguese arrived in Rio in January 1502 with an expedition led by explorer, Gaspar de Lemos. Thinking that he'd arrived at the mouth of a river, he named it the January

River, or *Rio de Janeiro*, but there was no River – just a cove. At the time, the region was inhabited by the indigenous people of Brazil the *Tupi*, the *Puri*, the *Botocudo* and the *Maxakalí*.

The French appeared in 1555 with 2 ships and 600 colonists. They took possession of the small island of Serigipe (known as Villegagnon Island these days – just 3 miles north of Sugarloaf Mountain) and decided to set up base there themselves. The Portuguese paid little attention to this and the French called for more colonists a couple of years later. 300 more arrived in 1557 and things carried on quite calmly until 1560 when the new governor-general, *Mem de Sá* (yes, that's a name), received order from the Portuguese government to expel the French. So, with 2,000 soldiers and 26 warships, he attacked. With the help of the natives, the French mostly legged it to the mainland where they continued their lives.

In 1565, the city was officially founded and named in honour of St Sebastian who was the namesake of Dom Sebastian (the king of Portugal and the Algarves at the time). The city was, therefore, named São Sebastião do Rio de Janeiro. Eventually, the São Sebastião was dropped and just the Rio de Janeiro remains.

In the 1690s, some Portuguese settlers (called the Bandeirantes) who were exploring Brazil found gold and precious stones in some mountains in the state of Minas Gerais. This launched the start of Brazil's gold rush (which is the term used for the discovery of gold along with other precious metals and rare stones and minerals). Rio was a major trading city and was a lot closer than Salvador – Brazil's capital at the time – so it became more practical to transport gold, diamonds, etc. from Minas Gerais via Rio than via Salvador, and eventually, in 1763, the capital was relocated to Rio. From there, it remained Brazil's capital city until 1960 when it was changed to Brasilia.

In 1808, the Portuguese royal family fled to Brazil to escape from Napoleon's attempted invasion of Portugal where they hunkered down for a few years and returned in 1821.

A couple of other events on the timeline: In 1887, slavery was abolished, and in 1888, after some disagreements with Portugal, Brazil declared independence and the two countries signed a declaration to that effect.

So, that was a tiny bit of Brazil's history and how Rio came to be Rio. There was loads more, including slavery, disease, pirates and pole dancers – ok, maybe not pole dancers – but I don't want to focus only on history and abstract concepts of royal families because I know that more than 3 lines bores many people to death – including me. Besides, history is written from someone's point of view, so although the events might be accurate, the reasons may be completely wrong. Put simply, history is a mix of truth weighed down with oodles of bullshit.

The guide walked us around some artworks and such and said, "ju yu knows what ees de nateural looking of a Brazilian porson?" We ran it through a translator – "What does a

BRAZILIAN person look like?" Well, I personally thought Brazilian women were all hot, tanned, slim and mostly naked. Not sure about Brazilian men.... Hmmm... tanned, thin moustache, pot belly and large overbite?

As it turns out, anyone can look Brazilian. The country over the years has had such a mishmash of cultures that it's almost impossible to tell what a true Brazilian is anymore. It's true that the Tupians were around initially – I suppose they were tanned and mostly naked, but somehow, it doesn't quite hit my g-spot. Also, I guess the 'Red' Indians were indigenous to the United States, but if I were to ask you what an American looks like, you might picture a fat white man with a milkshake in one hand and a gun in the other, yelling... "Ahm gonna sue yer".

So, Brazilians can look like anyone. This is just as well really because the elections are coming soon and there are hundreds of posters plastered around the city in Rio (as well as in Foz) of the nominees with plastic smiles and the look that – like Boris Johnson – says, "I'd say or do anything to get elected, but once I'm in... you're fucked."

And all these posters have very different looking people on them. White, black, tanned, bone through the nose, slaughtering a chicken, sacrificing a white virgin... ok, a couple of those are made up, but the gist of it is that these candidates/criminals – however you look at it – are all Brazilian and that's the norm. There is genuine multiculturalism here from what I can see... unlike a lot of western countries that just pretend to be and feel forced to pay lip service to it. I look forward to the day where I see a black leader of the conservatives in the UK.

In Rio, the average salary is around 1,300 reals (about £600) per month. The average salary of a twat… I mean, politician here is 15,000 reals (£6,800) per month. Small wonder why money-grabbing tosser criminals want the job. It's free money for doing nothing and being able to ignore laws.

The guide walked us around the streets. We went to the oldest coffee shop in Rio, but far from being a cosy little place that's a bit run down, it was huge, shiny, glorious and bloody expensive… we didn't buy a coffee. We bought an expensive cake which was ok but overpriced and then we scarpered. Visiting places like this on free walking tours seems a bit pointless and forced, but the guides have to take us to some of these places as they get some kind of commission. I guess it adds to the flavour.

Outside the city centre area, it was actually quite nice and less commercial. It was the more commercial bit where people walk around the shops that I found grimy – just look at any town centre in the UK. It's the general public area where you'll invariably see a fat woman in Lycra waiting for a fat man in Lycra outside the public toilet and a little old lady sitting on a bench with her legs open. Outside of all this, it was quite nice, and by quite nice, I mean edifices with clear history to them, lovely architecture and less overtly commercial. We stopped at the Escadaria Selarón. This was a staircase covered in an arrangement of colourful tiles.

Jorge Selaron was an artist who moved from Chile to Brazil and literally lived right where we were standing. Part way up the staircase to the right there was a door into a building and that was the entrance to his house. One day, he looked outside his front door and thought the staircase was ugly so he started to lay down some tiles to smarten it up a bit, and over time, bit by bit, the entire staircase was tiled in lovely colourful tiles – it really does look spectacular. There are pictures in the tiles, pictures and writings made up of tiles, tiles up the wall next to the staircase and the whole place looks like some kind of insanely decorated bathroom. It is so – well – for want of a better word – cool. People would bring him tiles to stick up and the staircase became renowned throughout Rio. Unfortunately, he was found dead lying on his decorated steps in 2013. The cause of death was either not known or not made public.

This is exactly the kind of thing you could never do in England. Some overpaid mouth-breathing nobody who left school at 16 with 1 GCSE in drama – grade E – finds a random job for the council and, somehow (via the mysteries of how councils function in the UK), ends up being given too much authority and would look at the beautiful staircase with incredibly dopey eyes and make up some health and safety excuse to have the tiles removed.

Council nobody – "Erm... the tiles are a danger because they... do... ca... pr... erm... they reflect too much light and people walking up them might be blinded and fall down the stairs. The colours might also upset older residents, so we want them grey."

Older resident – "but we like the colours."

Council nobody – "no... sorry, this is a democratic process and people prefer grey."

Other older resident – "I like the colours too."

Council nobody – "No, the decision has been made. Grey it has to be. It's for your safety."

Another older resident – "No, but I like the colours too, and they're fine to walk on."

Council nobody – "No. I have democratically voted for everyone. Grey it is."

All older residents – "But we don't like grey, we like the colours!"

Council nobody – "You voted for the councillors and this is how democracy works. Grey it is."

All residents – "But in your manifesto, you said you'd listen to people. You lied to us."

Council nobody – "I am listening to you. You're a minority group. All the other people who haven't said anything are clearly happy with grey."

All residents – "They have no idea about this. They are all shopping in Primark. You haven't asked them. There has to be a vote."

Council nobody – "Grey it is."

That's how democracy works.

Ironically, I'm just bitter I didn't study drama and got an E in geography instead. Otherwise, you never know, I could have been councillor nobody working for the council, earning a good salary and doing nothing for it.

The walking tour ended in a restaurant (as they often do) where they serve traditional national dishes. In this case, the dish was called *Feijoada*. This is a typical Brazilian dish made with pork, beans and kale in some kind of a dark sauce. It came with rice and had some garlicky powder on the side. It was, at best, edible. I wouldn't order it again if there was something else on the menu. I was quite surprised actually. I'm pretty good with food and I'll try almost anything once – not that I'm the Bear Grylls type who would eat raw musking elephant testicles and dung beetle arseholes, but I was (and still am) surprised that with some of the best beef in the world and great weather for barbecues, one of the national dishes was a type of stew. Although, having said that, stews are all the rage in Persian cooking too, so it's pretty clear that the whole 'stews in winter because they warm you up and salads in summer' is somewhat of a myth. Maybe it's because typical stewing vegetables traditionally could be picked in winter – like carrots, parsnips, sprouts, etc.

One of the really good things about these free walking tours is that you get chatting to random people, usually from different countries who are all sharing the same experience as you are – and everyone has a different story to tell which is always great to hear. With the number of destinations we were visiting over the 3-week period, ours was the one people were most interested in – even if I do say so myself – but that's only because of the time frame. Some people had been travelling for a few months and had visited a number of countries, so they had incredibly interesting stories to tell too.

Although it was a free walking tour, it's customary to leave a tip at the end. I can see how this is a nice little earner for the organisers and a nice little extra for the guides who might be doing this in their spare time.

On leaving, we went – as quickly as we could – to the Copacabana/Ipanema area on Rio's south side to try to catch another free walking tour. The first was in and around the city centre, this other one was on the southern beach area.

Our guide this time was a short bloke from Chile who had come to Brazil for a holiday and decided to stay here. I'm always amazed and, in some cases, a bit envious of people who do things like that. There are loads of airy fairy people who consider themselves to be *free spirits* because they walk with no shoes on and have multiple sex partners, but I consider people like this guy from Chile a more genuine free spirit. A guy goes on holiday and doesn't return because he preferred his holiday destination to his home. I'd love to be able to do that.

A few years ago, I went out with a girl for a few weeks. One evening, she looked at me and said, "I see you as a free spirit", which felt really amazing. It made me feel like I had become the person I wanted to be – and then she dumped me. Hmmm... but I did find Vesi, so in this circumstance, all's well that ends well.

With this tour, we walked up Copacabana Beach and then onto Ipanema. These beaches can be recognised by the patterns on the paving slabs on the path in front that separates them from the road. There's no use describing them because they are nothing more than patterns. If you're interested, I recommend looking them up. Perhaps type 'Copacabana pattern' or 'Ipanema pattern' into your search engine and you'll see them. They're nothing special, they're just patterns that would make you think... aha, Copacabana... or aha, Ipanema. A bit like the 666 squiggle that's the sign of the devil... Nothing special, but it's recognisable.

Copacabana district has a 4km stretch of beach which is one of the most famous in the world. The area was named after a chapel was constructed with a replica inside of the *"Virgen de Copacabana"* – virgin of Copacabana – who was the patron saint of Bolivia. Before that, until the mid 18th century, the area had been called *Sacopenapã* which was Tupi for "the way of the socós" – the socós being a type of bird. Why the difference in spelling? I don't know. Maybe the Tupians pronounced them sacos.

The chapel, which we walked around on the tour, was built over by something that is much closer to our hearts as human beings... a fort carrying guns and cannons and weapons. Back to one of the human race's 2 principal loves. You can just picture it now:

"Hmmm... ey, Pedro?"

"Yes, Pedro?"

"Ay no like de chapel... it look too moch like de symbol of de peace."

"Ay agree, Pedro. Bot what are we going to put een iis pleice?

"Ay don no, Pedro... Ohh wait a meenute... Ay no... Gons... Lot of gons."

"Yes, Pedro... Ay like eet. For de keelleen and de morder and de warring. Ay like, ay like."

"Yes, yes... jou getting me now... Excellent, Pedro. Bot, Pedro... Ay Jos 'ave won question."

"Yes, Pedro?"

"Why jou have a Mexeecan accent?"

Ok, I'm paraphrasing a conversation there... in real life, it's possible that one of them might not have been called Pedro.

The beaches are divided into sections with numbers. The numbers denote a particular 'posto' which is a lifeguard post. From what I understood on Ipanema beach, the sections between these lifeguard posts informally denote people's particular preferences too. Posto 7 (life guard post 7) is for surfers and the favela, Posto 8 is for families. Between 8 & 9 is the gay section. Posto 9 is the young and hip area and then Posto 10 is for the richer people.

Postos 1 & 2 are Leme beach which is in the Copacabana district and blends into Copacabana beach. Then up to Posto 5 is Copacabana beach. There isn't really a Posto 6 it seems. I didn't see one and there doesn't appear to be one on the map and Ipanema beach starts at Posto 7 and goes up to Posto 10. Then the Leblon district starts past a small canal and Leblon beach passes Postos 11 & 12. Leblon is a very affluent place apparently – i.e. plastic perky tits only.

I'll be honest, I have absolutely no idea what all that means. Maybe I didn't stay on the beach long enough to see a tanned guy mincing towards me, or see people smoking tobacco through a 100 real note, or catch some coolios doing some flipmungotastic whizz popping beechams on their shibams (maybe you have to be under 15 to understand that, and pretty clever too because I just made it up). But, basically, there were people on the beach… and that's all I could tell.

And after these sections of beaches, which appear to get richer the further you go, and finally reaching Leblon, the world changes and you get the Vidigal favelas.

Now, there is a lot to say about the favelas but I'll try to condense it a bit. I'd hate to think that I'm culturing you to the point where you are so numb that you don't even realise you're bored.

The favelas are, as everyone (apart from people who read The Sun) knows, Brazil's slums… The equivalent in England would be a lot of whatever southerners think is north of Birmingham.

We were given two stories about the rise of the favelas – I'll tell you what they were in a couple of sentences but I had to go and look it up on the internet… yes, ok, I cheated, but hey, I don't want to give you false information… if it's wrong then fine… let me know and I will happily change it.

Story 1 – When the Portuguese Royal family came to Brazil, people living in the houses were given 24 hours to leave their homes, and so having nowhere else to go, they ended up in the surrounding areas, which is how the favelas were effectively born.

Story 2 – Following the Canudos war (1895-1898) – Brazil's bloodiest civil war which was a conflict between the Brazilian state and some 30,000 settlers in Canudos (northeast Bahia –

northeast Brazil) – soldiers were brought back to Rio de Janeiro and were all promised homes. However, the Brazilian government pulled a Greece and said, "sorry, we're skint now. No money for houses but you can still hang around in the surrounding areas and build your own homes," and so, the favelas were born.

And to give an explanation of what I found out (by cheating and looking on the internet), it turns out that the second explanation might be more correct... or at least correct by my research standards. In the end, who knows which part of History is right or wrong? History is written by the winners... i.e. the ones who killed the others. Doesn't mean they were right. As a kid, we used to play cowboys and Indians and the Indians were always the bad guys. However, as we know, they were not the bad guys, they were the good guys, and that's a history we know about. Imagine if Hitler had won the 2nd world war, then he'd be perceived as the good guy and the Americans would be history's bad guys.

The Canudos war itself started because the president at the time, Prudente de Moraes, believed that the spiritual preacher, Antônio Conselheiro, who had gathered a mass of followers (mostly farmers), might try to attack the city of Juazeiro in the Bahia region, so he sent soldiers to crush the uprising. This failed, so a larger army was sent, then they failed and so another army was sent until, eventually, the uprising was stopped, but not before around 25,000 of Antônio's followers and around 5,000 soldiers were killed. Although, some historians believe that the number of Antônio's followers who were killed was more like 15,000. Maybe one lesson there is that if you're going to go to war, proper weapons are preferable to pitchforks and eggs. But on the flip side, you can't eat a gun.

On the soldiers' return, they set up camp on the outskirts of Rio whilst waiting for the government to house them... which they never did. Kind of an 'I'll relinquish my humanity and risk my life in your war, and after that, you can forget I did that for you and do nothing for me in return' arrangement. A bit like the army today, except I don't think in those days recruitment to soldiery was done by showing kids a video of people camping and going windsurfing with beautiful big-breasted girls.

So, in the end, they remained in the surrounding areas of the land they were promised and made their lives there. The area supposedly reminded the soldiers of the location in Bahia where they had gone to war and where an indigenous – skin irritating – tree grew. They nicknamed their home on the hill in the outskirts of Rio *favela* (after this particular tree), thus calling them favelas for the first time.

Then, as people moved further South from the North to work in Rio's growing industry, the favelas organically increased in size. They were classed as an urban 'underclass' but they grew in size, and because the government pretty much ignored them and didn't provide them with amenities, they started to provide sanitation, transportation and medical care for themselves and for the community around them.

Put simply, there was a housing shortage in Rio and the government – because it's a government – couldn't be arsed to resolve it.

Unfortunately, because these communities were largely ignored and uncontrolled, they descended into a culture of drugs and violence.

Fortunately, though, some favelas have been pacified, and because of the outrageous prices now in South Rio, they have become somewhat of a status symbol and people actually want to stay there. Some favelas in more northern parts of Rio are still riddled with drugs, murders, prostitution and politicians, so they are caked in filth, corruption and degradation (...like 10 Downing Street and the White House).

And you know the saying that goes something like – you can take the X out of Y but you can't take the Y out of the X... e.g. you can take the farmer out of the countryside but you can't take the countryside out of the farmer. It's a saying to suggest that a person deep down does not change even if his life circumstances do. Well... David Beckham has bought a nice little shanty retreat in Rio's Vidigal favela – maybe for the times that he misses parts of Manchester. This isn't 100% confirmed but it wouldn't surprise me.

The guide we had is living in a favela at the moment. They have gone from being the slums to being housing for ordinary people and, in fact, the ones around the Ipanema/Copacabana (Vidigal) district are pretty posh and very expensive.

The Vidigal favela is pacified and so ok to visit, but as I said, I don't really fancy visiting the Brazilian slums even though they are quite a tourist attraction. It feels too voyeuristic and regardless of how touristy it is, somewhat disrespectful. It reminds me of the Banksy artwork of a fat couple in a 2-wheeled carriage smiling and taking a selfie whilst the carriage is being pulled along by what looks like a small African child dressed in rags. Look it up – it's really good and very poignant.

Still, renting a place in this favela costs around 300-700 (£150-£350ish) reals per month which is not very cheap considering it's meant to be for the poorest people. On the other hand, rental prices in the main town are more along the lines of 1,000-2,000 (£450-£900) per month for a 2-bedroom flat which is what you'd expect to pay in any city of the UK– including Birmingham. We were told that to buy a property in South Rio, it would cost between 1 & 5 million reals (£400K-£2.2 million).

So, as I mentioned previously – but I think it's worth mentioning again – this is why most people live at home for much longer than would be considered standard in the UK or even in most of Europe. It's just too expensive to move out. It is also why there is great demand for motels like the Panda Hotel where you pay by the hour. Our guide was saying that there is lots of infidelity in Brazil. Many Brazilian women try to find non-Brazilian men because they don't trust them, but it swings both ways. Our guide was Chilean and, at one point, he had a Brazilian girlfriend with whom he got on really well. He met her parents and thought things were great and that she might even be 'the one'. But it turned out that she'd been seeing numerous other men at the same time. Apparently, he'd never told her that they should make it an 'exclusive' relationship so she'd been going about her business as normal in a Brave New World-esque manner. She didn't even try to hide it apparently, which is why his episode with 'the one' lasted just under 2 months.

The tour of the beaches also took us to the Veloso bar near Ipanema where it is said that Antônio Carlos Jobim and Vinicius de Moraes were inspired to write the girl from Ipanema song. I'm not really one for being impressed with locations where a famous person was said to have been, or where a particular event was said to have taken place. Saying that though, take me to Hiroshima and I'll be impressed... but a place where someone sat and wrote a song about a girl... hmmm, not so much. Show me a picture of her naked then I'll be more impressed. It's like when people are amazed to sit in a chair that Arnold Schwarzenegger once sat in. Not my thing but we all got a free shot of Cachaça out of it which was a nice touch, along with a little bit of advertising.

The tour ended in the late afternoon with the group sitting down by Lagoa Lake to have a chat as opposed to going to a restaurant or an eatery, which was a nice refreshing change from other free walks we'd been on. Afterwards, most of the group walked back together to the Copacabana area before disbanding.

The beaches are a big part of Rio's culture. It's totally different here in Brazil to how it is in many other countries – or at least, many of the other countries I've been to. The difference is somewhat intangible. Everywhere else I've been to with a beach seems to have it as not just a focal point but the raison d'être for the town. The existence of the beach in these places literally *is* the lifeblood of the town/resort. If the flip flop wearing, towel holding, red-shouldered, nose peeling, camera-toting tourists were to disappear overnight, so would all the businesses, souvenir shops, beach paraphernalia shops, bars and restaurants in a matter of days.

However, in Rio, the beach is not just a place for tourists to go and spend 2 weeks getting spit roasted (no sexual innuendo intended), buying inflatable dolphins to take into the sea and spending the hours of the midday sun sat inside a restaurant café. The beach here is simply part of the city. On one side of the road, there are the usual small fruit juice shops, bars and restaurants, etc. But, on the other side, there are expensive homes and office blocks where people go to work for their daily crust of bread. If all the tourists disappeared overnight, then of course there would be significant closures of attractions, shops, etc. but Rio wouldn't die because the beach is part of daily life for the locals too. Some people leave the office at the end of the afternoon or go out for lunch and go to the beach which is just across the road... literally. The beach here is like the equivalent of living in London and going for a walk in zone 1 on a Saturday on a sunny day or lunching in Hyde Park on a Monday.

Later on in the evening, Vesi and I took a stroll through the Rio night street market in front of Copacabana Beach to have a look at and potentially buy a few nik-naks. You know what I mean, those bits of crap you feel you have to buy when you're abroad but when you get back home they end up at the back of a drawer only to be found a few years later and given away as a present to someone you don't actually like.

The market was really extensive and, like all similar markets, it was full of bits and bobs and nifty little souvenirs along with complete and utter shite that makes you wonder how the hell these people stay in business by selling coloured strings with knots in them and ping pong balls with googly eyes.

We walked past a stall with some really beautiful and colourful paintings on a canvas. Paintings of the favelas or sunsets behind the Christ the Redeemer. They weren't beautiful in the sense that they were picture perfect, precise and accurate. They were beautiful because they were really lovely and colourful and looking at them was fun and enjoyable.

We asked the guy at the stall how much they cost and he said he was looking for the equivalent of £200. We stared at them for a while longer – almost contemplating it – but then we walked away, still contemplating it.

10 stalls later, we came across another guy with very similar pictures. They were just as lovely and colourful, but these ones only cost £15. Hmmm... slight difference? We wondered whether there was any difference to these paintings. They were all actual paintings, not prints or copies, so were they any different to the ones costing £200? Yes, they were different...

these cost less than 1/10th of those other ones we saw. And it turned out there were quite a few similar stalls selling these paintings for £10 - £20.

You cannot imagine the sigh of relief that went through us as we woke up to the fact that the first bloke was simply trying to rip us off massively. Quite clever really. I almost felt like going back to shake his hand, telling him how clever he was – then setting his stall on fire – for the cunning plan of placing himself near the beginning of the market where people walking in from one particular direction would stop first, maybe buy one of these expensive paintings and then, 10 minutes later (when it's too late), realise they had been ripped off. Thing is... this guy didn't count on meeting Sergio and Vesi who are always so indecisive that sometimes we even struggle to buy food when we're hungry. Besides, getting ripped off like that makes you feel like a complete sucker. I once got ripped off for 90p by a homeless person selling the big issue magazine. Never again. Put it this way, if they can afford to smoke, they are not hard up enough to be hobos.

Clearly... given what I just said above... we bought nothing and went back to the air Bnb place, stopping to buy some sandwich ingredients and fruit.

Back in the room, knackered and pleased we hadn't been ripped off, we went to sleep.

Tomorrow night, we leave for Manaus and the... tsk... Amazon... the bloody Amazon. Secretly, I'm not really looking forward to that so much, but we still have tomorrow day. It should be a good day before we get barbecued by some cannibals or eaten by some disgusting creature that loves nothing more than to suck your brains out. Still… you've got to laugh, eh?

Day 7 – Rio de Janeiro

We were up early again to the sound of horns and traffic jamming outside our window, but it didn't matter, it was sunny. Crikey, how often do we wake up to sun seven days in a row back home in the UK? Maybe a couple of times a year, and then they declare a drought. In all honesty, I even start to worry that our reservoirs will dry up if it hasn't rained for 3 days. I've started to join in with the 80-year-olds in saying, "ooh, too warm today," when it's 15 degrees and I'm still wearing a jumper.

I opened the windows to take in a deep breath... Ahh warm, polluted air – it just doesn't get better than this. Admittedly though, there were a few wisps of cloud and visibility wasn't great, and that's not just because there was another building right in front of us.

Today, we were meant to go to Christ the Redeemer but as Vesi and I sat down outside on the front step to the house, she started sending and receiving a number of text messages.

I was thinking – what the bloody hell? We're on holiday and she's on her phone. Seriously? Have we reached that point where being on her phone is her entire existence? Is this it? I've been in several situations in Autumn/Spring on a sunny day at work where someone has asked, "is it cold outside?" and people have picked up their phones and said, "it's 15 degrees outside... Oh, and my phone says it's raining." Well I guess your flipping phone is right then. Rather than stand up and walk 5 metres and put your hand out of the door… best consult with a device created by intelligent people, operated by average joe public and observed by some cowardly unseen forces.

"We're here about to go and see one of Rio's most impressive monuments and you're texting?" I asked. "You have another family or something? Do they know you are in Brazil right now? Are they going to be ok without you for a couple of weeks?"

"No," she replied. "I'm trying to arrange a surprise for you."

"A surprise? For me? Oh my god. That's so sweet."

She handed me the travel guide and asked if I could guess what it was. I rifled through the little sticky labels… restaurant? No. Hostel? No. Another restaurant? No. Beach? No. Then I saw it… Hang gliding! Hmmm, I thought. Vesi knows about my obsession with aeroplanes and flying as well as my obsession with water and water recycling – she could either be arranging a hang gliding experience or perhaps a trip to the local sewers.

I felt a bit naff for thinking bad thoughts about Vesi on her phone, but realistically, how often does the head down in the phone mean your girlfriend is looking to surprise you and not just checking Facebook to find out what a friend had for lunch and watch a video of a dog wearing a pair of sunglasses? God, have we lost the meaning of life? I should write a book about it. I know just what to say in it too. It starts with 'Get off your fucking phone' and ends with 'don't ever trust a politician'.

Next thing I knew, Vesi had whisked me away from it all and we didn't come to rest until we reached… an appropriate bus stop.

Vesi pointed to where we were going on the map. A different part of Rio… not a huge distance away but far enough for me to say, "Well, Vesi, we won't be in Kansas anymore". I was pretty apprehensive. This part of Rio was a lot more run down than where we were staying in Botafogo, so even though I was putting on a brave face, I was actually making sure I knew which direction I could run away to, dragging Vesi along behind me.

Two dodgy feeling bus journeys later (where we looked like a couple of chickens at a turkey convention), we reached a spot near a lovely looking beach. I do and always will be amazed by Vesi's ability to know where to get off a bus in a place where we have never been.

I have to admit, hang gliding is something I've always wanted to do. It was on my bucket list. I've been bungee jumping, parachuting, I have trained for my private pilot's licence and basically done a whole load of things which involve me being in the air. Hang gliding was something I hadn't done and still really wanted to try – it's not the only thing I'd love to do though. I remember seeing an advert once where a guy was skiing down a mountain, and when he reached the end of the piste, instead of stopping, it went off the edge of a cliff – he skied right off the edge whilst wearing a parachute. I've never forgotten that. I would love to do something like that too but I can only just ski and I'd need to be a proper skydiver. I guess accountancy will have to do me for now – oh god, how did I go so wrong?

The weather was a bit touch and go. The wind wasn't quite in the right direction and the guy named Paul who Vesi had been talking to was not keen on taking us up as he wasn't 100% comfortable with the wind conditions.

He asked around and some other guy volunteered to take me – he was as big as me so that would have meant almost 30 stone in weight hanging from a hang glider. The words 'plummeting' and 'rock' sprang instantly to mind.

We were driven up a long road and when we reached the top, we were faced with a 10 or 20-metre wooden ramp that sloped down off the edge of a cliff into the great big nothing. Looking at it was pretty frightening. Not the kind of place you'd want to hang around the edge of on a windy day.

The main instruction for me was, "once we start running down the ramp, don't stop running or the glider will swing across and the momentum will drag us over the edge and we will probably fall to our horrible, gruesome deaths." (Ok, I added the words 'horrible' and 'gruesome' in myself for effect – but it worked, didn't it?) What a prospect, with the instructor, I had to run off the edge of a cliff which instinctively is against our nature because running off cliffs usually results in a grim death... on the other hand... once we started running, if we tried stopping, then we'd probably fall off the edge in such a way that it would probably result in our horrible and gruesome deaths. Loved the choice.

In all honesty, though, I wasn't really nervous. In the past, I've stood in a little cabin that was numerous metres above a car park, watched by hundreds of people who expected me to jump off and hurtle down towards a Ford Escort before being twanged back up by an elastic band. I was also nearly killed under a parachute on only my third jump when it didn't open properly (1 in 10,000 that one). And also, I am a mediocre and badly paid accountant, so for several hours a day, the possibility of shifting off this mortal coil would feel like a promotion in life. Ergo, in all honesty, running off a cliff was not particularly scary.

We ran down the little ramp. Thoughts of stopping or the urge to stop didn't even enter my mind and I ran like a chronically depressed Jihadi lemming anxious to get his 72 lemming virgins in the afterlife. However, the ramp didn't stay under our feet for very long. Within a few short steps, the hang glider lifted us up and off and out over the beach and towards the sea.

Wow. The wonderful feeling of gliding slowly through the air is the closest thing I can think of to flying like a bird... much like underneath a parachute which travels even slower. There was no engine to make noise and I wasn't hurtling towards the ground at 100mph. I – we – were flying... turning left and then right and then left again and then right again and the scenery was beautiful. It was sunny and we were flying over the beach with the sea in front of us and grassy hills to the side which had been divided up into fields.

The flight was all too brief though. We circled in over the beach like an aeroplane approaches the runway. When I've got these feelings, I don't like to let them go, so in my mind, I kept repeating to myself, "still flying, still flying, still flying, still flying" right up until the moment my feet touched down in the sand and we fell into a crumpled heap on the beach – a part reserved for hang gliders to land I assume. I'd had thoughts of landing on top of a topless middle-aged sunbathing woman... or her husband... or worse... someone's barbecue.... But fortunately, we had that bit of beach to ourselves.

I stood up, cool as a cucumber (even though I hate cucumbers), brushed the sand off my t-shirt and shorts and walked to the side to wait for Vesi. I was cool on the outside but inside I was thinking... wonderful... wonderful... wonderful, and again... wonderful. I had managed to do one more thing I'd always wanted to do and I'd done it in Rio de Janeiro off a cliff, out over the beautiful blue sea and came in to land on a white sandy beach with very few people on it.

It was a good 5-7 minutes before Vesi came in too. In that time, I did get the terrible feeling she'd been kidnapped by some drug-pushing Juanitos... whatever that means, but it fits the sentence nicely, so I hope you get me.

Luckily, it was just my overactive imagination and I saw her and the instructor floating down, circling around and coming in to land just a few metres away from where we landed. I ran over to her and gave her a big hug. Had I been a bit more of a sissy, I'd probably have cried... but I'm not, so I didn't.

Back at the hang gliding kiosk, we saw that Paul bloke who asked if we wanted to buy photos of the flight. The hang gliders all had cameras installed and took a load of photos for people to buy if they wanted memories of the experience.

Vesi bought some. 60 reals was pretty steep but she'd never done anything like this. I've still got a video at home of my first ever parachute jump. A video camera had been installed onto the wing of the aeroplane that had taken us up... £15 and the only interesting part – i.e. where I jump out – only lasts about 4 seconds. I loved the idea but like a truly beautiful sunset, no photo will ever capture the absolute majesty of the live experience. Paul was shocked but I declined the photo set. Vesi's would be enough.

The bus back felt just as dodgy as the bus on the way there, but a) we were feeling pretty good by that point and b) we had a couple of hundred fewer reals to nick – so we relaxed. It was about 2pm when we got back and our flight was at 8pm, so we didn't really have time to go anywhere. We packed our bags and left for the airport, stopping to pick up some lunch at a supermarket on the way and I think I started to understand why the Brazilians are beginning to plump up like Americans. Sugar upon sugar upon sugary crap upon artificially flavoured plastic sugary crap. Fat women buying coke zero and a big pile of sugary crap. To buy something with "natural" ingredients was really extortionate. Fortunately, we had no desire to buy a £5 (equivalent value) Terry's chocolate orange, and it begs the question... who the hell does? I know I said all this before but I find it staggering, so I had to mention it again.

We went to the underground station. We'd not seen it during rush hour and it's an experience I'll never forget. I mentioned the buses in Foz... well, they were first class seating compared to the metro during rush hour in Rio. This was the single most crowded location I have ever experienced in my life – ever. NEVER have I been more cramped ANYWHERE and I've been to see Lionel Richie at Glastonbury festival. I can only imagine this is what babies feel like a couple of days before they are born... that's how cramped it was. The people were crammed in there like a whitehead zit that was ready to burst. I didn't even have to hold on to anything (apart from my wallet and my testicles). We were so crammed that even when the metro was slowing down, I barely moved, although I did feel sorry for the girl standing in front of me who wasn't even tall enough to reach my armpits... I kept thinking she should have brought a snorkel – especially since I farted a couple of times.

Fortunately, half the underground had cleared out by the time we reached our stop. Unfortunately, this meant that there were still more people in the carriage than a taxidermist could have squeezed in and, equally unfortunately, the door was on the other side of the train to us, which would have been ok had we not had luggage. Clearly, we made it and we reached the airport, but trying to get out with our luggage was a bit like how I'd imagine a race trying to escape a big vat of super glue

– you have just a few seconds to push your way through before it closes you in. We felt quite lucky that we'd had nothing stolen but just thinking about this for a second made us realise, these people were just trying to get home from work like millions of people do every day. They weren't thieves, they weren't pickpockets, they were ordinary people living ordinary lives. Bloody TV propaganda strikes again.

Manaus next... a 5-hour flight away rested the home of some of the most repugnant creatures outside of a parliament building... Ok maybe not *that* bad, but still pretty grim and disgusting all the same.

As I sat at the airport, I pondered... what have I learned about Rio?

1 It's very divided. The northern half is grim and is not the kind of place you'd be proud to show your parents. The south side, on the other hand, is the side that the TV shows you when they want to show Rio in a good light. The northern part is where they show you if they want to show it in a bad light... In short, the TV is very biased.

2 The southern favelas are pacified and are not the shanties people make them out to be, and to be honest, they are even too expensive for a lot of people on ordinary incomes to afford. To buy a property on the south side of Rio is almost

impossible unless you are a proper drug pusher who can afford it.

3 Favelas in the north of the city are cheaper for people to live and many people who can't afford south side favela rents live in the north, and although not all have been pacified, they are still filled with people who simply live and work like anyone else.

4 Rio is a wonderful city with amazing history and was the capital city before Brasilia.

5 They have a strange accent in Rio compared to the rest of Brazil... personally, I didn't pick it up.

6 There are many more beautiful women here than there were in Foz, but there is a definite push towards obesity.

7 The basic ingredients of food are meat, vegetables, and fruit, so are a lot cheaper than other supermarket food which is filled with sugar or artificial rubbish.

8 The beaches are just a part of life in Rio rather than the only focal point of the city – the same way parks might be in the UK. Beaches just happen to attract a lot of tourists too.

Manaus

Day 8 - Manaus

This was it. We were on our way to Manaus.

I was pretty nervous and worried about this trip to the Amazon. I said it before. Who wants to go to the flipping Amazon? It's not like in Tarzan. I'm not going to be going around in a loincloth befriending elephants and lions, swinging from vines, staying in a beautiful tree house with running water and miraculously clean toilet facilities. It's the jungle. It's hot and hostile and nothing there is your friend.

I even took the liberty of looking up some of the creatures of the Amazon. There are Caiman crocodiles that can grow up to 6 metres in length; anacondas – the subject of possibly one of the worst films of the 20th century but still vile and deadly. Candiru, that apparently loves to swim up your pee hole; Piranhas – lil buggers can strip the flesh off a chicken in a few seconds; some fish called Payara – aka the vampire fish with teeth long enough to pierce through the entire width of your thigh; and a host of other grim and disgusting creatures, none of which, may I add, actually like you. Everything in that river wants you dead – if you're lucky.

There are freshwater dolphins in the river too but they are rarely seen. They are pink and pictures of them make them look like foetuses - friendly but a bit grim-looking really.

Manaus is a city in the middle of the Amazon that grew as a result of the boom in the rubber trade. It was also one of the cities that hosted some games during the World Cup in 2014.

Going with no knowledge of the place, what images does a city in the middle of the Amazon rainforest conjure in your head? For me, it conjured images of a city with dirt tracks or narrow tarmacked roads and areas of jungle dotted around. In my mind, I fully expected to see monkeys roaming free.

During the World Cup, the TV was showing images of Amazonian tribes going about their daily lives in various areas of the jungle. Then they showed a rather misplaced football stadium which I thought would look a bit funny placed in the middle of the rainforest. I could picture people returning to their beaten-up cars after a football match only to find that they had been stolen by some baboons or been crushed and swallowed by an anaconda. Suffice to say, my image of Manaus was that of a hot and humid placid city with jungle surrounding it; a bit like being in a park surrounded by trees, only bigger and with a few more buildings. A place where we'd be approached by some natives gnawing on a human shin bone who would look strangely at our mobile phones and try to sniff them or something.

After a short sleep on the floor at Galeão airport, we were ready to face the 4.5-hour flight to Manaus. We untied our luggage from our limbs at this point because sleeping at the airport in Rio, there was the expectation that we'd go to sleep with our luggage near us and wake up with no luggage and wearing nothing except a post-it note with 5 reals stapled to it and the words 'For de baying of som cleen pants'.

I learned something new too. I didn't realise that small aircraft like Airbus A320s were used for what are technically long-haul flights. We flew 4.5 hours on an A320. I was impressed, making me what some people would consider to be a sad individual – but what do they know eh? I was almost as impressed with the plane we flew on as I was standing on the top of Sugarloaf Mountain looking down at the majesty of the southern coast of Rio de Janeiro at dusk. I am either easily impressed or extremely difficult to impress. I'd like to think the latter.

I performed my little touching the outside skin of the plane ritual and we took off. It was pretty cold on the plane actually. I don't know if it's because it's always so hot in Brazil that people leap at the chance to feel a little cold or because someone forgot to wind their window up before take-off, but it was definitely colder than it should have been in my opinion – not unbearably cold, maybe 2 CDs cold.[3]

We landed at 1am, which, according to our body clocks was 2am because we were on Rio time and Manaus is 1 hour behind. As we were landing, I was feeling the anxious sense of 'oh dear, here we go; we'll be attacked by mosquitoes and raped by some horny monkeys as soon as we get off the plane. I must pay attention to where we are going. I don't want to

[3] CDs cold. This is a modern measure of temperature that, I'm sure, will one day replace Celsius and Kelvin. CDs cold describes nipple stiffness and how many CDs could be hung from them. E.g. 1 CD is a little cool whereas 5 CDs is freezing. Anything more than 10 CDs is Siberian Winter and a recommendation that you get checked out by the doctor for having unfeasibly large nipples

turn the wrong way and end up getting eaten by cannibals … my mum would not approve.'

I drenched myself in mosquito repellent as soon as I could, thinking, 'ha, these idiots around me are going to get sucked dry as soon as they step out.' As we shuffled towards the exit, it felt like the moments before my first parachute jump; nerves twined with hints of excitement (I don't know where the excitement came from. Must have been because the first few days had been better than expected so I was secretly hoping this part of the holiday would be too).

As we walked out, I braced myself for the onslaught, but a couple of seconds later – nothing – no mosquitoes, no monkeys, no rampaging rhinos and not a cannibal in sight. Cool, I thought, and then the whack of humid heat hit me. It's something you never get used to. It's both amazing and horrifying at the same time. Amazing that I'd gone down from 2 CDs to 0 CDs in a split second, but horrifying to think that if this is what it's like at 1 am, what the hell will it be like at 1 pm?

As I walked across and down the staircase, I felt like I was moving in slow motion, like in those 1970s and 1980s films where the actors were pretending to move in zero gravity – just without the outer-worldly music. By the time I reached the bus, I was already starting to get sticky but I started to feel ok about it. I realised that the mosquitoes here were unlikely to be some kind of super species that would enjoy hanging around airports.

Poor Vesi though. She booked this because she wanted to see the jungle, and to a certain extent, I was curious too but she suffers the heat a lot more than I do and was a bit worried about how she would cope with the daytime heat. This kind of heat gives her headaches. Admittedly, she drinks less water than a Saharan sand lizard, so it could be dehydration, but if I tell her that, I get a bit of a tongue whipping for moaning at her.

We were picked up outside by some guy. He was holding a sign with our names on it. His face made him look like he could be tribal but he was in jeans and a t-shirt so the images I had of being transported to our hostel in a bamboo carriage pulled by crocodiles was looking unlikely. But I held on to that glimmer of hope until we reached his car; clean, modern and with air conditioning.

He drove out of the airport and tanked it out and down some very quiet but modern tarmacked roads. In fact, they were huge and everything was lit up. Triple lane carriageways, traffic lights (European style) and massive buildings. Boy was I mistaken about Manaus. The drive seemed to go on forever and even at the speed he was going, it took more than 30 minutes to get to the hostel. I was quite glad there was no crocodile-drawn carriage as it would have taken a lot longer. Manaus is big.

We reached the hostel at around 02:30. We had to meet up with the Amazon Tours people at 08:30 so we were looking at less than 6 hours sleep. We tried to explain to the guy on the front desk that we were going on this Amazon trip in the morning and we didn't want a room for the night, but he didn't want us to hang around for the next 5 hours. He didn't even want to let us snooze in the lobby on the floor or a couple of sofas. A room would have cost us 80 reals each. That's about £22 each. £44 in total to sleep in this place for 5 hours? No chance. We could have probably found a cheaper brothel. We'd said we'd rather sleep on the pavement outside like a couple of tramps but he told us not to as it's not safe, even just outside. Blimey, I thought to myself, we're in Manaus. This is a city in the jungle. Up until about an hour before, I thought everyone here would be running around in loincloths, have lip plates and earlobes so long that they had to keep them tied in a bow under their testicles. Surely, he didn't mean we'd get picked up by some cannibals and dumped in a stewing pot, did he? Nah, just local yobs. There I was thinking the most dangerous thing in Manaus would be a stray poisoned dart from tribal warrior and it's a bunch of kids beating people up. Manaus dropped in my estimations at *that* news.

He tried to fob us off when we said that the guy we're meeting will be coming from a particular hotel and he suggested we could sleep in their lobby. Luckily, Vesi had the bright idea to get him to call that hotel to ask if they'd let us. Result was that they wouldn't. Not even 5 flipping hours. That's the equivalent of a Lord of the Rings film + trailers + adverts at the cinema, or one 20-minute sitcom episode + adverts on American TV.

In the end, Vesi had the even brighter idea to call the guy who was leading the tour. Luckily, he answered the phone and told the bod on the front desk that we had a room booked there anyway. It was part of the tour; you get a night in the hostel included. Phew – screw you, little bloke on the front desk.

We were shown to a dark room. On entering, we could see 3 bunk beds and could hear the whirring of a couple of fans to cool the place down. In the 2 other bunk beds, there were 2 other bodies, clearly other travellers. I tend to feel a bit uneasy in these situations so when we jumped into bed, I slept clutching my rucksack.

It was somewhat like when I went to Ireland with a friend from university. We were really pleased when we found a hostel for £8 per night but were a bit shocked by the whole sleeping with a bunch of strangers thing at that time, and I remember my friend literally walked into the room and jumped on a bed clutching his bag as tightly as he could. I, at least, had the dignity to take my shoes off first.

Even though we went to bed at about 3am and had to get up for breakfast for 07:45 – which meant getting up at 7am so that we could shower, which meant actually getting up at 06:30 in case we had to wait for the shower and so set the alarm for 06:15 – I woke up naturally before my alarm. 3 hours of sleep and that doesn't include putting on the mosquito repellent and actually falling asleep in a room with 2 strangers who could have been potential weirdos or serial killers in a 30-degree and 90+% humidity room with no air conditioning and just a couple of fans to keep us cool. (Thank god it was only 30 degrees. We dreaded a power cut.)

I went for a shower at 06:20 after realising I wasn't going to fall asleep again. The shower felt good even though I knew I was just going to put on the same dirty clothes afterwards. On returning to the room. I noticed that one of the bodies in the room had actually gone and when I caught a glimpse of the other one in his bed, he turned out to be a man in his 50s with a beard who slept naked with a bed sheet only half covering his nadgers. However grim the sight, you have to respect the boldness.

He woke up a few minutes later though and I did manage to talk to him. It turned out he was French and I love the opportunity to practice my French when I can, but this guy spoke very quickly and in really short sentences. Most of the conversation with him seemed to revolve around what we were doing and how much it cost.

Me – (in French) "Our trip is London to Madrid, São Paulo, then Foz do Iguaçu, then Rio, then Manaus, Rio, Salvador, São Paulo then driving around a bit before returning home."

French bloke – (in French) "That's expensive."

Me – (in French) "We're paying £X which is €X for the whole thing."

French bloke – (in French) "That's not very expensive."

Me – (in French) "Well, the alternative was to buy a ticket with a load of different destinations on it."

French bloke – (in French) "That's expensive."

Me – (in French) "And a ticket including Manaus was difficult to find so we ended up buying a load of internal flights."

French bloke – (in French) "That's not very expensive."

We seemed to have a good conversation going.

I didn't learn why he was in Manaus. I thought the only reason people went was to go to the Amazon, but he wasn't going so I wondered what other wonders Manaus had to offer.

The 3 of us went for breakfast. That's Vesi, me and the new mosquito bite on my leg that was the size of the palm of my hand. The French guy went by himself (appropriately covered up).

Breakfast was on a roofed terrace in the open; something that would be quite impossible in the UK. It included self-service fruits, melon, papaya, watermelon, bread, self-cooked eggs if we wanted them and a couple of different fruit drinks – not juices, unfortunately – but some form of cordials, slightly chemical I think but still nice. The guava was delicious.

Breakfast in this setting was absolutely wonderful. Looking out into what was actually a pretty huge city. There were birds chirping in nearby trees and it was still very quiet. It was as warm as a hot summer's day in the UK at only 8am and this was almost the end of winter. What an incredible experience. There were no doors leading down the stairs from this eating area meaning it was permanently open. Again, an alien concept to me; at home, we need doors and double glazing to keep the cold out but not here. Designing a building like this shows 100% complete confidence in the weather. It would be like organising a barbecue 2 weeks in advance in the UK and feeling 100% confident that it would not rain. I mean, yes, the doorway leading downstairs was under the same cover we were sat under. After all, it does rain a lot in the Amazon, but that was the only protection.

Other travellers were sat at different tables eating their breakfasts, including the interesting French guy who, by the way, was actually married. I'd love to have asked him why he was travelling without his wife but between him asking me how much things cost and then following up by saying, 'that's expensive' or 'that's not expensive', I didn't get the chance to. Also, I didn't want to get into a discussion about how his wife sends him on a holiday by himself a few times a year – maybe so she can go out shopping without being told things are very expensive and others are not very expensive.

We were picked up at 08:30 by one of the organisers, which was the guy Vesi called in the middle of the night. He didn't even remember the call. He said he thought he'd dreamt it.

He took us to the main office where we had to sign all these disclaimers. I'm not a fan of disclaimers. It's a 'we can do what we like with you and get away with it' card. Yes, ok, I accept it's my responsibility if I am eaten by crocodiles, or have an allergic reaction to something that lays its eggs in my brain, or I get lost in the Amazon River and only my bones are found after having been used to bang bongos in a blood-curdling cannibalistic ritual. Plus, surely they have to take some kind of responsibility. After all, what if the guide kills us and eats us himself? My mum wouldn't approve of that either.

Then the main guy at the office explained a bit to us about the ecosystem and how it's in a really delicate balance and deforestation along with the politician-approved building of dams has and will cause more species to become extinct, including various species of monkey that live on opposite sides of one of the river's tributaries. It was all very sad – I was expecting him to jangle a collection box under my nose after bringing us to the brink of tears, but he didn't... which was nice.

Then he explained about the rivers of the region; the Amazon River and the Rio Negro and the Rio Branco, and how they meet and that we'd be passing over where the Rio Negro and the Amazon Rivers meet. It was an interesting talk. I wish I'd kept detailed notes but the others in the group were already waiting for us, so we had to get a bit of a move on.

We were loaded onto the car and taken to the port. In the car, we met our guide for the next couple of days. Some 23-year-old who was part Brazilian, part Guyanan and who was raised in a tribe called Wapishana. Fortunately, they were a friendly tribe. Some other Amazonian tribes hold them slightly in antipathy because they are so friendly to the outside world which is actually going in and destroying their homeland. I was expecting his name to be Nimbakabuktu or something equally tribal, but no... Shaun... Like the sheep from Wallace and Gromit.

We had a chat in the car and he *was,* in fact, very friendly. Very smiley and his English was really good. I still reserve judgement on whether I'm pleased he was in jeans and a t-shirt as opposed to a loincloth with a bone through his nose. I don't know. Maybe it would have felt more authentic that way and given my lack of trust in many people, it would have made me believe more that he knew what he was talking about. This way, he'd have to earn my trust. But I suppose, on the other hand, too authentic and it probably would have been a bit freaky to be driving in a car with an open window and watch as the wind caused his lip to repeatedly slap him in the face and his earlobes stretch to the back seats and flick me on the nose. To tell the truth, I don't know what I was expecting, so Shaun in a t-shirt, no bone, no long dangly earlobes and no huge flapping lip was good enough for me.

As we drove, we got a bit of a better look at the city of Manaus. For a start, as I said, it's a lot bigger than I thought it would be. Second, it looks like a really shabby city. Large buildings everywhere, filthy roads, rubbish everywhere, graffiti, and from what the bod at the hostel's reception said the previous evening, it's not a particularly safe city. Clearly, it's very industrial and it turns out that to keep industry alive after the years of holding onto a monopoly in the rubber trade, the government allows for goods there to be made and purchased tax free – I laugh when I say government because, like in most countries, governments are made up of lunatics who would gladly tear their country apart if it meant they would get a brand new shiny penny for it.

I got the chance to wear my green hat with the rim around the whole edge. I think it makes me look like Indiana Jones but Vesi disagrees. She thinks I look like a bit of a prat. But I was convinced I looked like Indiana Jones when I tried to wear it in Foz but *there* I really *DID* look like a prat so I flipped back to the baseball cap. Here, the brimmed hat felt right so that's what I wore. Oh, and I did eventually catch sight of my reflection in a mirror and I did look a bit crap... but no... even the mirror lied. I *was* Indiana Jones.

We reached a little port. Not the main port of Manaus. The main port is huge with large container ships going in and out and is pretty amazing in itself. I believe it is the only port in the world that sits 1,500km away from the actual open ocean. There is no equivalent European distance because there is nowhere in Europe that is so far away from an ocean or sea – not even in Russia I don't think. Historically, it was the only way in or out of Manaus and only exists thanks to the rubber boom that began in the 19th century. Manaus became very wealthy and, for decades, Brazil held a monopoly on rubber exports until 1876 when an Englishman called Henry Wickham smuggled some rubber tree seeds out of Brazil and managed to make them grow in some of Britain's colonies like Malaysia, Sri Lanka and tropical Africa.

Thanks to the new competition, by 1912, the rubber boom in Brazil was waning and pretty soon after that, the state was in a deep recession with high unemployment rates.

Henry Ford of Ford motor cars tried to revive this in the 1930s by planting a load of rubber trees in a zone (new city) he called Fordlandia, where he attempted to recreate the Brazilian rubber market. The crop of trees fell victim to leaf pests and the whole effort failed. Fordlandia is still there but it's a ghost town that people can still visit.

There was a second rubber boom between 1942 and 1945 during the second world war when the Japanese took control of various areas that included British colonies' rubber plantations. Brazilian rubber became popular again for a period coming to an abrupt end again at the end of the war because... well... the Brazilians were crap business people and thanks to corruption, excessive greed and terrible treatment of slaves who were harvesting the rubber, they lost control again. I don't think that's a particularly bad thing – being crap at business – but if you're the greedy type too then it's a bad amalgamation. You can't be crap at business but all the while be greedy and then expect a good deal from those you negotiate with. It's like hoping to be a great runner when you have little stumpy legs so you try to win by taking obvious shortcuts around the track.

The rubber boom also created slaves of many indigenous people living in the region. One plantation started off with 50,000 Indians working there and, by the end, there were only

8,000 left. Profits before people at any cost? Fine if you're a psychopath (see current banking practices).

After the end of the second rubber boom, Manaus went into decline and only started to revive itself in the 1950s when some kind of renewed development took place. Then, in 1967, the Brazilian government made Manaus a tax-free zone to attract new investment. It worked. A load of companies went there (best analogy I can think of is like flies to a fresh cowpat in a field of stinging nettles) and for the first few years, Manaus became like a big shopping centre to all Brazilians and, even today, people can still buy cheap white goods. Personally, I wouldn't spend £200 to fly to Greece to buy a fridge for £80 cheaper than you can buy it in the UK, or a TV for £40 less when you have to pay extra to transport it back too. Guess times have changed. Either that or they were really dumb. Or maybe, I've just got the wrong end of the stick of how it all works.

So, the port we were at wasn't the main port, it was much smaller and it had a really strong smell of fish. The expanse of water in front of us was pretty large. I always pictured the main bodies of rivers to be narrower; something like the Thames at London Bridge, but this was much wider. It was more like the *mouth* of the Severn where the bridge distances that cross from near Bristol to Wales are counted in miles; except we were nowhere near the mouth of the Amazon.

Shaun, the guide, took us around the port area to show us what kinds of fish are caught in the Amazon. Yes, I love saying

'The Amazon'. It actually feels quite exciting to think that I was close to the Amazon River. I imagine it to be the same feeling that a chav would feel standing close to a 'celebrity'. There were lots of different types of fish there, including some pretty large ones and when I say large, I mean about the length of my leg... i.e. the best part of a metre. I didn't make a note of the names, I should have really.

There were also a couple of shops where we bought bottles of water – under Shaun's recommendation as it tends to get quite hot in the Jungle. We then jumped on a boat and jetted off over the river. We were on the boat with a couple of Italians, English, French, Americans, and a Brazilian guy.

Ten or so minutes into the crossing, we came to a stop in open water at the 'meeting of the waters' point. This, I was not expecting and it left me with my mouth open. It was a truly incredible sight. This is where the Rio Negro meets with the Rio Solimoes to form the actual Amazon River.

The Rio Negro – or 'black river' – is a large tributary of the Amazon that flows down from Colombia and Venezuela and meets with the Rio Solimoes (The Amazon) at Manaus. The Rio Negro is so named because it looks black, which is due to decomposing organic matter inside that give it that colour, which is actually more like the colour of tea.

The Rio Solimoes – or 'river Solimoes' – is the upper part of the Amazon River, in northwest Brazil. This part of the river is, for want of a better word, light brown. They call it white but it has more of a dirty, muddy puddle look than white. The name Solimoes is just used in Brazil really – and possibly not even everywhere in Brazil. Everyone else just calls it the Amazon River. The Solimoes part is a corruption of the name of the regional aborigines who lived in the area – Soriman.

The meeting of the waters is where the Rio Negro and the Solimoes waters come together. It's a spectacular sight. The dark water and the light brown (white) bump into each other but the amazing thing is that they do not mix immediately. There is a clear and distinct black and light brown divide between them which runs for just under 4 miles before they finally do mix and become the light brown (white) colour we think of when we think of a silty river – If you haven't seen it, I truly recommend searching for pictures of it... Search for Amazon meeting of the waters. You can even see it by using some online global maps, although some are better than others.

The reason they don't mix is because they actually have different properties. The 'white' Amazon River is silty and completely opaque. It's the kind of river that would be quite frightening to jump into because you don't know what's lurking below. The water here has a pH of between 7 and 8. Acidity is measured using the pH scale. The scale is from 1 to 12 where 1 is acid and 12 is alkaline. Water is neutral and has a pH of 7, so along with the water here being quite neutral, the Amazon (Solimoes) flows at around 7 km per hour and has a temperature of approximately 23 degrees Centigrade.

The Rio Negro that meets it has a pH of between 3 and 4 so is more acidic. It has a similar pH to red wine so not flesh-meltingly so, but more-so than the Amazon. This is because after the parts of the year when the rains come and the river floods, some land and a lot of organic matter is pulled inside where it decomposes. I don't know why it doesn't happen in the Amazon (Solimoes) too – or maybe it does but with different plants. The water of the Rio Negro flows at around 3km per hour and has a temperature of approximately 28 degrees Centigrade. Apparently, the fishing is better on the siltier Amazon side, probably because the water is less acidic.

These differing factors keep the waters separate for a good length of the river and the overall effect has to be one of the most spectacular natural phenomena I've ever seen. I put my hand in the water (after Shaun suggested we should try) on the Rio Negro side as we slowly crossed into the Amazon. It may seem stupid to be impressed with something so seemingly banal as water changing temperature, but it's actually amazing to feel the water change temperature over such a short distance. There is something poetic about it that I just can't describe.

Around 25 minutes later, we reached a small port on the other side where we got off to take a minibus. It almost felt like travelling back in time. There were loads of little shops selling fish, fruit and various other things. I say it was almost like travelling back in time but it's actually pretty difficult to go anywhere in Brazil without seeing a Coca-Cola advert sign. I made a pact that I wouldn't touch a drop whilst out here –

admittedly, I don't drink the stuff very often at the best of times so it wasn't going to be a difficult pact to maintain. Anyway, this is Brazil. Home to some of the most amazing and delicious fruits and juices on the planet, what kind of a lowlife drinks Coca-Cola out here when there are so many more delicious beverages?

The minibus journey took over an hour. No air conditioning so it was hot and sticky – and it was only 10am. Apart from the road, we were in the jungle proper now. From my preconceptions, this was what I thought Manaus would look like – dirt tracks, areas of jungle and some (but not many) rundown buildings. We stopped in various places on the bus trip; a toilet, to refuel, to look at some naturally occurring giant water lilies and to drop some guy off with his shopping. I'd seen these giant water lilies before at Bristol University's botanical gardens in their tropical greenhouse, but never had I seen them in the wild. They grow to almost 2 metres in diameter with enough strength to support the weight of a human baby and they were in front of me, alive and in the wild; a totally different experience to seeing them in a greenhouse. It's like the difference between seeing caged and wild lions – except if you touch the lily, it won't eat you. I recommend searching for pictures of 'Giant Amazon lilies' online.

The houses we went past were all raised onto stilts. This wasn't to avoid crocodiles but the whole area floods at some point during the year and it's simply to stop the houses from flooding too. All the trees had marks on them where the water had reached, so I can hardly imagine what this place would be like during the flood season. Suffice to say that, here, a boat is more useful than a car. The houses were not secure like they have to be in the UK, they were mostly made of wood and, instead of glass in the windows, they just had mosquito nets. It's completely unfathomable to us in the UK where the seasons change and you can literally experience all 4 seasons in a day.

We reached another small boat port – well, it wasn't so much a port as a place where little boats could stop. 12 of us climbed into this long, narrow wooden motorboat and we jetted off again. This water was tea coloured – like the Rio Negro – It was another part of the Amazon River. A small tributary called the Arara River.

10 minutes later, we reached a little pier where we disembarked. This was where we were staying. There were some plain and simple huts. We were literally in the jungle; sounds of crickets and birds and other animals all around us. Not a single engine sound, not a whiff of smog or exhaust fumes. This was the jungle and we were on the Amazon. I had to pinch myself to fully believe this. It was nothing like I'd expected, even though I didn't know what to expect. I'd not been eaten alive by mosquitoes. I had survived the boat journey in crocodile and piranha-infested waters. I allowed myself to love the moment. Yes, I was loving the moment.

I had been a bit apprehensive about Brazil on the whole, a bit nervous of going to Rio, nervous about Manaus and the

Amazon as the jungle is an inhospitable place, but everywhere Vesi and I had been so far had been completely different to my expectations. I was genuinely impressed and gave myself a moment to not be worried or suspicious and allowed myself to calm down.

Somehow, the 2 Americans had enough luggage for 10 people. They instructed Shaun to take their cases off the boat, to which I felt like saying, "oi, you dozy fuckwits, you're in the jungle not the fucking Ritz, pick your own fucking bags up, you fat lazy bastards." But I didn't, of course. I just smiled sweetly and judged them.

Vesi and I had opted for the true jungle experience, i.e. the cheaper option, so we got to share a hut with 5 other people, some of whom had arrived a couple of days earlier. As with the houses we passed on stilts, the huts had no glass in the windows, just mosquito nets. We, who chose the cheaper option – ahem – the true jungle experience – didn't have beds either. We were going to sleep in hammocks for the night. The hammocks had a mosquito net tied to each end, so unlike in films where you see beds and a mosquito net hanging from the ceiling draped over the sides and ends of the beds, our faces would be within a few inches from ours.

We lunched in one of the large huts with tables and a canteen; again, no windows, just mosquito nets and there was absolutely no breeze. The canteen was like an oven. Actually, it was a mix between a steam room and an oven.

After lunch, we had about an hour before we went on a boat tour so we could just potter around. Shaun said, "if you want, feel free to go for a swim." "Haha," I laughed... swim? In the Amazon? With crocodiles and piranhas and big toothy fish and electric eels and those things that swim up your willy? Was he serious? He was serious. The crocs come out at night, the piranhas tend to stick to certain coved areas, and the rest of them... well, the dangers are massively inflated by the western media to make people watch sensationalist crap on television. In actual fact, creatures tend to steer clear of people.

That was enough to convince me

Apprehensively, I stepped into the water. It was lovely and warm so I tentatively stepped a little further. It was quite slimy underneath my feet which felt weird, so I stepped a bit more quickly and, pretty soon, I was swimming. But where was I swimming? I was swimming in the Amazon River. I'll say it again... I was – swimming – in – the – Amazon – River. I even *peed* – in – the – Amazon – River. Nothing wiggled up my willy. Nothing bit me, nothing electrocuted me. I was – swimming – in – the – Amazon – River. This was the most incredible experience. I know that swimming is swimming is swimming, but I was swimming somewhere I never thought I'd ever swim... ever. Again, words fail me and it would take the mind of a master poet to describe the experience in words rather than feelings. After all, it's only swimming and people swim every day. I think it's the contrast. I was swimming in what I pictured to be the most inhospitable place and where just a few hours earlier, I was almost afraid to come. A place where I pictured everything as a threat that either wanted to kill me or bury itself inside my brain or something. Clearly, I watch too much crap TV… not quite as crap as sleb nonsense (celeb TV) but programs that fill you with dread. I felt a bit like Truman in the film The Truman show where everything around him was discouraging him from leaving Seahaven. Watching television programs can fill you with a sense of incredible awe but also unimaginable dread. We've only just moved into a new house. I think we'll forego getting a TV licence when we get back and try to have more of a life instead.

Vesi took some photos of me before coming in herself. I've seen them and I look genuinely happy in them; no fake smile, no pretend anything; just a look of serenity and a real smile to go with it. I don't know when I last felt like this – I guess all I needed now was a coconut. Thank you to my beautiful Vesi.

When she came in, I think she was even more apprehensive than I was. I guess she's seen the same crap TV shows I have. I don't know whether she experienced the same feelings of awe and amazement that I did and I think she felt a little nervous throughout the whole swim, especially when I got out of the water to take some photos of her and she was the only one left swimming, but she looked happy too and that was enough. Overall, only about 4 of us went swimming. I was the first… I don't know whether that makes me brave or adventurous or just a bit gung-ho.

We showered after the swim because the dark water left a load of mucky residue on us that looked a bit like dust. The shower water was cold – no mod cons there. In fact, it was more of a dribble of water than a shower but the fact that it was cold water and nothing more than a dribble made the whole experience feel even more real. And it didn't matter anyway because it just felt fresh in the hot and humid heat. Had it been from a waterfall, that would have been the ultimate experience but that might have been pushing the jungle experience beyond reasonable expectations.

After having cooled down slightly, we went for a boat trip on the Amazon to see what we could find in terms of jungle wildlife. 10 of us in a narrow wooden boat with a little motor in the back cruising over the super still waters of the Amazon. We saw a couple of parrots flying past. Real life macaw parrots, the colourful kind you imagine when you think of parrots, except these were flying in the wild. Shaun also pointed out some açaí palms – no berries on these that we could see but I still took a photo so it just looks like a regular palm. We saw some wild toucans too. I've grown to love toucans more than ever in the past few days given we've seen so many and even more since our little experience with the black beaked toucan at the bird enclosure in Foz. We also saw 2 sloths. Sloths are among my favourite creatures ever. They are so relaxed and they look like they are constantly smiling. Basically, they are chilled out happy little dudes that look stoned and when they move anywhere it just makes me think… ahh, they've got the munchies. They're going to the petrol station for some crisps and a spicy curry Pot Noodle.

The first sloth we saw was a bit of an experience. Only a couple of people said they saw it so we were a bit doubtful. "Yeah, sure... that little blob 50 metres away is a sloth? Pull the other one." So, the boat was stopped and we pulled up to the bank. We all got off, Shaun went to one of the trees, jumped on it and started climbing up like one of those guys who climb coconut trees, i.e. by grabbing the tree with both hands, then his feet would grip the trunk, push himself up, then he moved his hands up, grab the trunk with his hands again, bring his feet up... etc. and he shuffled up the tree in about 20 seconds; seriously impressive. I used to be a pretty nifty climber as a kid but nothing compared to that.

Down below, while we were wowing, the mosquitoes gathered around us like a bunch of pissed up yobs in a pub and, within a few seconds, 7 of us found ourselves doing gymnastics, street dancing and fighting the invisible man to try to get rid of them. At the top of the tree, Shaun was giving the sloth chase and although sloths are not known for their swift escape tactics, somehow, this one managed to do a runner before it was caught. Some of us remained sceptical there ever was a sloth.

The second sloth we saw was real though. It was climbing from one tree to another and all of us saw its unmistakable lethargic movements as it lazily reached for one branch of a tree with a slow arm, then a slow leg and then another slow arm and then disappearing as it let go with the other slow leg – no doubt off to the petrol station for a chicken pasty and a packet of Doritos. We all got to see a real-life sloth! What an amazing adventure. Down over the water we even saw large sheets of sleeping grass. This is a plant that closes its leaves when touched. It's not carnivorous or dangerous, but as soon as it feels contact with something, the leaves fold in. Not slowly either, it happens within a couple of seconds. Why it does this is not really known. 'THEY' (whoever 'they' are) suggest it might be a mild defence mechanism but it's just a guess really, and to be honest, it's not much better than my random guess that it's trying to communicate with creatures from other planets.

It's quite remarkable to watch though.

I used to have a little plant of this type in my room for a while but I didn't take care of it well enough because I took it somewhere to show around and must have forgotten about it because I found a sad, frozen little plant with its leaves all closed up underneath my car seat at the end of one particular Winter. It was one of those – "oh, so that's where it is... I was looking for that," moments. I thought it had grown legs and run away to start a folk band with some other things I thought I'd lost – a half-eaten Twix and some compostable tent pegs. But it was such a cool plant. If you can look after exotic plants, I recommend getting one. They're a great conversation piece for when the in-laws come and you've got sod all to talk about (especially if they're foreign).

As we went past a house – also on stilts – it got me wondering, what on earth do people do to live here? If they commute to Manaus it would be pretty stupid living out here. Turns out, they fish, forage, and make money by picking and selling Brazil nuts (they just call them nuts out here in Brazil though). Such simple lives; I'd love to have talked to one of them to ask what they thought about their lives; how happy they were, what they pictured life outside of the Amazon to be like and a load of other things. We stopped to get some drinks at a riverside shack. One thing was certain, there were no Coca-Cola adverts around here. There were some local children jumping into the water, swimming around and playing. Sitting there with my feet dangling off the edge of a little pier, next to Vesi, drink in hand, looking out over the silent, still waters of the Amazon, watching as the sun started to redden, I felt all I needed was an ice-cold coconut and it would have been my nirvana.

We were going to hang around to watch the sunset at around 5-5:30pm-ish but the sun was about to hit some clouds and we wouldn't have seen it go down properly, so we went back for dinner. At the start of dinner, around 6pm, the generator wasn't working so we ate by candlelight, but they managed to get it started by the time we finished eating.

Dinner by candlelight in one of the huts is an experience in itself. There were bugs, cockroaches and even bigger bugs and even bigger cockroaches both flying around and climbing on the insides of the hut. For people who hate bugs, this would have been like being in Dante's ninth circle of hell – the place reserved for corporate bosses, their lawyers and politicians. The show, however, really started when some of the bugs dropped from the ceiling onto our table, plates, shoulders or heads.

It's freaky to be on a table of 10 people who are eating and chatting calmly when, all of a sudden, one person throws their hands up in the air, screams, dives backwards and starts rolling around on the floor. Before we realised that the bugs were falling from the ceiling, I was wondering whether there was a case to be put forward on a potential feedback form that these trips should include a resident exorcist. However, after this happened a number of times around the room from the groups on different tables, I thought perhaps a ghostbuster might be better.

One of the other groups had gone piranha fishing earlier and they ate their catch. The look on the piranhas' faces said it all... The irony of them being eaten themselves was not lost on them. The wide-eyed look of surprise along with the open mouths that said, 'oh boy was I suckered'. Ok, so that's what all fish look like but the teeth gave their expression that extra dimension. We were lucky enough to try them too. I was expecting a different flavour to carnivorous fish, but no, they tasted like ordinary, tasty fish; perhaps even less fishy than I expected as they were freshwater rather than salt water.

After dinner, while it was pitch black, Vesi thought it would be fun to mention crocodile spotting. Within 10 minutes, the whole group plus 3 guides went out on a boat again looking for caimans. Now, I know a little about crocodiles, not a huge amount, but enough to know that they are one of the few creatures in the animal kingdom that actually see us as food rather than a food substitute when their regular food is scarce. E.g. sharks do not. Neither do lions, tigers, etc. Sensibly, I took my lesson from Tarzan who had managed to make friends with pretty much all jungle animals but not crocodiles – that in itself has to say something.

Crocodiles look at us and think, 'I want to eat that' – conversely, many people think that about crocodiles too but people will eat everything from mushrooms to tarantulas to birds to dogs so I'm going to keep humans out of this. Also, I've seen videos and I know how fast crocodiles can move. They pretend to be tree trunks, sneak up to unsuspecting victims and in the blink of an eye, fling up out of the water with their mouths open and drag the poor unsuspecting prey to their inevitable doom.

Considering we were in a boat where the only light was coming from Shaun's torch scouting for caimans and a little moonlight, our surroundings were pretty black. The water was terrifyingly black and to think the sides of the boat were around 15-20cm from its surface and somewhere in the black, black water, were some crocodiles, needless to say, as inexperienced crocodile hunters, we were slightly on edge. Vesi, for all her bravery, was openly saying how she was shitting herself – and it wasn't due to the piranhas we tried at dinner. Had it not been for my own excitement, I'd have agreed.

We pootled along slowly with Shaun at the front making crocodile sounds (which happened to sound a little bit like the dying giraffe from the South Park movie if you've seen it) and shining his torch around to try to see the reflection in a caiman's eyes. We'd approach the riverbank sometimes in the hope something had been spotted which was actually quite nerve-wracking, but at the same time, astonishingly beautiful. There were scores of little green glowing bugs resting on the grasses growing out of the water – like carpets of randomly dotted little green LEDs. It's utterly magical. The problem was that to get closer to the bank, the boat had to go through areas of thickening vegetation and tree roots just below the surface of the water. The scraping sounds from under the boat as we traversed these areas were terrifying. We went through a patch where the boat slowed right down and pretty much came to a stop. I think all of us felt a shudder at that point. Shit... what if we get stuck? What if the propeller breaks or gets clogged up and overheats the motor? There would be a healthy buffet for crocodiles just sitting in the dark water unable to go anywhere.

To the relief of everyone on board, we didn't stop for more than a few of seconds and the boat managed to push through into vegetation-free water. There was a moment of genuine panic though.

A couple of minutes later, Vesi's complained that her feet were getting wet. Initially, I ignored it, putting on my pirate accent saying, "Aye, lass. That be bilge water" and telling her that boats are always wet on the bottom. But after a couple of minutes spent investigating the very obvious pool of water at our feet, we realised that it was larger than previously thought and it was getting deeper too. It turned out our boat was sinking. Now, this makes for a fantastic story but not a fantastic experience. It's one of those things you can laugh about afterwards but at the time you think… I'm never going to see the light of day again… I should have been kinder to my parents… I should have told that guy I hate to fuck off… I shouldn't have gotten on this bloody boat… what the hell was I thinking going to look for crocodiles in the Amazon in the dark in a boat that offers as much protection as an inflatable ring?

To the sound of prayers, quiet sobs and incoherent vocalisations of last wills and testaments, Vesi scouted around for and found the hole where the water was coming in from (we were all looking but Vesi was the one who found it). Shaun jumped into action blocking it with his finger (like the little Dutch boy did to the dam). He then started scooping water out with a little container that they kept on board. At this point, given we were on a sinking boat, the consensus was it was time to head back.

Ok, freeze time for one moment to focus on what was happening… What a story. We were in a small wooden boat on the Amazon River in the pitch black with just a torch and the moon to light the way. We were looking for crocodiles but the water was also home to carnivorous piranhas. We were several hundred metres away from where we left and the boat started sinking. Isn't that a story worthy of Hollywood as either a tragedy or a comedy?

But in reality, can you imagine the icy chill that went through everyone's spine when Vesi exclaimed, "the boat is sinking!"? Thoughts of swimming to the closest pitch black bank just 20-30 metres away were tarnished with fears that these dark-skinned crocodiles might be lurking there, waiting – or that whilst swimming, an initial sharp pain in the ankle would be quickly followed up by being pulled under the water and into what is lovingly called the crocodile's death roll – or perhaps, a sharp nip on the leg could have quickly turned into a piranha feeding frenzy that didn't need to last any longer than a minute or two.

As I mentioned… it's a good story but a frightening experience. But hey, aren't frightening experiences that end well always good stories… afterwards?

As our boat was being turned around, one of the guides at the front spotted something in the water. There was some commotion at the front, a bit of thrashing and within a couple of seconds, the torch was shining on him and he was holding a small 3-foot-long caiman crocodile. It was so quick that I thought he must have come out with it stuffed down his trousers and whipped it out at the moment when it would look the coolest to a bunch of nervous tourists. However, with a split second's thought, it would probably be unwise to keep a crocodile hidden underneath his clothes – especially given that the biting end would have to be close to either his throat or his gonads. I had to concede that he had actually been so cool that he actually scooped the crocodile out of the water with his bare hands.

Just 10 minutes later, we were back by the huts. We all took it in turns to hold it, stroke it, poke it, and prod it (gently). Everyone was stupendously impressed. Not just by the crocodile, but by the guy who caught it too; everyone clapped at his bravery and skill but as we know, fame is a fickle thing and he was forgotten as soon as the applause ended and the star of the evening was definitely the little crocodile.

Its back was tough and scaly, whereas the underside, although the skin was kind of scaly, was actually very smooth. It was cold to the touch (well, it is a reptile) and it had a bit of a pungent and unpleasant smell. Clearly something Mrs crocodile doesn't mind, but it made me think, 'wow, if my partner smelled like that, it would put me off mating.' Admittedly though, if a crocodile tried to mount me, the last thing I'd be worried about is the smell.

The crocodile looked positively stunned while we were holding it. I'm not surprised really. Maybe it thought that if it didn't move, we wouldn't see it. Same tactic I used to use with my gran when she came to stay with us and I used to crawl into her bedroom at night and try to hypnotise her – unsuccessfully I might add – but the tactic was, stay still and she won't notice me.

Eventually, when we let the crocodile go, it didn't move for a good 30 seconds until it was prodded back into the water by one of the guides; it still looked pretty shocked as it hesitantly crawled back into the water. Poor little geezer.

We hung around and talked for a while after that. I only realised how many mosquitoes were around when I looked at one of the outside lights. It literally had a cloud of mosquitoes buzzing around it. I looked around and the other lights did too.

I got to chat with Shaun too on a one-to-one basis. He'd had an interesting life. He'd caught malaria at one point but the doctors initially mistook it for dengue fever so he nearly died, he had a Swiss girlfriend (she'd done one of these jungle trips) and was going to visit her in November and he actually wondered about where his life was going. He seemed so... well, the best way I can describe it is... pure. He said his girlfriend's parents (understandably, I guess) were worried that if he ever made the move to Switzerland it could be just to make use of their benefits system. But he looked at me with a look of cluelessness and said (and I'll never forget how he said it), "I don't even know what that means". And he said it with complete sincerity too. Then I was curious as to what kind of job he might be able to do in Switzerland and he said he'd be up for pretty much anything... manual work, milking cows, etc. which is quite endearing given that I don't think much hand milking goes on anymore. I also asked him how he handles the cold and he said he'd never felt it. I am always amazed when I talk to someone who has never felt the cold before. He seemed so incredibly genuine and humble too – I kind of wondered whether introducing him to a crowded European life where people's primary purpose is mostly to accumulate money and stuff would have been a bit of a cruelty to him. I hope it works for him.

We hit the hammocks at around 9pm, which seems early, but it was completely pitch black outside and we were getting up super early the next day.

What a day. In just 1 day I had learnt so much about some of the creatures of the Amazon and I love animals – apart from mosquitoes. In the grand scheme of things, I didn't learn a lot, but enough to look back on what I thought I knew and completely change my mind about most of it. The Amazon *IS* a romantic place and although it has grim creatures living in it, the most annoying ones are actually just the mosquitoes... and you don't have to travel to the flipping Amazon to get bitten by those buggers, you can find them in France. Ok, you won't catch malaria or dengue in La Rochelle, but still, they are a pain.

Piranhas, although frightening and deadly, are not found just anywhere in the waters of the Amazon. Caimans are less aggressive than many other crocodiles and, in general, most animals tend to stay away from you – except for bloody mosquitoes.

Going to sleep in a hammock was new for me. It's normally nice to lie in a hammock for a while but to know I was going to have to sleep in one the entire night is a different experience altogether; especially having to get through the hut in the dark because the nearest generator-driven light bulb was about 20 metres away. I was worried I'd get into the same hammock as one of the French girls (well, not too worried)... or worse... the Brazilian guy (yes, I was worried).

We had sheets and thin blankets, but realistically, it was too warm for that and I slept with my clothes on but no sheets or blankets. It felt like I was in the army or something, except I wasn't about to jump up to kill anyone – I was covered head to foot with anti-mosquito spray. Incredibly, I wasn't tired. We'd slept all of 4 hours the night before and we'd had a very busy day of adventure. I thought I'd crash out immediately but I didn't. I lay in my hammock listening to the beautiful sounds of the rainforest and they were as wonderful as I'd imagined them to be... except for the generator.

I was so worried about letting mosquitoes in under the netting. To get into the hammock, I crawled under the net, trying to keep it in contact with my skin as much as possible so as not to let any mosquitoes slip in. When I managed to climb in, I remained extremely aware of my surroundings, listening closely for that unmistakable high-pitch buzzing sound to go past my ear because just one of those little bastards buzzing past my ear is enough to keep me awake for the rest of the night. Luckily, no high-pitched buzzing.

Even though I wasn't tired, I managed to drift off eventually, waking up occasionally because of the new environment and to uncrick my neck.

Day 9 Manaus

The alarm went off at 5am. It was pitch black outside so I was a bit surprised I got up as quickly as I did.

At around 05:30, the group boarded a boat – similar to last night's boat but without a hole. We were going out onto the Amazon River to watch the sunrise.

We paddled out so as not to make any noise, using Hawaii 5-0 style paddles, and came to a stop about 500 metres away. As we paddled, the river in front of us was completely and totally still. It was like looking at a reflection from a sheet of glass. This was the most serene, peaceful and beautiful sight I'd seen since I don't remember when. *This* is where the romantic image of the jungle comes from. These were the exact surroundings Tarzan would be proud to show Jane to convince her to live with him.

Tarzan: Jane, come live with me

Jane: I can't, I hate mosquitoes

Tarzan: Mosquitoes no problem... just roll in dung

Jane: Well, it's tempting but I also have a job

[Tarzan shows Jane the majestic panorama of a still Amazon River]

Jane: My god it's beautiful and so serene. When can I move in?

Tarzan: I tell your workplace already... here your P45.

We came to a stop in the water. Behind us were the fading ripples from where our boat had passed. We could hear crickets, the occasional chirping of birds and then the sun started to rise.

The water had now become almost perfectly still again and we sat in a motionless boat facing some trees through which the glow of the sun could now be seen. Then, from being just below the horizon, it shot up in about 3 minutes and started to warm the jungle. Again, all I can say is, it would need the words of a master poet to describe how exceptionally beautiful along with what an amazing experience this was; the quiet, the surroundings, how everyone on the boat sat in awe at the majesty of an event that happens every single day and has done so for billions of years. Sugarloaf was pretty impressive, I'll be the first to say, but it's crazy how those 'Cariocas' aren't interested in seeing spectacles like this.

No sooner had the sun completely cleared the horizon than we paddled back – and fast. The sun had started to beat down on us and given that we hadn't become accustomed to jungle temperatures in just 1 day, chances were that before long, we'd be knackered and sweating like a politician on a lie detector.

Back at the huts, we had a breakfast of pineapple slices, other fruits, fruit juices (those chemical cordials again), dough balls and a couple of other little bits like cheese and the like. It was here we'd heard that the American couple had left. They originally planned on staying for about 3 days but the wildlife wasn't enough for them apparently. Not surprised really, they started complaining from the moment we got on the first boat at the meeting of the waters. You can't come into the jungle expecting room service and then complain when the animals you are hoping to see don't make an appearance when you want them to. So, all I can say is good riddance to them and their enormous luggage.

At 08:00, we went for a hike through the jungle. (I LOVE THE FACT THAT I JUST SAID THAT – after all, when am I ever going to be able to say it again?) Long trousers and a long sleeve top were recommended. This was to keep mosquitoes at bay and to make sure ticks would not latch on. Ticks are little blood-sucking parasites that latch onto people. Multiple ticks can be referred to as POLY (to mean many). Lots of blood-sucking parasites = poly-ticks... So, now you know what politicians are involved in: poly-ticks.

We all dressed appropriately and stood outside to wait for Shaun. He appeared dressed in a long sleeve coat with a collar, army trousers, wellington boots and was carrying a machete. I was in a paper-thin cotton top with long sleeves, long, thin trousers, low trainers and was carrying a camera. It's enough to make you think that if we were chased by some grotesque beast, I wouldn't fancy my chances. I think some swings of a machete would be better protection against a monster that drools unspeakable horribleness than a couple of photos with the flash. Everyone else was dressed lightly too, like me. We all looked at each other and muttered, "Holy Christ. What the hell have we just committed ourselves to?"

We walked from the huts down a tiny little path that led straight into the jungle. This tiny path turned out to be our entry point to a 3-hour hike, stopping at various points of interest.

Within the first few minutes, and I have absolutely no idea how she spotted it, Vesi saw a poison dart frog; a tiny orange thing, not much bigger than a thumbnail. Seriously, a tiny little frog... it wasn't even one of the most colourful poison dart frogs – and just to emphasise again – it was tiny. How the hell did she spot it? Admittedly, I can't really try to compete, I'd have been the last to see a brontosaurus if it crossed our path. Meh... good thing Vesi's on our side. Pretty soon after that, she saw a line of ants. I'd seen this before on documentaries and cartoons and it reminded me of the start of the film 'A Bug's Life', where the ants are all carrying little bits of food when a leaf falls to the ground interrupting the line and the first ant behind the leaf stops and shouts, "I'M LOST." Then another ant comes to their rescue, guiding them around the leaf and back to the line. These little ants were following the line in exactly the same way with little bits of leaf or seeds or something to take back to the nest. Then, Vesi dropped a leaf on the line to see what would happen. Pretty quickly, a build-up of ants appeared behind the leaf and a very clear and obvious confusion swept them all. But unlike the cartoon, they did not find the line again. I mean, I'm sure they did, but not in the few seconds that we were there anyway. We scrambled away feeling a little guilty that we'd... woah... what do I mean WE... that VESI had interfered with the ants' line.

We walked past a number of trees. Occasionally, Shaun would hack off some bark with his machete and get us to smell it. There were all these varieties of recognisable smells; Vicks, Deep heat & lemon, amongst others. He made me a bracelet out of the lemon one which was pretty nifty.

Now, this may seem obvious but walking through the jungle was not massively different to walking through a normal forest in the UK. Yes, of course, there were some differences. Firstly, the heat and humidity, then there is the constant fear of the mosquitoes in the shadows, but unless you can identify trees and plants properly, many look pretty much the same. The biggest difference was the huge banana tree-like leaves on some of the plants and some of the tree roots. They definitely don't grow them that big at home.

Throughout the whole walk, even though we all had loads of anti-mosquito spray on us, there were lots of the little buggers flying around and occasionally someone would get a little bout of what must have looked like Tourette's syndrome with the jerking, self-slapping and loud involuntary swearing. I picked off a small leafy branch and walked along waving that around like a pair of nunchucks to keep the mosquitoes away. It worked beautifully.

We stopped at the base of a tree where Shaun coaxed a tarantula out of its little hole. With his bare hands, he pinned it down and picked it up for us to look at. I actually got to stroke a tarantula's hairy leg. Ok, it's not quite like stroking a girl's leg – unless she's Greek – and it did not have the same effect as stroking a cat or a dog. It neither purred nor got an erection. To be honest, I'm not sure the tarantula liked it. It sure as hell didn't show any gratitude – unless you call poking its fangs out a show of gratitude.

Just above the tarantula hole, at about shoulder height, we saw what looked like some kind of hornet's nest with the hornets clinging to the outside in a position of readiness. Shaun looked up from holding the tarantula in an arm lock and calmly said, "those are hornets. They are in attack position". I guess it was because Shaun was calm that we all remained calm, but deep inside us, it was definitely brown trousers time. The particularly worrying thing was that we could have inadvertently walked into the nest and worked the hornets up into a frenzy or they might have just attacked as a pre-emptive defence. However, fortunately, they've not been paying attention to the 'first world' western culture of pre-emptive strikes and then telling their mates we were the ones who were *going* to attack them – honest guv.

We left them alone and they left us alone – as it should be in these circumstances.

We passed some Brazil nut trees – they are massive. I didn't know this but the nuts grow in a large pod about the size and shape of a coconut, and then when it's cracked open, it is full of Brazil nuts packed so neatly in their shells that they would be an attractive centrepiece on a dinner table. The nuts are actually the seeds of the tree, and in Brazil, they are called Castanhas (translated – chestnuts).

On the walk, Shaun told us how he is also the guide for jungle survival courses too. He says that a lot of the people he gets on these courses are Israeli soldiers or ex-soldiers but many of them don't actually manage to make the full course and duck out early. Personally, I found that really interesting. Here we have a 23-year-old guide, born into a tribe, guiding around a bunch of soldiers trained in survival and in all manner of 'outdoor activities' (let's call it that) and a lot couldn't take the jungle. I think that comparison is quite remarkable.

A couple of hours into this walk, we were all sweating profusely, and although it didn't seem like it, we'd actually gone full circle and reappeared at the gap that we entered the jungle from. I'd managed to avoid the mosquitoes with my little pair of nunchucks and I didn't feel as though anything buried itself into my body and made a nest in my brain – which was nice.

Poor Vesi came out with a terrible hot weather headache. In some respects, I was pleased for her that we were leaving after lunch because she does seem to suffer the humid heat and you don't get much hotter and more humid than the jungle. The unfortunate thing here is that Manaus – the general area – is hotter in Winter than it is in Summer. The rain in Summer tends to cool the air a little, whereas in winter it does not, so, unfortunately for Vesi, we caught the Jungle at a bit of a bad time. Although, admittedly, hot and humid is better in my books than slightly less hot and pissing rain. But, I suppose that if this is the hottest it generally gets, then the weather is not totally unbearable – although Vesi did spend a couple of years living in Thailand and she said she never got used to the humid heat because it always gives her headaches.

On the other hand, we were sad to be leaving because we did not get the chance to go piranha fishing or spearfishing or even spend a night out in the jungle itself in a hammock put up by us, which I would have loved but I think Vesi would have thought twice about given the mosquito biting during the jungle walk and the general heat. Also, we were sad to be leaving because of the amazing experience of it all.

As we sat on the decking by the edge of the water waiting for our boat, we got talking to a weedy-looking local – late 40s, early 50s. I say talking, I really mean we were gesticulating and speaking to each other in a variety of languages, most of which none of us actually knew how to speak.

He was telling us about his job as a caiman crocodile killer. He controlled the population of caiman crocodiles by killing off the larger ones. Frankly, I think he was pulling our chain. He weighed about as much as one of my elbows and had fewer teeth than a one-year-old. Still, we had fun pretending to understand what he was on about. It was a bit like pretending to understand the old guy who corners you in a pub and talks at you, telling you a whole life story; not his own life story, someone else's. But you don't figure that out until the very end, when it also happens to be closing time in the pub.

On the boat back, there was another American with a bag large enough to lose a pregnant hippo. He was quite friendly but I'd still like to know what the fuck these people need such big bags for. He wasn't even particularly overweight.

Both Vesi and I were sad on the boat on the way back. We had so many memories from such few hours and, a few sad hours later, we were back at the hostel. I saw the French man there again and had chatted to him again. I told him about the jungle trip and, of course, how much it cost (he hadn't remembered a thing from our last conversation) to which he replied, "that's not very expensive," – of course. I still didn't understand what he was doing there. He hadn't travelled around Manaus and he wasn't there to do a jungle tour. He had hung around the hostel and the local area for the last day and a half.

I kind of felt like we'd outstayed our welcome. The same guy was on the desk as when we arrived and I was getting the uncomfortable feeling that he wanted us to leave. He didn't say anything, I just felt it... call it a sixth sense I have. We didn't really like him, so I guess it was fate that individually, both Vesi and I inadvertently managed to block two separate toilets before we left. Some small satisfaction I guess.

We went to a bus stop and just being there convinced us that Manaus as a city is pretty horrible. Most of the areas smelled of urine and there was graffiti and smog everywhere. There is so much traffic for somewhere in the middle of the Amazon. I must admit though, as we waited for a bus (a 1-hour wait), we must have seen over 100 drive past. There's a lesson for the UK. If they can get *that* many buses into the middle of the jungle, why the hell can't the Brits get them into our cities?

Our flight was at 3am. We reached Manaus airport with 8 hours to spare. Sticky from having been in the jungle, we washed in the toilets. We also tried sleeping in various corners but didn't manage. Believe it or not, the airport was actually quite cold. We ate some pão de queijo and eventually boarded the plane back to Rio. There was also a gate change and slight delay that Vesi heard (luckily). I'd still be there now otherwise. So, we ended up taking off at about 4am.

On take-off, we took a last look down at Manaus and the jungle but it was pitch black so we had to imagine most of it. However, on the horizon, the faint outline of the tops of the trees was just visible against a very dark sky. Vesi and I held hands, both sad to be leaving but grateful we'd been, and if it hadn't been for her, I'd never have gone, so as the aeroplane climbed and the jungle got harder and harder to see, I turned to look at her and said, "Thank you".

What I learned in Manaus:

1 Manaus itself is a dump. At least, it's an industrial city with loads of graffiti, smog and much of it smells like piss. I'm sure there are some nice parts

to it but we didn't hang around long enough to find them.

2 The jungle, although inhospitable, is nowhere near as inhospitable as I thought.

3 There is less blatant colourful wildlife than I expected; but then again, I have spent my life watching documentaries on TV that focus on the most colourful and unusual wildlife.

4 TV about Manaus is only a half-truth... and that's mixed with a half non-truth, so excluding mosquitoes, my preconceptions about the jungle were incorrect.

5 Piranhas are not as mindlessly vicious and widespread as I thought. I've swum in the same stretch of water with them now and even though I'm sure they would still go for me if I were in the wrong place at the wrong time, they are not the constantly hungry devil fish I originally assumed.

6 Crocodiles. This was my biggest fear in the jungle and they are still, but I've learned that they are not as aggressive here as I thought they might be – not caimans anyway. They do actually avoid noisy areas where, for example, there might be boats and such. Noise is not always the dinner bell for these animals.

Rio De Janeiro

Day 10 - Rio de Janeiro

On our way back to Rio, I had a chance to examine the mosquito bites on my feet, ankles and in any other non-fungus ridden areas I felt compelled to scratch. It turned out that my little twig and leaf nunchucks only protected the top half of my body and completely missed the bottom half. How stupid was I to not imagine that mosquitoes – bastards that have been evolving for millions of years specifically to be bastards (a bit like the Tory party in the UK) – would not be able to bite through some cotton socks?

I counted them… they were packed so tightly that I lost count at around 40. 'My god,' I thought, 'how much of my blood have they had? Do I have any left? Have these buggers injected me with some disease?'

On landing and after a total of 8 hours of very broken sleep, we made our way back to Botafogo. I'd not really noticed before but there are so many women here with tattoos. All up their arms, down their backs, on their necks, it's quite disconcerting actually.

I used to dance a lot and this one woman I used to dance with had really broad shoulders and tattoos all over her chest i.e. the visible part between her massive Adam's apple and her pectoral muscles. I can still remember the fear I felt the first few times I danced with her. She was – dare I say – fairly toned. I thought 'Christ, if I step on her feet she'll pull my arms off and beat me to death with a few wobbles of her Adam's apple'. Luckily, she was actually really quite nice and I still have both my arms. There were a lot of women with tattoos. Ok, now I don't consider myself a prude but what kind of impression does the tattoo of a Rottweiler on your arms give off? It's like those T-shirts with slogans like *'I'M A VIRGIN'* and then underneath it has, *'(this is an old T-shirt)'*. Who looks at themselves in the mirror before going out and says, "yes, that's the image I'm pleased to be giving off," or perhaps a mother looks at her and says, "yes. I'm proud that's my daughter." Am I being strange here or something? Is there something I don't see that others do?

Anyway, lots of women with large tattoos that I bet they'll sure as hell regret one day – but I'll never find out.

Back in Botafogo and back to that same hotel/Airbnb place we stayed in a couple of nights ago, we were put in a different room. This one was bigger and was in a small apartment with a communal kitchen. Fortunately, we had our own toilet. I've never been a fan of communal toilets (and I've been to Glastonbury festival) as there is always a stray pubic hair resting on the porcelain... ok, I admit that it's usually mine, but still – I don't like it.

Lunch consisted of local supermarket fruit – guava, watermelon, papaya, a couple of massive passion fruits and a giant avocado – around 2kg of fruit for the modest price of £3. We didn't eat them all at once though, we'd still be on the toilet if we had, but we had enough for a day or 2.

After lunch, we went for a walk and ended up at Ipanema beach. It was 16:30 and the temperature was perfect; high 20s with a nice breeze. We stopped to get a 3-scoop ice cream on the way. The flavours were passion fruit, avocado and gorgonzola. Yes, you read that right, gorgonzola… the blue-veined stinky cheese that makes your fingers smell for hours and forces you to keep sniffing them every couple of minutes.

As expected, the avocado ice cream tasted of absolutely nothing. It was like eating a lump of sugar except it was worse because sugar doesn't give you brain freeze. The passion fruit was quite nice but, ironically, the gorgonzola ice cream tasted the nicest. It was a bit of a twilight zone moment I have to admit.

We sat on the beach – the sand itself (euch) – to watch the world go by. In our tired state, that's all we could do really. We hadn't really slept the night before as it was partially spent lying in a hammock listening out for the faint yet devastating buzzing sound of mosquitos as they fly past the ears; that tiny little buzz that fills you with panic, has you fighting the invisible man in the dark and keeps you awake for the next 4 hours.

Sitting there watching the people and walking around, you can actually see the outdoor life and what it really means. The people on the beach sunbathing, not facing the sea but moving around with the sun as it arcs across the sky. Ok, not my idea of a fun afternoon but who am I to judge if people want to practice being dead? Anyway, who am I to talk? I was sitting there, stock still watching people lying down and doing absolutely nothing and there I was thinking they were crazy and wasting their time.

There were loads of people playing beach volleyball and some were using their feet to keep the ball up. Then there were other people running on the path that runs adjacent to the beach, people cycling, exercising, or even just walking... although the walkers were mostly tourists.

Personally, I don't like the beach but I could definitely imagine myself enjoying the outdoor life here. I could actually feel how the beach is an integral part of the way of life and not (as I said before) just the raison d'être for the local economy.

After a while, I think the stress of being on the beach was showing on my face and Vesi felt sorry for me, so we headed away from the beach to a bar on the side. The 2 main observations I made about the beach were:

1. As the beach is simply a part of life here, a lot of people are there by themselves so for the most part, they don't give a damn about the outside world, which is different to seeing oily parents shouting at their oily kids to get the lilo out of their sun whilst lying on rented sunbeds 1.5 metres away from their obese neighbours who are splashing bronzing oil onto their already half burnt, half orange bodies. Here... you don't get the feeling you're being watched by anyone or their ugly kids because they just don't care.

2 The beach had no seashells which is a strange one. I don't know why either. Maybe it's because the water is so cold that no fish are daft enough to live in it and prefer to hang out in warmer waters, or maybe the Brazilian authorities have paid someone to walk around before anyone wakes up and pick up all the shells, leaving a pristine white sandy beach. It's almost as though it were made for beachgoers. Walking on the beach, you never get that feeling that you're about to step on something spiny or sharp.

Sitting at the bar on the side of the beach, I fell into a moment of complete and total happiness once more. I had my cool, lush coconut and I was somewhere beautiful. My fantasies this time lived up to my expectations. We watched the world go by from there too; people jogging or cycling, people throwing nets into the water to catch fish and some kids jumping into the 12-degree water, although, admittedly, just watching them dive in was enough to make my scrotum leap up into my throat.

We didn't think we had stayed long but, somehow, we had made it to the early evening. We meandered through the street and passed through the market as they were setting it up before trying to go to a supermarket on the way back but, unfortunately, it was closing so we didn't manage to get anything and by the time we got back to our room, all we could do was eat the remaining fruit we had and go to bed hungry. So, our meals for the whole day comprised of: aeroplane breakfast, fruit for lunch, a sandwich with processed cheese a bit later, and then some fruit remains for dinner... a total intake of around 1,000-1,500 calories combined with a lot of walking around, so I think we lost some weight.

Back at the Airbnb place, on walking in, we noticed the light was on in the apartment. We hadn't left it on, so this was a distinct sign that we either had or had had intruders.

Holding Vesi outside, I walked in and picked up the only weapon available to me... a Rubik's cube... and crept in further. Lo and behold, a stranger walked out of a room holding a sandwich and said hello to me in a funny accent.

I was so shocked that I didn't know how to react, so I offered him the Rubik's cube. At the time, it hadn't even occurred to us.... well... me... that some other people might have actually moved into the empty room opposite ours. Silly really as we had a communal living space and kitchen, but no, I was convinced we had a murderer walking in our room.

Fortunately, we laughed about it and ended up having a brief chat with the COUPLE in the room opposite. They had a funny accent so we spoke to them in pigeon English and it wasn't until they asked us if we were Dutch that we thought something was a little funny, then we discovered that they were from South Africa... and their English was absolutely fine.

A lesson in how to look like TWO cheeks of the same arse on a first impression.

Day 11 – Rio de Janeiro

Christ the Redeemer at last. This is one of the things you have to do when you come to Rio – I think it's the law, it's got to be done – a bit like eating a kebab in Greece, suing/shooting someone in the USA or pickpocketing someone in Naples.

Was I excited? Well, after having seen an amazing waterfall, a sign that points to Argentina, swum with crocodiles and piranhas, slept in a hammock in the jungle, gone hang gliding and drunk water from a coconut, I think the bar needed to impress me had to be pretty high. In fact, I was thinking that I would only probably be impressed if the statue got down and did some break dancing.

We walked outside, mainly to get some food. We didn't eat much the evening before so we were pretty hungry. The traffic was unbelievable, but then again, it was a school day and as we found out from our hosts, there are so many schools in Botafogo that the building of more schools has been prohibited.

We left for Corcovado which is the mountain that Christ the Redeemer stands on top of.

The mountain – Corcovado – was originally called Pináculo da Tentação... no, you pronounced that wrong, not TentaKAO... it's pronounced TentaSAun. Come on, get it right... that's what all the squiggles, dots, blobs and bogey things are there for. Ok, let's be fair, the *ção* bit on the end is a bit tough. It's a bit like the GLI or the GN in Italian... you have to know it and there's no real equivalent sound in English on its own. But basically, the *ção* is the equivalent of the *TION* on the end of a word in English, like, in this case, tentação means tempta*tion*. In actual fact, the *ção* sounds a bit like *saun* (not saun to sound like sawn, but *saun* as in the first 4 letters of the word *sound*... just the 'soun' part). God, that's complicated... but at least it's not Welsh.

Anyway, Pináculo da Tentação literally translates to "pinnacle of temptation" by the Portuguese settlers. Why? Good question. Well, one story suggests (from Copacabana.info – yes, I cheated) that the name was a biblical reference to the story where the devil tempts Jesus Christ to leap from the tallest mountain (Luke 4:9 but also in other gospels) and God would send angels to save him (a bit rich of Luke I think as that same god didn't send angels to stop me from twisting my ankle when I was a kid and jumped off the garage roof with an umbrella).

The story sounds plausible what with Brazil being very religious, and even though the whole Jesus thing happened thousands of miles away near the middle east were the west are consistently starting wars these days, people tend to relate to things locally... so if Pináculo da Tentação was the highest mountain around to those who named it, then that's where Jesus was tempted. Screw Mount Everest... Sod K2... Pináculo da Tentação was where it was at. After all, I knew the story of Jesus as a child but I grew up thinking he was buried in a local graveyard.

The name Pináculo da Tentação remained for about 100 years before it was renamed Corcovado – "hunchback" for its hunch-like appearance. Not the most flattering name admittedly, which is probably why they tried to redeem themselves and stick a Jesus on the top, then name the nearby mountain "Sugarloaf".

It stands at just over 700m high, is situated within the Tijuca forest national park and houses one of the most recognisable sights in the world along with the leaning tower of Pisa, the Eiffel Tower and Pamela Anderson's cleavage... The Christ the Redeemer statue.

Name-wise, they could have just called it Jesus, but then half the Puerto Ricans would have thought it was named after them – "Oh, taaank jiuu soo berry berry match... exsep.... I no have dat beerd and I don' wear a dress." – so they left no doubt as to whom it is and what he did/does. It was Christ, and he was a redeemer. That was his job. Had he followed in his mum's husband's (Joseph's) footsteps, the statue might have been called the less impressive Christ the Carpenter... but he followed in his dad's footsteps who, luckily for him, turned out to be God. (Talk about getting a good start in life – but not such a great end.)

The statue is 30 metres tall and with its arms stretched out, it's also 30 metres wide – which is pretty cool considering we are actually about as tall as the total span of our arms. On the top of the granite mountain, it weighs 635 tons and is made primarily of reinforced concrete with outer layers made of soapstone so that it's smooth to the touch.

Originally, in 1853, there was a proposal by the French-born priest called Pedro Maria Boss (of course, Pedro ☺), who thought Corcovado was so beautiful that he sought approval from Princess Isabel (member of the royal family there at the time) to build a religious statue in her honour... although, when he said "sought" approval, he probably meant "sought" money and when he said it would be in her honour, that sounds like the kind of bullshit you peddle to rich chicks when you want something. She wasn't impressed by his proposal so she didn't fund it. So, I guess he got his 15 minutes of fame and went back to praying.

In 1921, the Catholic Circle in Rio began a privately funded campaign to build a monument and an artist called Carlos Oswaldo was commissioned to draw some sketches for what could be put there. His sketches included one of just a cross, one of Jesus carrying a cross and a globe and standing on a pedestal representing the world, and the final sketch was of Jesus with his arms stretched out. Guess which one they picked.

Then, Brazilian engineer, Heitor da Silva Costa (probably Pedro to his friends), drew up blueprints of the statue and French sculptor, Paul Landowski, was responsible for moulding the materials into shape. Between 1922 and 1931, the statue was designed and built and became the property of the Catholic church on 12 October 1931.

An interesting fact about the statue is that, originally, the head of the statue was going to be looking straight ahead, but during the construction, they decided to tilt the head forwards so that it looks like he's looking down over the city. However, this meant redesigning chunks of it because it would have otherwise upset the balance, putting too much strain on the body and it might have either broken or eventually toppled over, doing a lot of damage to structures and people alike – Christ the Redeemer would have become Christ the destroyer which, I must admit, has a ring to it but then would only receive visits from army obsessives, DC Marvel comic fanatics and politicians.

Knowing how busy it was going to be, we managed to get there super early and were actually the first people to queue up for the train to go up the mountain. There was the option to walk up too but it was not recommended. In fact, as well as being warned off it by the free walking tour, it was also in a British newspaper that walking up was not recommended – although the media is not always a very reliable source of truth and/or the full story. In all honesty, if the British media is anything to go by, I should have been killed in São Paulo, resurrected, then skinned alive in Rio and then had my innards sucked out by some gooey squidgy thing in the Amazon... so I take their word with more than a shovel full of salt.

However, I couldn't help but laugh at the irony of the prospect of being beaten up and mugged whilst going to see Jesus. It's a little like the more serious irony at the Hajj on the pilgrimage to Mecca where millions of people go, and very often, a few thousands die in the crush of the stampede.

So, we took the train up to the top – by which time, of course, a bunch of other people had joined us. The journey took around 20 minutes and the ride up was actually a lot more pleasant than I expected. I kept my arms inside, stuffed our money down my pants as a deterrent and kept a keen eye to the outside in case any muggers were hanging around the train tracks with hankies over their faces in order to commit a great train robbery-style heist.

On entering the little carriage, I scoped out the seats and we sat in what I thought would be the most appropriate for using a screaming woman as a human shield before grabbing Vesi and jumping out of the window to safety. Now, you tell me... are there any more heroic ways of running away?

As it turned out, the ride up was quite pleasant with some steep parts to it and some flat parts. A lot was actually surrounded by trees as though we were travelling through a forest – part of Tijuca forest national park I guess.

However, I couldn't help but notice that there was only one rail track and, intermittently, it would split in 2 for about 100 metres before joining together again. But then again, I shouldn't be surprised, this train was opened in 1884 and I doubt they thought that 130 years later this monument would see hundreds of thousands of visitors every year. I think the conversation between the engineers was like this:

"Ey, Pedro,"

"Jess, Pedro"

"Ay tink we shoull mayk de two rail line"

"Wha' fou? Wance evrywan has seen dee statue, wance or twaice, dey will get bored an' jou can be sure da' eet will be tekken down an' a shop will be bilt heer."

"Jou tink?"

"Of course, Pedro. Eet like de weemen... Jou see de same wan evry day, an' you ge' bored. Ees why we so promiscuous in Brazil. Ploss... two rail is twaice di work... I 'ave my new girlfriend Pedro to see for the next month."

"Oh.... Jou so smart... an' so tru... I see my wife Pedro evry weekdey an' my 2 gorlfrien's Pedro and Pedro at di weeken'."

"Jou see?"

"Ay see... Bot, Pedro..."

"Jess, Pedro,"

"Jou steel have di Mexican accent."

OK... so although almost accurate, there is an outside possibility that one of them was lying about having more than one girlfriend – but the rest is good I'm sure.

At the top, we took in the view and it was spectacular to say the least. I guess it doesn't matter how many crocodiles you hold or astounding waterfalls you see, an amazing view is still an amazing view.

Under these circumstances, you can never take too many selfies – until you look back at them when you get home and realise that you are going to spend 15 minutes scrolling through hundreds of copies of exactly the same photo. BUT, while you're taking them, it's never enough in the hope of capturing that perfect moment where you get some lovely scenery behind you, neither of you is blinking, you both look good and you don't have someone's arm or head in the frame.

Stereotypically, this would have been the best place for a marriage proposal, but as I mentioned before, to me, it would have been the most tasteless and most kitsch proposal and would have deserved nothing less than a big fat, "NO... take your cheesy proposal and stick it up your arse." I.e. a proposal that could only have been worse if I proposed to her whilst sitting on the floor in the bedroom in my pants during an online advert whilst watching porn. (I'm sorry about that, Vesi... it really was research.) Ok, just kidding... but it is the kind of place I'd expect an accountant to propose to his girlfriend.

We were one of the first people up the top which was fab because, for the first 10 minutes, we didn't have to battle against the hundreds of people trying to squeeze into the viewing and selfie spots for a photo-bomb free shot.

Naturally, we also took loads of photos of the statue itself... which, thinking about it is a bit of a dumb idea because there are hundreds of much better photos that you can download from the internet. Our own photos can never look as good. There will always be some flaw whether it's the top half of some fat woman posing with her arms sticking outwards to mimic the statue, or some dirt on the camera lens making Jesus look like he has a bogey hanging. But still, it's the thrill of saying, "I took that shot... no, I don't know who that guy is... or those other 20 people, and yes, the colour is crap because I took it at the wrong time of the day, but still... I took it. And here's another photo where I waited until there were only 10 people in the way... And here are another 500 photos of exactly the same flipping thing."

We only stayed up the top for about 25 minutes because by the time we had taken in the view and taken 502 photos, including those with poses mimicking Jesus, the area had become pretty crowded so we decided to go back down with another thing ticked off the bucket list of life. Yes, it was impressive and the view was great but Jesus was exactly what we expected, just closer up – and Pedro was right... we're not going to do it again.

On the way down, we realised why the track split intermittently... it was to allow 2 trains travelling in opposite directions to go past each other – quite obvious when you think about it.

Back down, we stopped to get some lunch briefly and saw on the news that there were riots in São Paulo. Police were throwing tear gas and people were smashing up shops and looting them. It made us think... shit... we'll be back there in a few days and we were only there a few days ago. Blimey, if we had we hung around there a few more days we might have been caught up in this... we could have had some free loot... oh well... life is 99% right place at the right time and 1% action, so we reluctantly had to accept we would have to forego a new sandwich toaster this time.

We didn't quite understand what the riots were about at the time but looking at the news in English, they said it was about the government taking back a hotel that had been abandoned for 10 years and had been used to house the homeless. A pressure group had been trying to get the government to build affordable homes, but who knows what will be done with it and who will be in there to cream the money from the top. It's hardly surprising given the disparity between political wages compared to those of the ordinary person. You just have to look at the Northern part of Rio and compare it to the Southern part to see the disparity between rich and poor.

On our way back to Botafogo, we stopped at Ipanema beach for a sit down. Vesi knows I hate the beach but we couldn't visit Rio without spending a little more time visiting the most famous beaches in the world.

There were very few people on the beach because it was quite windy so only we gringos who didn't care about having sand blown around were prepared to walk and sit there – even though it meant later leaving the beach looking like a sugared doughnut.

Actually, it was a little cold but I'd promised Vesi I would touch the water while she paddled… which I did… and instantly regretted. I can see exactly why all those people died on the Titanic (or Chitaneekee as they call it in Brazil). The water was so cold they didn't even get a *chance* to swim the couple of thousand miles to shore. I shrieked like a girl which was probably not a great move as we were at Posto number 8… next to the gay section.

Fortunately, the Brazilians were even wussier than I was and had stayed away so I managed to sit down to wait for Vesi without incident and the only people I was bothered by were those bastards trying to sell stuff.

I can't say that I loved the beach part today. While Vesi was trying to brown herself, I passed the time watching the pigeons and seagulls (there weren't enough women on the beach at that point to do any other kind of 'bird' watching). For a moment, I thought that some of the pigeons were cold by the way they walked with their heads sunk into their bodies and exaggerated head nods, but it turned out that they were males courting the females. Watching one go after all these different females and being rejected reminded me of when I was at university and how I was so crap at pulling girls that I didn't even bother trying for long. Watching this one pigeon, I was almost envious. 'Look at this guy', I thought, 'he has tried it on with at least 5 birds (literally). His only 'pulling' move is that stupid little walk he does... they reject him... he tries again... rejected again... tries again... no shame... no fear of rejection, he just goes for it. I bet he ended up getting laid in the end. He found that one loose slapper pigeon who found his dumb little walk endearing or sexy and just went for it. Little bastard. Why couldn't I have been more like him at university? I've got a stupid little walk too... I can even dance and some might say I have a sense of humour as well, but NO, it turns out I wasn't even half as cool as that little pigeon. This sad little event made me feel a little less manly.

The day had worn on a bit. We were actually fairly tired from walking around since early in the morning. We had been to see Christ the Redeemer, pottered around a bit, lunched, I was almost killed by a bus (I'll not go into that) and it was starting to get a bit late. We didn't really have any plans for the rest of the day but we were both exhausted. I looked over at Vesi to see if she was changing from pink to brown but I guess she was starting to feel the cold too because she'd gone from pink to pale blue. So, we left.

By the time we had stopped at a supermarket and meandered back to our room in Botafogo, it was fairly late and we just sat chatting to anyone in the local vicinity. It would have been better had we understood more of what they were saying.

Before going to bed – ok, I don't need to tell you this but it was a part of our journey that will remain with me for the rest of my life, and I plan to tell any kids I have so they can tell their kids and so forth until the human race expires or is drastically culled... which could be anything from 32-117 years away (but that's another story) – I needed a poo. So, I took one. Now the thing about some countries is that they don't always have a sewage system that can support wads of toilet paper so they ask you to throw it in a specially provided bin. You might be familiar with this practice if you go somewhere like Turkey or other holiday destinations on the outskirts of Europe or outside.

To some 'westerners', this is a disgusting notion – meaning we westerners have been spoilt since our sewers can take a lot... which is good but it doesn't always prepare us for throwing away used toilet paper into bins.

Although here in Brazil, I'm not sure if it's the sewers that are the issue or the toilets themselves; the U bend is somewhat thinner than the ones we have in Europe. Ours are pretty hefty U bends and you could probably flush a small cat down the toilet... not very easily, but still.

So, as you can probably guess by now, SOMEHOW, when I flushed, the bowl filled with water and it wouldn't go down – or it did... but very, very slowly.

At 9pm, this is a problem and it's a problem I don't think enough public places address. In fact, this style of event can be so traumatic for guests and people in general that I have purchased a plastic bin for our bathroom at home so that it can be filled up with water and used for potentially embarrassing occasions. I call it Buster.

So, the toilet blocked and there were not enough cups, mugs or bowls on the premises to make a difference – no plungers, no utensils... and so I had to be a man about it (screw you, pigeon with the funny walk).

Making sure I had trimmed fingernails and with an appalling look from Vesi, I plunged my hand down... Well, I say hand, I mean arm. In these situations, it's always a case of the toilet paper blocking the toilet so you have to clear the toilet paper away.

I must have pulled out several handfuls of toilet paper... 'I didn't use that much toilet paper,' I thought. But I should explain that, by this point, the water was not... opaquely tainted. It was not like putting my hand in raw sewage. I had flushed a number of times and although the water was not completely clean, neither was it opaque brown.

So, to cut a longer than it should be story shorter, I dug out a lot more toilet paper than I thought I'd used and realised that, in actual fact, some git had blocked the toilet before we got anywhere near it and had legged it, leaving it for the next poor buggers to deal with, and those poor buggers were.... well... me.

What a sucker I'd been. Still... I was in it up to my elbow so all I could really do was try to finish off unblocking it, but as I found out a few handfuls of paper later, I had reached as far as my hand could reach and there was still paper to be extracted.

I did the only thing I could: I took my arm out, washed it a number of times, then had a shower, then washed it again, then again and then I went to see Vesi who was looking at me as though I'd just had my arm down a toilet... so I went back to wash it again before doing everything else that evening with my left hand.

In the morning before leaving at stupid o'clock, I wrote a note to Giuliana, the owner, and told her that while innocently having a wee, we realised the toilet was blocked but it hadn't been us, and how we'd heroically tried to unblock it.

I left the note somewhere she'd find it... and legged it to the airport.

My observations for the remainder of Rio are as follows:

1. People seem to just mind their own business here. They do their own thing, running, cycling, volleyball, beach volley or just sunbathing. To them, it's very much a screw you I'll do what I like attitude – which is actually admirable.
2. The beach has no seashells that I could see. It's as though they made the beach specifically for beachgoers.... How they do it, I have no idea. Unlike the UK, they don't have Polish immigrants ready to do all the jobs that the English think they

are too high and mighty for and (wrongly) feel there is more dignity in claiming the dole.

3 I learnt that my tropical fantasies of sitting somewhere beautiful, drinking from a coconut and maybe eating a guava or nice papaya actually do live up to my expectations.

4 We saw the glimpses of corruption from the images in São Paulo and the countless plastic smiles on the dodgy faces of the people putting themselves up for election.

5 A lot of people here are pretty fat… but looking at the ingredients on a lot of the foods, it's quite easy to see why.

6 Having said that, some of the women are very pretty and have great bodies but their facial expressions seem to say, "don't you dare talk to me," so I guess they are bugged a lot by men… even though, secretly, they might even like the attention, else why would you put more of your flesh on show than many other women (but that's another topic of conversation)?

7 Overall…. Rio is a fabulous place. But I would not like to live here.

8 Their U-bends are not as wide as ours – Grrrr!

Salvador

Day 12 – Salvador

The day was still very young. We left the Airbnb place at 06:40 and walked through ridiculous traffic to get to the station. We were kind of hoping for a bit less traffic as it would have made the journey over the really bad pavements a little easier... but no... it was nose to tail all the way. I thought it was New York that never slept. Guess Rio sleeps just as little, and whereas, in some countries, the procedure to turn a corner in a car is mirror, signal, manoeuvre, here it seems to be manoeuvre, get beeped at, beep back and swear at the other driver.

At the airport, we were pretty impressed with the recharging stations for phones and plug sockets for laptops. There was also a point with numerous adaptors for various different phones that were all free to use. How cool... in the UK, these would be charged out at £X per minute if they existed... which they probably do... but I've not paid attention so I don't know.

We were on our way to Salvador. The 3rd largest city in Brazil after São Paul and Rio de Janeiro, it is also known as São Salvador, Salvador da Bahia and Salvador de Bahia.... Even with 3 possible names to choose from, they all still sound nicer than Skegness. Salvador is the capital of the state of Bahia and used to be the capital city of Brazil before Rio.

I took a 1.5 litre bottle of water on the flight with me. I guess they don't think terrorists will travel on an internal flight.

We landed in Salvador and our immediate impression was that it was a bit different to Rio and the other places we'd been to so far. It took several sets of directions to find our way outside and to the bus stop. Finally, we managed to get out and walk through the 'any which way you want to drive is good' car park. On our journey through it, we must have been approached at least 8-10 times by random people asking if we wanted a taxi. I've learnt about this... I've seen the Simpsons.... You don't get into a random, unlicensed taxi with a random person who is offering to drive you out to the middle of nowhere, rob you and leave you for dead... ahem – sorry. I mean, offering to drive you to the destination of your choice.

So, we went to the bus stop and sat down. Sitting there was a guy walking up and down, yelling, "AGUA, AGUA, AGUA GELADA, AGUA GELADA," which translated to WATER, WATER, COLD WATER, COLD WATER... and every couple of minutes, some random guy walked past asking if we wanted a taxi.

Oh, one thing I should have mentioned... we were pretty much the only white people there, and not just slightly lighter in colour... I mean, it was like Nairobi. I think this is where the African slaves settled after the Portuguese brought them over.

Now, before some random holier than thou reader starts getting ready to whip out the racism card and encourage creationists and flat-earthers to jump on the bandwagon just because I mentioned people of a different skin colour... just think for a second, if you can. We were there, in a foreign country by ourselves with no tour guide other than a book that highlighted some of the nice things in the city along with a warning not to take a taxi from unlicensed drivers, and we stuck out like an Israeli newsreader with a tattoo of the swastika on his forehead. When something is THIS new and we look SO different, one can't help but feel a little apprehensive.

30 minutes passed… no bus. We saw several numbers pass on numerous occasions but not ours. I started to feel like a small group of Italian kids I once saw who were waiting for a bus in Bristol and had been for about an hour. The sign said that number 99 stopped there but I knew that it didn't. I was pretty worried we were in that same situation and we'd be spending the couple of days in Salvador at a bus stop at the airport. "Where the bloody hell have we landed?" We both said to each other.

"AGUA, AGUA, AGUA GELADA, AGUA GELADA," we'd been there longer than everyone apart from that guy selling water. People came and went… no bus… "AGUA, AGUA, AGUA GELADA, AGUA GELADA" – god he's annoying.

The reason we actually came to Salvador was because it had been recommended by my sister-in-law who said we'd love the people who are so jolly and the whole place is rhythmic and full of music – it's like a carnival all year round. Well, apart from her description of the place and the words she used to describe it all… everything else so far had been correct.

"I'm going to get back, and I'm going to kill her… Unless I die out here first."

FINALLY, after an hour of waiting, OUR BUS ARRIVED. We stood up as it circled around and came to a stop in front of us. At last.

But, NO... the bus driver stopped and switched off his engine. I laughed nervously thinking he was being environmentally friendly. Then the bus driver came out. I laughed nervously again thinking he was being welcoming... he looked at me, gave a half smile and pissed off somewhere.

We were back to square 1.

“AGUA, AGUA, AGUA GELADA, AGUA GELADA” – little bastard.

Helplessly, we waited a further 45 minutes for some git to come back to drive the bus.

We boarded and off we went, and now... this was Vesi’s dominion. Had it been for me, I’d have gotten off somewhere random and died 2 days later of dehydration not knowing where the hell I was, screaming for the git with the AGUA GELADA to rescue me.

She knew how far to go. She knew which road we were on at any time... and she was just following a map in the Lonely Planet tour guide and matching the road names to the ones we were on. How she does that, I say again, I do not know. I couldn’t even see the road names half the time. I just kept staring outside at the city... it was a bit like the northern part of Rio, grubby buildings, graffiti everywhere, people looking miserable. “Oh god, where the hell have we landed?”

I was so hoping that at any moment, like in Rio, the grubbiness would stop and we would enter a zone like South Rio where everything was sparkly and shiny and lovely... but then I heard words that made my heart sink. "Our stop." "What? You mean where that biker gang are waving chains or where that guy is sleeping in his own filth?"

"Gang with chains..."

"OH NOOOOOOOOOOOOOO!"

"Just kidding..."

"Phew"

"Filth guy..."

"OH NOOOOOOOOOOOOOO!"

We got off the bus just next to a square. Grubby rundown buildings, graffiti, groups of people staring at us and into space... I clutched onto Vesi for dear life in such a way that made it look like I was protecting her more than I was scared to death. Turns out she was doing the same to me... Our hands wouldn't have separated in a hurricane.

And I say again – holier than thou types ready to brandish the racism flag. When you are among a handful of white people and you're in a strange place where you don't know a) what people are like and b) exactly where you're going, I don't care who you are, you're going to be nervous. You don't want to walk down a wrong alley that you don't know the reputation of... hey, this is Brazil not the frigging Vatican. You're unlikely to be assaulted by a cardinal even if he is wearing a funny dress and, however unlikely we were to be assaulted or mugged or whatever, fear of the unknown was clear and present in our sweaty palms.

Having said all this though, there was music in the air. There were people smiling in certain places... not in the square we had crossed just after getting off the bus, but in the alleys with shops and market stalls and restaurants and the like. It was almost an idealised version of New Orleans (pre-Katrina) – like in the film the Blues Brothers. I was expecting Aretha Franklin to appear in her apron and break out into song, and although she didn't (I don't think she knew I was there), within a few minutes, we calmed down and started appreciating the place a bit more. Ok, so it looked a bit grubby and dirty, and ok, as white people we were in a massive minority, but beneath all that, it didn't actually feel dangerous. I can imagine walking through Harlem and even if it might present itself similarly, it probably feels different. Of course, I don't know as I've never been, but I've been places where it didn't feel safe. I was starting to accept Salvador more than I had when I got off the bus next to the man in his own filth.

We walked through the streets and market and bought some food – fruit and the like – as we were going to our Salvador Airbnb place and we wanted to have some food there.

The food was about half the price it was in Rio, but then again, it was also half the quality. We bought the usual fruits like avocados, watermelons and complemented that with some vitamin drink and some biscuits and local bread products... they were a bit stale, but hey... when in Rome.

We made our way to the Airbnb place which was down a really dodgy looking road, but again, maybe the dodginess was part of part of Salvador's charm... or perhaps I was only beginning to see it as 'charm' because we are here for 3 days and to *not* see some charm in amongst the grime would make for 3 very depressing days indeed.

We knocked on the door... SHTUM... THWING... SLIDE... CLICK CLACK CLOCK... (they were the locks and bolts to open the door). "Hmmm, safety first... Charming". A fairly young, very dark – and I mean Ethiopian dark – and quite pretty lady appeared. She was wearing a pair of glasses and initially had an extremely suspicious look on her face. On telling her who we were, her expression changed and she smiled – thank god.

She was the wife of the guy who had put the room up on Airbnb. She kindly welcomed us in and showed us the room we were staying in, along with the kitchen and what we were welcome to and what belonged to the family.

We've done Airbnb a number of times and it still gets to me how we just turn up at a random person's house and sleep there. People who do their own thing during the day and effectively ignore the fact they have some complete strangers rummaging through their fridge and walking around their house wrapped in nothing but a towel, or worse, a fig leaf.

There is something incredibly refreshing about it whilst feeling really wrong at the same time.

Before trying to book a place in someone's house, we – like most people, I guess – look at the reviews and if they are good then that's encouraging. However, someone has to be the first person to stay there and that takes bravery, so I take my hat off to that person. They have no reviews to go on... just pure faith that the people whose house they're staying in are not going to drug them and harvest their organs for the black market. Yes, ok, it's very unlikely anything bad will happen, but then again, it's very unlikely someone will win the lottery but people still play in their millions and someone usually does.

The room we are in is quite nice; simple with a double bed in the middle but no window. In all honesty, it's nicer than we expected given what we had to walk through to get here, and by that, I mean the dodgy looking streets with grimy and grubby buildings, so for £40 for 2 nights for 2 people... frankly, it's a pretty damn good deal. Maybe I am actually scared to death of this place but because we're here, we have to make the most of it, so the fear inside me has been temporarily numbed until we leave and when we get on the plane. Then I'll probably start to cry.

The lady doesn't actually speak any English but we caught her name and it was something *like* Alquila (but not exactly). Speaking slowly, we could understand her Brazilian Portuguese... (that's the luck on our side of being able to speak Italian). Of course, Vesi understood more than I did... but then again, her brain is incredibly tuned into words and the details in them. So, when Alquila said a word in Portuguese, it was picked up by Vesi and when I said, "huh?" Vesi repeated that word to me with a more Italian slant and I had that eureka moment... I said it once, I'll say it again. Maybe I'm just a bit thick, but in reality, Vesi... kicks... arse.

After the pleasantries, we actually stayed in the room for a couple of hours to sort some stuff out before eventually going for a walk to see the local sights of Salvador. We can visit Salvador properly tomorrow, but for today, we thought we could just get acquainted with the local area and get some dinner at the same time. We had seen a couple of busy restaurants on our way here so they looked ideal. I wasn't sure if I wanted to take a camera but I wanted to show my sister-in-law where she had flipping sent us.

We were told that to access the restaurants, the market, bus stops and things we might want to see, we had to turn left on exiting the house. To the right there was nothing of interest. It felt like a "stick to the path, steer clear of the moors" moment. If you've ever seen the film 'An American Werewolf in London' – giving the impression that going on the moors was a bad idea. And it was. The 2 guys accidentally steered onto the moors and one was killed by a werewolf while the other one was scratched, thus cursing him.

So, we turned left outside the house, walked around the local area to explore it a little, and that's all I have to say about that – I'm gonna kill her.

Dinner consisted of the remains of the bready products that we had bought earlier in the day and we returned to the Airbnb place where we met and had a chat with Alquila's husband. He was a short white American guy called Mark who owned a music shop just around the corner from the house. He had originally come to Brazil to do some capoeira dancing but he met Alquila, got married and settled here.

Now, for those of you who don't know, capoeira is an Afro-Brazilian concoction between dance, martial arts, music and acrobatics. I'm sure if you threw a frying pan into the mix they could include pancake flipping into the mix.

The name capoeira has mysterious origins... i.e. nobody is exactly sure where it came from but there are 3 possibilities:

1 Tupi-Guaraní... of course... like the origin of so many things in Brazil. The CA possibly coming from the caá or kaá to mean vegetation/underbrush/area with shrubs and growth. And then coêra, poêra or puêra which is the past tense, suggesting that it is no longer there... i.e. very basically growth that is no longer there... we'd call it deforestation or privatisation under the bastard Tories.
The theory being that the slaves used to use capoeira – the martial arts side I assume, not the dancing side – to evade recapture once they escaped.

What's the likelihood of this being true? I have no idea. I can't see how it links into dancing and I can't see how clearing forest stuff links in with fighting. So, this could be true just as easily as it could be complete bollocks.

2 From Portuguese, and I must apologise, I took this straight from a website. It looks like such gonads that it would be like summarising the workings of a monkey that had been banging on a typewriter for 20 minutes.

From capoeira-connection.com – *"Big basket or cage in which capons and other birds are kept. From capão [capon, a male chicken castrated when young] + the suffix eira. This etymology suggests that slaves bringing cages of birds to sell at the market used to pass their time there by playing capoeira"*

See what I mean? – utter shite. When I first read it, I thought it was a long anagram.

3 From African Kikongo – spoken by some people in the democratic republic of Congo and surrounding area, including Angola – coming from the word kipula/kipura, it refers to sweeping ground movements used in martial arts.

In fact, if you watch capoeira, there are a lot of sweeping movements and even the basic step looks like a sweep with its forward, side and back motion.

In the end, I've tried to look up the origins of the word and the dance and it's not entirely clear. Basically, it may well have been lost in the sands of time. I've tried to read up on what linguists and the like believe and they all had differing opinions, so I don't think I'm wrong in saying that people don't necessarily know, even if they claim to be certain they do. So, if you ever feel like bluffing, pick one of the above, say it with conviction, add a couple of the buzzwords like "Kipura" or "Kipula" or "From the Tupi- Guaraní language", etc. and even the most ardent expert won't have grounds to challenge you, especially if you begin the conversation with, "well, from my research...". Even though saying "*well*" means you're about to talk complete tripe, it somehow adds an air of authority to it. Just listen to a politician next time he/she pretends to answer to a simple yes/no question in some half-arsed interview. "*Well*" suggests you have something to say... even if you don't. THEN, if you can shoehorn in the word "*juxtaposition*"... Christ, a newspaper would call you "an expert," which these days, if the media mention it, it means absolutely nothing.

So, Mark ended up staying, opening a shop and starting a family. In fact, a 9-year-old boy strolled in called Arturo, he was really cute, cheerful and playful even though he didn't have a clue who we were, which was kind of endearing. He was literally a mix of the two parents. Brown with dark eyes and an American accent – although he could speak Portuguese too.

Turns out that Mark didn't let him outside the area to play with the other kids which made me feel really bad for him, but at the same time, I kind of understand. If the area is a bit dodgy, then you don't want him falling in with the wrong crowd. However, the idea of keeping him inside almost seems like he's missing out on a childhood with friends in the neighbourhood. It's a really difficult one to call and I'm not placed to judge... what would I do as the father if I were in a similar position?

We also met Effie that evening. She's an Australian girl who was doing a gigantic trip and was here at the moment by herself... brave girl. She was really nice and we all got on really well. In the end, we went to bed feeling fairly positive for the following day. Mark gave us a few areas to avoid... such as turning right outside the house, but apart from that, the area was actually pretty safe.

Roll on Salvador.

Day 13 – Salvador

Up early again today and it was off to the historic centre of Salvador. Breakfast of passion fruit and watermelon and a cold shower later, we started walking to the centre.

Looking around, the district we were staying in was not very attractive at all, but by the time we reached something resembling the historic centre, we couldn't walk 30 metres without being hassled by someone asking if we wanted a tour guide, someone begging, someone trying to tell us about God or just someone trying to show us a shop they own. What an incredible pain in the arse. It felt like being in Tunisia, but I guess a lot of these people are descended from African slaves so it's not a major surprise – however annoying it might seem, it really is rather entrepreneurial.

We saw some fairly nifty things and learnt some history along the way when we stopped in little museums and the like.

Very briefly:

In 1549, Salvador became the first capital when the Portuguese settlers came under Brazil's first governor-general (i.e. the head honcho), Tomé de Sousa. He brought with him 400 soldiers, 400 settlers and a statue (royal I guess). Included in the people he brought along, there were a number of priests (maybe because he was a goodie) and prostitutes (maybe because he was human).

On top of a cliff overlooking the Bay of All Saints, in a defensive position, he plonked a city and then surrounded it by walls to keep out the nasty natives of the land. Bloody natives… always getting in the way of the righteous invaders.

The city became a major port, initially for the slave trade and sugarcane industry, then later for exporting tobacco and then they introduced cattle ranching before trading gold and diamonds. The city was super wealthy and the architecture is said to reflect that… hmmm, looking at it now, I guess you had to be there.

The city is divided into 2 sections due to an "escarpment" – basically an 85m-high cliff in the middle of the city – Originally, the upper part of the city was used for residential purposes as well as containing administrative and religious districts, while the lower part was more the commercial centre with the market and a port close by.

Salvador remained Brazil's capital city for a couple of centuries until the decline of the sugarcane industry and, from there, along with the gold rush, the capital moved to Rio de Janeiro in 1763. I've already talked a bit about the history of Rio.

We went through the town and stood on the edge of the 85-metre escarpment and looked out over the area of Salvador that led to the Bay of All Saints. The bay itself looked lovely with nice looking water and expensive looking boats, but below the escarpment and leading off to the side as far as the eye could see were high rise buildings… lots of them… and these did not look so nice. In fact, they looked really run down and the sight was positively grim. Many looked condemned.

Even the buildings that did not look condemned or filthy were just plain ugly. It was as though some of the worst council-owned buildings from the UK in the 1970s had been dumped there... badly. It was a really pitiful sight to see what were once likely to be incredible looking buildings peeling or stained on the outside with massive amounts of damp or black dirt that ran all the way up the 15-20 storeys.

They were so horrendous that I looked at Vesi and said, "thank god we don't live anywhere like this." I took some photos in the same way a person would take a photo of a car accident. I class it as morbid curiosity so that, one day, I can look back and remember how it felt to stand on the edge of the escarpment and think that wherever I end up will hopefully NEVER be as bad as any of the buildings we could see. I can't liken it to anything I've ever seen before. The area looked like it was just decaying. I've seen places where one building looks awful but it's surrounded by nice looking buildings. I've seen the building works around buildings like these to try to give them a facelift. Here however, a facelift here would be ineffective. This part of Salvador would have needed the surgical equivalent of a facelift, liposuction, breast implants, a nose job, hair transplant, ears pinning, botox injections, a penis extension and anal bleaching all in one – and that's before euthanizing it and starting again.

On turning around and still with a disgusted look on my face, we saw two women dressed in what I guessed to be carnival clothes running towards us. They tried to get us to pose with them so that they could ask for money for the photos... Haha!

Not fooling ol' Serge, my luvvies. I remember the days of the bastard rose sellers in England who stalked poor young couples sitting down after the pub closing time for a romantic late night kebab… seeing the grateful looks on the boys' faces when this saviour of theirs held out a rose-laden hand and was about to ensure they got – at the very least – a snog by the end of the evening, all thanks to this miracle flower… and then the crushingly awkward look a split second later when the bastard asks for £3. Of course, by that point, the guy feels compelled to buy one so as not to look like he doesn't care, so he starts rifling through his pennies for several minutes before ending up paying with a £20 note. Then he makes a mental note not to accept anything from these pigs again.

A lot of people go through that moment, but are rarely suckered in twice, which is probably why you don't see them anymore; people wised up and started giving them a berth wide enough to make it look like they had bubonic plague.

I never got suckered in but I don't think that makes me look good, it just made me look like the guy who didn't get a date often enough… I was unwittingly good. I used to go to where these bastard rose sellers never went: a restaurant. But because I was a jobless sixth form student, I'd take my date out for a pizza with a voucher that let *this* lothario buy the cheapest pizza for just a penny, but that's another story.

But back to Brazil. So, in the end, we sent the women dressed in carnival gear packing…. And just to rub it in, I took a photo of them from a distance and *didn't* pay for it… ok, it wasn't a very good photo. One of them was looking at the underside of her shoe and the other one was scratching her arse, but still, I got a free photo and the last laugh… I have now deleted the photo.

We then descended the escarpment and went to an undercover market in a large warehouse-type building… well, I say warehouse in the sense that it was a big building without separation walls like a warehouse.

Inside, there were lots of little market stalls selling all kinds of shite. And when I say shite, I mean shite. There were some lovely pieces of artwork and beautiful wooden sculptures (mostly sculptures of fruit), but they also sold a whole load of crap too, including pointless trinkets that look funky when you look at them the first time and then their lustre fades as soon as you hand over the money and remorse sets in… especially when you realise that you can't just put it in your pocket because it will break or bend. They had those trinkets that looked like paperclips folded into names or crap shapes. The only crap thing that was missing was the walnut shell with the googly eyes, although they had other bits of crap with googly eyes.

We were drawn to the artwork. We considered buying a couple of small paintings to take back to the UK. There were some really beautiful 3D paintings with painted backgrounds and raised detail like bridges and wooden houses made of real bits of wood, beautifully shaped and perfectly stuck next to trees with the trunks also made of wood and the leaves of some funky material.

I really liked those. They would look super stunning on our wall at home, but crushed in a suitcase and transported on several more flights, I severely doubted they would make it back in one piece, so in the end, we decided on and haggled (90 reals down to 60… not bad) over a couple of thin pictures with wooden frames on the back. One of Salvador from the sea which Vesi liked and one very orange one with 3 Capoeira dancers painted on.

We left the market to walk around the historic centre passing by some churches on the way, which were very beautiful both on the outside and inside, as always, but I still find it amazing and grotesque how churches take money from the poor with the same impunity as banks – ok, donations rather than theft but it's all based on lies. In fact, between the church and banks, scandals are 10 to the dozen… shame not enough people seem to care about this either.

We walked to the Pelourinho, known as Pelo to the locals, which is the historic centre in Salvador. From what we read, Pelourinho means 'whipping post' in Portuguese – not in a brothel kind of way – more a slave punishment kind of way. They had various places/posts around the city to expose and punish offenders. This was also the location for slave auctions back in the day when slavery was common, or, more to the point… accepted (it still goes on but under the cover of zero-hour contracts).

When slavery was outlawed in 1835, over time, the city fell into disrepair. So, in effect, Salvador was all glitz until it lost its status as the capital city and then, after slavery was banned, it was abandoned and left to become a bit of a shithole. A lot of repair work was done in the 1990s to try to revive the city's old glory and it has, in fact, become a tourist attraction.

We walked around the area. Cobbled streets that were very quaint, lovely colourful houses, tat for sale as well as lots of nice little restaurants and little eateries. Annoyingly though, we were hassled every minute by someone wanting to sell us something or offering their services as a tour guide of the area and, believe it or not, that does take the magic away somewhat.

We stopped for lunch in a cooking school. It was really good actually. They did food by weight which I am starting to like the idea of in all honesty.

But even with all the music, quaintness, colour and the array of friendly people, the feeling of the place did end up getting a little more menacing when we were about to walk down one of the roads that leads off of the main route where a couple of guys called at us and warned us not to go down there... And what was menacing about it was that it looked no different to any other road. There were some guys a couple of hundred metres away who didn't look menacing from a distance but could well have been for all we knew. Had those guys not been there to stop us, we might have walked down there. It was a shame because, up to that point, we weren't feeling threatened at all.

We left the Pelhourinho after stopping for a coffee. I had a coconut water but the effect was not the same. The scenery outside of Vesi wasn't beautiful and the coconut was ambient temperature, i.e. about 28 degrees... so my fantasy of happiness still stands... it has to be coconut water in a beautiful place... but to add to it now, the coconut water has to be cold.

Under the circumstances, I think I'd have preferred to spend a couple more days in the jungle, fishing for piranhas and setting up camp out in the jungle – which were a couple of the other activities we could have done but, unfortunately, due to time constraints, didn't manage.

We went back to the restaurant we had seen before that was full of people and sat down, it was a semi rodizio restaurant. There was a load of meat on chopping boards available and a number of bowls of vegetables. But instead of coming around and cutting pieces off, it was all self-service and you then paid by the weight of the plate, giving the beef the same value as beetroot, which is unconscionable in the UK – or virtually anywhere else for that matter.

The food was pretty good... admittedly, the chopping boards with the meat looked less than sanitary but you know... when in Rome, etc. etc.

The evening was spent back at the Airbnb house just chatting to the family and playing with their 9-year-old son who was really quite fun. The dad, Mark, was actually appreciative of the time I spent with him because he didn't have many children to play with.

I also tried to teach him the importance of mathematics in the world, so we played a game – a bit like angry birds – where you had to knock down a structure with things shot out of a cannon and when these structures came down, I'd look at him and say, "you see. That structure came down like that due to *mathematics*," and then after a few more stages in the game, he'd knock something down, look at me with a cheeky little grin, point to the screen and say, "mathematics" with his little American accent... I had to admit, it was very cute.

It took a while to get to sleep. The outside was pretty noisy and it reminded me of those films where someone might be trying to go to sleep in New York, they turn their music off to sleep and the sound of music is immediately replaced by sirens, screams, people talking, shouting, glasses breaking and gunshots... ok, it was not quite like that but there was a low flying aeroplane, cars parking, people outside the house talking as they went past, dogs barking and people playing music, so it was hard to get to sleep.

The night was then further interrupted by numerous rumblings in my gut and several visits to the toilet... sitting down at 3am cursing the restaurant. And for that matter, the Romans. In the UK, we are wusses... our guts can't take this kind of abuse.

Vesi joined me in lavatory do-si-do a couple of times and we ended up having a less than pleasant night.

Day 14 - Salvador

Woke up 8:30 with a hungover belly. Fortunately, I'd stopped needing to go to the toilet by this point but my belly was behaving just like a guy who wakes up one morning in a park, naked, with a stinking headache, clutching a traffic cone and says to anyone who approaches, "oh god… just leave me alone."

Vesi pretty much felt the same.

"Last day,"

"Last day."

"We can do this!"

(You can choose who says what there)

Vesi and I got together and Vesi decided unanimously for the both of us that we were going to the beach.

Yes, the fucking beach. I'd like to take everyone who likes the beach and drop them in the middle of the Sahara for a few hours and say, "THERE'S THE FUCKING BEACH… LOVE IT!"

So, with dodgy bellies and poor Vesi suffering from TOTM (Time Of The Month) pains on top of that, we boarded a bus and off we went to Barra (a neighbourhood in Salvador). On the way, we picked up some dry bits of food – some crackers and dry baked goods.

In all honesty, we didn't feel like doing anything but we knew we should. Once off the bus, we stopped to watch a couple of guys in the street doing some Capoeira who had attracted a bit of a crowd.

We took some photos and, admittedly, the frozen photo actions look good but, overall, the dance itself looks quite pointless and I sincerely doubt that any of the origins remain. Two guys… one in his late 50s/early 60s (good on him, really active guy clearly – high kicks, handstands, cartwheels, etc.) stepping and then occasionally a leg would fly through the air, catch the other guy off-guard and whack him on the chin. Somehow, stopping to apologise for kicking someone in the face when you're actually trying to kick him in the face has a slight stench of absurdity to it… but hey… the photos I took look really good.

We stopped for an açaí smoothie – mainly so that I could go to the toilet. It was one of those toilets which they lock up so you have to ask for a key. Not a big fan of that and although I'm not overly private, I don't like to announce to people I'm going to the toilet. Then, afterwards, there's the awkwardness of having a queue outside when you open the door to leave… denying you were responsible for the smell and trying to tell them to take the key back to the bar when they are done – all in a different language. It has the same level of dignity as bungee jumping in a mankini.

Luckily, none of that happened and I was able to take the key back to the bar myself.

We then made the effort to sit on the beach for a little while. I hate the beach... and this one in particular. To say it was manky was an understatement. It was more like an industrial dumping ground. Dirty, sooty sand, grime in the corners where there were mini stone piers. If they really have given Salvador a facelift, then we were definitely still in the saggy jowl area awaiting the second operation.

On our way back to the bus, we stopped for some food as we were both a little peckish, and I think this place was our final testament to Salvador... Genuinely unfriendly staff.

I hate to say this but, fortunately, we had to leave to go to the airport.

By 5pm, we said our goodbyes, washed our hands a couple of times and headed for the bus to take us to the airport. This took about 1 hour and a half. The bus started off completely packed and I was already quite used to having some woman's face in my armpit and some random guy's bottom resting on my crotch, so it didn't even feel unusual.

The only thing is, the airport to the bus did not have the word 'Airport' on it which was unlike every other bus we'd been on in Brazil... so going only by the number on it (as mentioned in the lonely planet guide), we were a bit nervous that the bus was going to take us somewhere else. The driver was impossible to reach as he was behind 15 layers of people and probably some bulletproof glass, so we couldn't ask him, therefore, we had to rely on the words of some of the passengers... and if you've ever asked anyone for directions anywhere, you'll know how unreliable random people can be.

"Oh, yes. Go down the road, ignore the building on the right and the second turn on the left and there is usually a drunk with a shopping trolley who lies on a bench there around this time on the left-hand side opposite a bus stop near a grey house. Well... ignore that house. Then it's 100 metres... no, wait... 2 miles... no... 100 metres... oh... hang on... well, it's between 100 metres and 2 miles after that house, then there's a turning on the right and that is where you want to go. Stonecold road... yes."

"ok, so down the road and it's first right on Stonecold road?"

"Yes,"

"Ok thanks."

"Oooh, wait... no. I think I might be wrong. It's actually in the other direction. Ok, so go up this road where you'll see a fork... bla, bla, bla."

In the meantime, we opened the crackers we bought and Vesi looked at the ingredients and noticed 4 words that I've never wanted to see: 'contains genetically modified ingredients'. This argument could fill a whole book in itself but there is one phrase that sums the whole GM thing up... "They don't want to feed the world, they want to control the world's food supply," purely on the trumped-up lawsuits that these GM companies get involved in... i.e. suing everything and anyone... frankly, I don't want this shit anywhere near me if I can help it. Is the food safe for everyone in the long-term? I don't know, possibly... but that's not the argument. It's when NON-GM farmers get their crops *accidentally* pollinated by a neighbouring GM field and either have to pay for use of patent rights or they are sued. Bluntly, I find that behaviour abhorrent and that is one of a number of reasons I am against genetically modified foods at this present time. Another is that with all the chemicals used in terms of weed killers and herbicides, it's not good for the soil and it could spark the birth of 'superweeds', just like the overuse of antibiotics creating superbugs. On top of that, in 2011, WikiLeaks revealed how the American ambassador to France went back to his government asking them to retaliate and cause "some pain" against European countries who rejected GM food. In essence, there is so much filth and corruption underneath the whole GM story that I am totally against it and fight it at every turn. And to put to bed the main myth... NO WE DON'T EFFING NEED IT. Put it this way, would you be happy to be fed food by a company that made agent orange, makes nuclear weapons and tried to defend the use of DDT saying it was ok? I.e. a company whose business model is based around killing stuff? In the end... people can argue anything they want in favour for GM but not against the primary motivations: control and profit over everything else.

End of political rant.

So, what did we do with the crackers? Well, we had already bought them by accident so throwing them would not have done any good... not buying them would have been better. Sorry about bringing the subject up... it feels I've tainted this diary with talk of genetic modification... It's the literary equivalent of looking at a naked woman with a nice body but seeing a giant oozing wart on her nose.

So, we were on the bus travelling to the airport. One thing that amazes me around here is that beggars are ok to get on the bus for free. Then they tell a story to everyone on the bus and walk up and down collecting any money from anyone willing to give them anything. Had we thought about it sooner, Vesi and I could have reached the airport free of charge just by carrying a bowl onto the bus and giving the people on board a long speech – well, long enough to reach the airport – about how the education system was so bad, we never learnt Portuguese, how we have no home or job in Salvador and have had to spend the last few nights in the houses of other people... hey, at least it's all true.

They sometimes also sell little bags of sweets, which is quite a nice idea as it feels more like a two-way transaction rather than a one-way thing. Of course, the sweets are overpriced but that's ok. You know they are homeless... hang on... where do they get the sweets from? Do they mug kids for them or ask politicians to do it for them if they aren't low enough to do it themselves?

It's quite impressive though, they always manage to collect from quite a few people. I'd love to know what they say. I'm guessing it's better than the line in the UK... "spare any change to get into a hostel please?" Maybe it's something like... "I know where you live and if you don't give me money, I'm going to come to your houses and take your children away." Then those with kids give money and those who don't, give nothing. I don't know... I don't speak Portuguese. We didn't manage to give anything because here in Salvador we made sure that all our money was stuffed down our trousers and even a homeless guy would probably have found it a bit grim to be given a handful of pubic hairs along with some loose change.

We reached the airport at around 18:40. Realistically, a very welcome sight given we weren't entirely sure we were on the right bus. And compared to the city, it looked very modern. I like old style buildings but not so much that they look like they were condemned by a previous generation.

I think the final act that depicted the people here perfectly was that as we walked *towards* the airport with a clear sense of purpose, about 30 metres away from the entrance, some bloke approached us and asked if we needed a taxi. I almost felt like saying, 'sure, drive us to check-in desk 27 please. It is upstairs so I hope your car is small enough to fit into the lift.'

Anyway, we made it to the airport with plenty of time to spare – 9 hours actually. Our flight was at 03:30 but I think we'd had enough of Salvador, so we opted to leave purely because we didn't really fancy going anywhere else. I'm sure there are some lovely parts of Salvador but where we stayed wasn't one of them, unfortunately.

As the aeroplane accelerated down the runway, lifted off and disappeared into the big black sky, I looked at Vesi's tired little eyes and said, "let's never go there again, please."

<u>My observations in Salvador:</u>

1. It looks like a massively run-down shadow of what certainly used to be a very impressive city.
2. It feels less safe than it is, but I think that can be said for many places.
3. As opposed to other cities we've been to, Salvador has a largely black population. Unlike Rio where people tend to be lightly tanned, and Manaus where the people are slightly more tanned – although there are still a lot of more lightly tanned people in other parts of the city of Salvador.
4. There is more poverty felt here than in the other parts of Brazil we've been to so far, and that includes Manaus which has portions of its residents living a couple of hours from anywhere, in a house that is on stilts, who make a living from picking nuts from the jungle and selling them.
5. The food and the music were meant to be an attraction of this city but they turned out to be rather disappointing – as was the street food. The music was confined to the more run-down areas of the city… and even then, nobody was dancing.

6 Even the nicer parts of the city that we visited were right next to some no-go areas which put a bit of a downer on visiting them. At least Rio was divided into sections: south side, north side, etc. But pretty much the whole of the south side felt ok and nobody warned us of any places we shouldn't go.

7 The beach was a let-down even though we only went to one. It put us off of going to another and there are meant to be some quite nice beaches in Salvador.

8 Overall, Salvador is not the nicest place to visit.

Bonito

Manaus
Salvador
Bonito
São Paulo
Rio De Janeiro
Foz Do Iguaçu

Day 15 – Travel to Bonito

Bonito... Why Bonito? Where is Bonito? What's in Bonito?

Well, we went to meet my brother and sister-in-law (Alessio and Priscila). That's the same sister-in-law who recommended going to Salvador. Good, I thought, I'd have a chance to talk to her while my belly was at the tail end of a hurricane. Not enough to make me race with the devil every time I need the toilet, but a solid and humbling reminder of the potential grip it could have over me.

Bonito is a little town in the state of Mato Grosso do Sul. It has a population of fewer than 20,000 and is where Priscila's (Pri) father lives. We will be staying in a caravan outside his house.

Yes... a caravan... in a little town owned by a man who spent his life being a farmer. I was not bowled over by the idea... I could picture it now.

Ok, now apologies to some of you on the subject matter in the next sentences, but it's still cleaner than talking about GM food.

Before landing, I heard an exquisite sound... that of a dry fart. It accidentally popped out when I was dozing and my initial feeling was one of panic. I'd spent the previous day with a dodgy belly and trying really hard not to fart to avoid my pants looking like a Jackson Pollock. But now I was back to passing just air... I say it regularly, feeling normal is one of the best feelings you can get. Think about it. When you're feeling ill, all you want to do is get back to a state of normality. If you're feeling great, that feeling cannot last and if it does, it becomes your normality… so feeling normal is the best feeling you can feel.

We landed in São Paulo at 06:40 in the morning after having had a couple of hours sleep on the plane… if that. This time, we landed at the other airport in São Paulo… Congonhas. This one was apparently slap bang in the middle of the city – however, the person who told us that was the same sister-in-law who recommended we go to Salvador, so we weren't overly trusting of its location.

We were pretty exhausted so we had breakfast at the airport… a ridiculously expensive breakfast too. We were almost considering going out into town again but we were so tired we couldn't face it. 49.30 reals (about £12.50) for 2 croissants, 2 pães de queijo (that's plural of pão de queijo) and 2 espressos – pretty cheap for UK standards really but here in Brazil, it felt like we were being taken for a ride.

It was a bit like the after-feeling from haggling for a souvenir t-shirt with some street seller in Tunisia when they're trying to flog it to you for the exorbitant price of £2.53… but over there, NO BLOODY WAY… I want it for 10p or I'm leaving… and you end up haggling over pennies and, in the end, you feel hard done by because you bought that t-shirt for £1.82 and not 10p. It's not until you get home that you stop seething and picturing horrible bloody revenge in your mind and realise you just bought a t-shirt for the same price you could buy half a finger of a pair of gloves in the UK. Then all is forgiven and you can get on with your life and remove the pins from the voodoo doll you made of the street seller who you thought had ripped you off so viciously. We didn't haggle at the airport but the overall feeling was the same, except for the voodoo doll.

The girl behind the counter was pointing to a glass that was next to her and saying something to me... I thought she was pointing badly at a nearby table and I did the very British thing of staring at her with a blank expression and pointing to a table, saying slowly, "Y E S, W E A R E S I T T I N G T H E R E" and stood back feeling proud that I'd successfully communicated with a native as she laughed and pointed at an actual glass. She then repeated what she had said earlier and I pulled an "aha" face... "No thanks," I responded... 'sorry, my dear,' I thought, 'but you'll have to get up pretty early in the A-M to pull the wool over my eyes and try to rip me off with your little add-ons.'

I only noticed when she held up 2 cups of different sizes that she was just asking me what size espresso I wanted. Ok, so I felt like a proper D cup, but come on, why not do that in the first place? Or say something like "GRANDE?" (pronounced something like GRANJI) or "PEQUENO?" (pronounced PEKENO). I asked for small (pequeno) but I guess I ended up choosing large because that's what came.

We sat down to wait – for about 6 hours. What a pain. I walked outside to see what part of the city we might be able to go to but I was faced with a massive grey building in front of any kind of view. I walked around a bit and behind the grey building was another grey building. We looked it up on the map... Republica (where we went to a couple of weeks ago) – almost 9 miles away – aww we really could not be arsed. We were both exhausted so we just sat down and snoozed for a couple of hours. Naturally, I tied everything loose to my body but I think by now that goes without saying.

Alessio and Pri appeared at around 13:30. We hung around the airport and chatted to them for a couple of hours before checking in and boarding a flight for Campo Grande (pronounced Kampo Granji). This time, it was poor Vesi to have the person in front tilt their seat back, but she didn't mind so much, which was good because it was Pri. Even I had to switch off my internal kill mode for the duration of the flight but it didn't stop my mouth from twitching.

In Campo Grande, we had a hire car waiting for us. It was a nice big saloon with a puny 1000cc engine. Jesus, I thought, my old Fiat Panda had a similar sized engine and I could barely get 60mph out of it. We set off for Bonito which was a good 170 miles away. Fortunately, we had a satnav because we didn't know where we were going – plus, it was going to start getting dark pretty soon and we were going to be driving much of this in the dark. Also, I must apologise to those of you who still believe the earth is flat... satnavs really do work in the southern hemisphere. You really don't know what you are talking about, but that is also another story.

With the satnav leading the way, it took us about six times longer than it should have to get to Bonito, but that's because the satnav thought 'hmmm, I think we should take this empty country lane as opposed to the main road.' That's what satnavs are best at, isn't it? But this wasn't just any country lane... this was a 30-mile pitch black dirt track surrounded by trees. And when I say dirt track, it was probably the worst quality road you could ever imagine. Frankly, it makes me wonder sometimes whether some satnav designers run underground networks of criminals and install routes that increase your chances of being carjacked. "At the end of the road, turn left into the abandoned car park, turn your engine off and wait five minutes." I know it's unlikely, but when driving down one of these roads, it doesn't half feel like it.

You know how some roads have potholes? Well, this one the satnav had guided us to had gouges – maybe a foot deep and about 2 metres wide. They were so close together that we were constantly bouncing up and down as though we were riding a galloping camel, so needless to say we couldn't drive much faster than 3 miles per hour.

It was one of the most horrendous journeys any of us had undertaken. 1 car, at around 8pm, alone, literally miles from anywhere in the pitch black, 100% reliant on a satnav that could have been hacked by a little Chinese person who was just taking the piss, on a road that could be mistaken for a freshly ploughed field.

I wasn't scared when the boat had started sinking at night on the Amazon River, I wasn't scared when I jumped off a mountain with some other bloke under a hang glider, but here, I could safely say that I was pretty nervous. Probably even more than when we boarded the bus to go through Salvador.

You know how when you're a little nervous, the smallest things can amplify your fear by immeasurable amounts. It's like when it's dark in the house, you're walking up the stairs and you reach the top where you are confronted by a pitch black landing with a few doors that are slightly open and all of them lead to a pitch black room. Those are the times I find it best to imagine horror stories to write... i.e. what is the most frightening and scary thing that could happen right now? And going through all the individual possibilities makes me quite nervous... where could a hand come from now? Who is standing where and what do they do? Do they just watch me and wait until I'm sleeping to pounce or do they pounce immediately and do they do it from the front, the side or from the back? I work myself up into such a state that I have to actually say to myself, "that monster from Scooby Doo was just a cartoon... and besides, it was the creepy caretaker," before I can walk further.

Well, this was exactly one of those moments... all our senses were heightened. In the parts where we had to travel at 3 miles per hour, we would not be able to go any faster without instantly damaging the car, so if some deranged lunatic were to come out of the shadows with an axe or chainsaw, we would not suddenly be able to accelerate to outrun him because we would instantly break a wheel or do something of equal devastation.

"What idiots would ever come down this road? You'd have to be insane," we were saying to each other.

On a lighter side, we had to stop to let a little armadillo cross our path on the 'road'. Whilst watching it scamper off, there was a sense of, 'hey look... this little virtually defenceless armadillo (apart from the suit of armour on its back – but what's that against the bog creature from Scooby Doo?) is out here. He's scared of real predators like coyotes, wolves, bobcats, raccoons and a host of other animals, not to mention cars with nervous idiots inside worrying that they're going to be chopped up by a nutter with a chainsaw who just happens to be hanging around in the middle of flipping nowhere at around dinnertime. They have a genuine reason to be scared,' and I can't deny it made me feel a bit better.

It didn't make Vesi or Priscila feel better though when I started trying to calm them down by talking about how unlikely it was that a chainsaw-wielding maniac was out there waiting for us. Somehow telling them that the armadillo wasn't scared of the notion that it was pitch black outside and that anything could be lurking there ready to jump out during the moments we were inching along...but probably wasn't, didn't calm them down. It made Alessio laugh though.

Both my brother and I were finding it quite amusing until we saw headlights behind us. Headlights that were getting closer and closer until they were right behind us. At that point there, my musings that it could have been a serial killer went down like a ton of bricks. Hey, it's not my fault… it was just one idea. Then I tried to make things better by looking out the back and pretending I saw someone in the car… I thought of something that was harmless, kind of like the stay puffed marshmallow man from the Ghostbusters film… "It's ok, it's just one person and they look like they are dressed as a clown." Ok, dumb idea. For a moment, I forgot that people going around alone dressed as clowns in dark places could actually be a pretty terrifying thought.

This turned the conversation to, "who do we sacrifice in the car so that the others can get away?" Codename 'lamb'. Initially, by 3 votes to 1, Alessio was chosen but he protested and, in the end, there was no clear winner so we discussed fighting techniques. "Ok, if Alessio and I get out the car on different sides, we can distract them. You girls can run out, grab a stick or something, then come back and whack them. I'm sure the 4 of us can take them. OR, we… as in the men… can sacrifice ourselves while you two can run away and tell people how we fought bravely to the end and were not simply bludgeoned to death by a couple of fat blokes whilst crying on our knees and pleading for our lives." Alessio reluctantly accepted that whether he was part of a group, partnered with me, or completely alone, one way or another he was going to be sacrificed. Aside from the occasional blubbing, he took it quite well.

So, the conversation got more and more animated with intermittent periods of contemplative silences and the occasional, "I bet it's just a couple of other idiots who followed their satnavs to try to save 20 minutes."

We tried to slow down (from 3mph to 2mph) to see if they would overtake, but they didn't… so that led us to the conclusion that they were probably just following us because they were lost – all the while searching for potential weapons in the car that we could use… or maybe they didn't want to go in front because it's actually easier to follow someone in the dark than it is to lead the way, whilst looking for torches and anything that could light up in case we had to run away.

A good 20 minutes after they started to follow us, we had fairly good strategies for both fighting and running away and a small arsenal of objects that could be used as weapons (satnav being the first obvious choice – it seemed a suitable sacrifice since the bastard led us here in the first place) and things to light our way (bastard satnav again being the main candidate in case the lights on our mobile phones all died).

A short while after that, I guess the car behind got sick of driving behind us and found a place to overtake. We all stared at them as they did and it was 2 quite elderly couples dressed formally, and by the brief glimpse of the looks on their faces, they looked lost. It's just that we were driving so erratically they must have thought we were either drunk or joyriders.

The unbelievable relief mixed with the incredible feeling of sheer foolishness washed over us. And the newfound feeling of confidence allowed us to stop on the side of the pitch black road so that Alessio and I could take a pee. The girls didn't want to though... I guess that the squatting with your pants down by the ankles position feels a lot more vulnerable than the standing with your willy out position.

Back in the car, we managed to accidentally crush the head of the satnav charger cable by repeatedly slamming the car door on it, rendering the already old and used satnav unusable once the battery had run out. Under the circumstances, we agreed that the only honourable thing to do when we returned the car was to say it was like that when we found it, complain to the staff and try to get a partial refund on the rental.

Pretty soon after that, we reached Bonito. In true satnav style, we appeared randomly from a road in the middle of nowhere into the middle of town... at which point Priscila shrieked, "OOOOH, I know where we are," which was quite a relief as it was about 9pm and we were all a bit sick of travelling on roads where no one knew where they were, being guided by a psychotic satnav that was going to laugh at us until its battery ran flat.

We drove around a bit towards where Priscila's father lives. Bonito, as per the name (pretty), was actually really pretty for real. It was a quaint little town with a small population. Few road markings, even at crossroads, people could park pretty much anywhere but nowhere was overcrowded. It was the kind of place you might fantasise about raising your children.... Until they hit their teens, are sick of building bases and dens everywhere and want to go out somewhere loud to dance, drink and do drugs.

On arriving at Priscila's father's house, we caught our first glimpse of the caravan we would be staying in.

Oh. My. God.

It was huge. It was a motorhome long enough that the people who were sleeping in the front would not be able to hear the people having sex in the back – and vice versa. This was not the clapped out rusty caravan I had in mind... it was a 6-person monster with an 8.5 litre petrol siphoning engine. This thing would have done gallons per mile, not the other way around. We did not have to temporarily evict any chickens or share with a goat and change the dung-covered straw for fresh straw and we were definitely *not* cramped. I always have a problem sleeping in beds because I'm just a shade over 6 feet 2 inches (around 1.89/1.90 metres). Surprisingly, I actually fit reasonably well. There was a shower, a place to eat, a bedroom in the back, and some sleeping quarters in front on top of the driver's seating area. It was awesome.

Priscila's dad, named Alcides – don't even try to pronounce it... just believe me – looked exactly like how you'd expect a Brazilian farmer to look... effectively like he didn't give a shit about anything that went on around him. The kind of person who'd wear flip flops to his childrens' graduations and stand at the back chewing tobacco and picking his nose. His partner, Fatima – pronounced Fachima – was more tanned with a hefty upper body that looked like it had been glued onto a pair of skinny legs. It was quite weird to look at.

It's like when you look at a thin woman with a huge sticky out arse... and the only way she can keep her balance when standing still is by keeping one leg in front of the other and leaning on that. And when she walks, she has to lean forwards to avoid toppling over or take such weird looking steps that she looks like she is holding in a bout of explosive diarrhoea.

I think they had a reasonable amount of money too. The mobile home would not have been cheap. They also took us all out for dinner that evening.

We went to a pretty plush restaurant where our hosts clearly knew the owners... either that or they had been so many times that they were at least familiar with them. However, in such a small town, it's one of those places where everyone knows everyone anyway so one way or another it wasn't a surprise really.

On the menu was salad with palm heart – which is a vegetable that is found growing in some palm trees, e.g. some coconuts and açaí palm trees. Apparently, palm hearts are very popular in South America.

Then, in true Brazilian style, oodles of beef – from cuts of fillet to cuts of sirloin – and we even got a chance to try caiman crocodile. All the food was really tasty, but then again, if Brazil is famous for something, it's not just the football and the transsexuals, it's also the meat.

After dinner, we were really tired so we went back to the house (the motorhome) and went straight to sleep. Our hosts had plans on keeping us entertained using the local area facilities. This was going to be interesting.

Day 16 - Bonito

Up at 7:15am. Breakfast outside consisted of papaya, melon, some cream cheese, and various types of toast, including 'shippa' which is some fresh bread. We also had fresh coffee, fresh cashew fruit juice and a bunch of other things.

We were told that Bonito is booming as a town... more people are coming to live here and they are trying to get more work in the region, but for now, fortunately, it remains a quaint little place where people can still leave their doors open, which in my mind stands out as quite idyllic.

Bonito rests just outside of the Pantanal. The Pantanal is a massive region of tropical wetland that is predominantly in Brazil but at an estimated 75,000 square miles (195,000 square kilometres), it is large enough to occupy portions of Bolivia and Paraguay.

Because it is in a gently sloping basin, during the rainy season, roughly 80% of the Pantanal floodplains are submerged giving rise to a massive collection of aquatic life. In general, although the Amazon rainforest is the well-known place to visit to get an idea of jungle life, the density of the trees and foliage make it more difficult to see the wildlife. The Pantanal, which derives its name from the Portuguese *pântano,* meaning bog/swamp/wetland/marsh, is meant to be better for spotting wildlife due to its open areas. In fact, people have been known to spot jaguars which are the largest cats in the Americas and are very rare.

Unfortunately, we won't get time on this trip to visit the Pantanal. Instead, today, we visited a farm. Ok, that sounds very flat... what's so interesting about going to watch some cows get milked and some guy in a tractor pulling a trailer full of fresh cow dung? But it wasn't that sort of farm.

This farm is in a place called Rio do Peixe. Rio do Peixe itself is a state park measuring around 19,100 acres and is actually on the internet as a good place to visit. Roughly translated (from what I found out) as 'fish river'. It might not sound particularly good in English... in fact, it sounds positively rubbish... but it's not meant to be translated. It's like the Ferrari Testarossa; sounds sexy as it is, eh? But how crap does the direct translation 'Ferrari *Redhead'* sound? Christ, it makes you think of a ginger kid about to break out into the singing of 'Tomorrow, tomorrow, I luv ya...' Or how about Fois Gras in French, which means Fat Liver in English? It sounds wrong, doesn't it? So, we'll stick to Rio do Peixe as opposed to Fish River.

It seemed more of an activity place than a farm, although they do actually produce all their own meat and vegetables, which is absolutely fantastic. In the end, farming is the most important industry on the planet... and before you think of something else, think of 1 thing... they feed you and have been for centuries. Water too, of course. Teach this to your kids before they think that something like fashion is the most important industry.

The owners of the farm had a pet tapir. Yes, that's right, a tapir called Gigi. I can't write how it's pronounced but it is like the non-existent 'J' sound in Dvorak as in the composer... If you find out how to pronounce Dvorak, both the 'Gs' in Gigi sound like the non-existent 'J' between the letters R & A in Dvorak.

One thing I learned about tapirs is that they are a lot bigger than I thought they were and heavier too. They can also swim really well. They are funny looking things too. They look a bit like big pigs but their nose droops a bit like an elephant's. And they move the nose somewhat like an elephant too... except it's much shorter and it can't really be used to grab anything.

So, I am now the proud owner of a photo with a tapir... I bet that's a statement that hasn't been used in the world very often. Like once when Vesi said to me, "we are dangerously low on nutmeg," I thought, 'wow... I bet that's a phrase that has never ever been used on the planet... EVER.'

With a group of people, we went on a trek through a forest with a guide. It reminded me of the trek through the Amazon but it had some differences. This trek was less hot and less humid. There was a slight breeze and a lot more light. Also, there were far fewer mosquitoes which was an immeasurable added bonus. There were even wooden pathways along much of it for people to walk on and wooden rope bridges so that people could get past various ditches.

We reached an opening with a waterfall – wow was it spectacular. It wasn't especially high, maybe 3-4 metres, but it was such a beautiful area. The area was surrounded by trees. The water tipped over a little ledge and fell into this lovely pool that looked beautiful and clear. The sounds in a place like that are simply sublime. All you hear is the sound of the water and the wildlife around it. In the UK, you'd probably hear some cars nearby, but there was none of that here.

We were given the go-ahead to go swimming if we wanted to... and it was so beautiful that it would have been insane not to get in the water. That was until I put a toe in it.

Because it was coming from a running source, it was absolutely freezing (at least that's what I have been led to believe about running water... I've put my foot/hand in pools reasonably similar to this before and the theory has generally been correct). I don't mean arctic freezing but water that makes your body scream "GET THE HELL OUT OF HERE" for the first minute or so, then you become accustomed to the pain but you never actually get used to it... like having a brick hung from your testicles (or labia for women). You can get used to it but it never becomes comfortable.

Ok, so yes, I'm a complete wuss when it comes to cold water. I don't like it much and I will avoid it if at all possible, which is always possible since I now live in a terraced house in a city. But when on holiday... sometimes I'm faced with the dilemma... get in, scream and cry like a 2-year-old for a minute, making myself look like a wuss OR don't go in and look like a wuss.

Under the circumstances, I had to go in. The surroundings were too lovely to enjoy only from the side. I've always chickened out of going in water like this but I had to go in… I could at least achieve one of my ambitions in life and, for one split second, feel like Tarzan.

I looked out to see that Vesi, Alessio, and Priscila were all in the water and swimming towards the waterfall bit to take photos with disposable underwater cameras. I bravely tiptoed in, inch by inch. Do you have any idea how difficult it is to inch your way into water this cold and pretend it's not an utterly horrendous experience? I kept stopping every few seconds and pretending that I'd seen something really interesting on the bottom, whilst inside I was screaming blue murder. Still, I managed to keep my fake smile and fake interest in the bottom of the pool going until the water kissed my testicles. Then, before temporarily losing the power of speech, I literally couldn't smile anymore. But, I couldn't let the others (or myself) down so I kept inching towards them, finding interesting things in the sky to look at too until I was behind them. Fortunately, the pool was only a bit more than a metre deep so I managed to keep the top half of my body out.

However, you know how it is… when you're there having fun and everyone is in the water except you and there is the usual banter going on – your so-called friends and family *will* get you wet. I think it's the law in some countries that they have to do that to you. If not, makes up one of the unwritten rules on how to be a bastard.

Needless to say, I screamed like a girl so let's just draw a line there.

After a couple of minutes of thrashing so hard to try to warm up that some of the others in the group thought I'd been grabbed by a shark, I managed to calm down and start swimming quite normally... well, normally for someone thinking that frostbite was setting into his fingers, was developing hypothermia and had gone numb from the waist down. So, besides thinking I was dying, I started really enjoying it. We took a load of photos with the underwater cameras, under the waterfall, under water and even behind the waterfall where there was a little cove we could all slot ourselves into.

I've always had this romantic idea about waterfalls ever since watching Tarzan as a kid – yes, he was pretty cool in my eyes, and not just because I wanted pecs like him. I think it was from him that my love of the jungle developed. (the fantasy of it before I went) Basically, Tarzan follows an elephant to behind a waterfall and there is an elephant's graveyard there full of bones. It was from then I thought that behind all waterfalls there was a secret area or secluded spot. So, this little cove for me was a really exciting and wondrous place – even though it was only a couple of metres deep.

That was a lovely, fun spot that we stopped at. I was really glad I went into the water.

The trip continued.

As we walked and whenever we stopped, the guide would tell us about the plants and animals living around the area. I wish I could have understood more. But as a good human, even though I barely understood anything, I couldn't help but look at him through squinted eyes and nod or aww in amazement as everyone else did (pretending to understand what the hell is going on). For all I knew, I could have been nodding to some bloke saying that it was the spot where they sacrificed non-Portuguese speaking tourists and the tree was where they hanged them from their earlobes. Luckily, it must have been genuine information because I'm here writing this... either that or he thought my furious nodding and awwing meant I understood him.

We carried on the trek. Overall, there must have been about 12-14 of us in the group... there was another group of friends from another part of Brazil here on holiday, as well as a couple of guys with their girlfriends – and they were what I had in mind when I imagined Brazilian women... they were genuinely hot babes. We got talking to them and they were quite friendly too.

The second stop was next to a similar pool but with fish. This fish, called piraputanga, is apparently quite bony but it is served in quite a few of the restaurants here, so it's totally edible. We got to swim around here with the fish and a waterfall. It was a little surreal having these fish swimming around us... they were almost like little circling sharks. It was strange to think that if these fish knew what we humans did, they could all gang up on us. We are relying on their lack of understanding and inability to form organised groups. To be honest, that's exactly like corporate controlled governments and the people of the country. They don't want us to find out what they're up to and try to stop organised groups from getting together because they can be dangerous to the status quo of power, which is mainly made up of old white men who throw a few shiny pennies at politicians and tell them to fetch... BUT anyway, back to the fish... if they'd had the knowledge and the desire to do so, they could have kicked my arse but they didn't have either – probably because they are fish.

The third place we stopped was more open like a river rather than the pools we'd been stopping at. The waterfalls here were more like small natural stepped ledges than proper waterfalls but they ran the entire width of the river. It was super beautiful. We could lean up against these ledges and have the water pour down over our necks and shoulders. It was almost like receiving a shoulder and neck massage. By the way, yes, the water was still really cold.

The fourth stop was at another pool with a wooden plank protruding from the edge that acted as a diving board. We all had our share of injuries from this. I tried showing off and doing a backwards dive but ended up going a bit too far and slapping my entire leg on the surface of the water, but I kept my pain in like a man... which meant screaming while I was under the water, not showing it when I surfaced and then moaning about it to Vesi. I had a nice long red mark down my thigh to show for it too. Poor Vesi though, she partially slipped on the diving board and went in face first while the diving board sprang back up and hit her knee... We laughed initially but then she came out with a limp and a brave face. Then when she showed me her knee was both bruised and bleeding, I felt absolutely rotten for laughing.

After the tour, we all gathered together for lunch. Priscila's father and his partner joined us for this.

Lunch was pretty awesome actually. We were sat on long benches outside but under cover to protect from the sun. Overall, there were probably about 60/70 people lunching at the same time. This place was definitely a good attraction. It was a buffet lunch with loads of vegetables and a number of meats. I even got to try armadillo... probably not the one we saw on the road, but a mate of his. See, I told you he had a right to be more scared than us.

It tasted kind of weird... I thought it was a bit like chewy beef, however, it was shredded so that's probably not the best way to comment on a texture. Still... my verdict is that it was very nice.

During lunch, we saw monkeys. When the first one appeared, it was a massive attention grabber for all the people having lunch, standing up to look at it, taking photos, etc... but then another appeared, then another... then some came down from above... it was like a monkey ambush. They were climbing on the frame all around us and were really cute little things – I think they were brown capuchin monkeys. The brown capuchin monkey is native to South America, particularly Brazil, so it would make sense if that's what they were.

They didn't get too close to us and kept a close eye on everything from a distance. If someone went up to try to stroke them, the monkeys would scarper without letting themselves be touched. But then, if one of the groups of people left the table, there was suddenly a monkey melee around the plates to see which monkey would be able to grab the best bits from the leftovers.

Brown capuchin monkeys are omnivorous so they would eat pretty much anything, unlike some of their more fussy counterparts that only eat vegetables.

We were taking the lunching process so slowly that we almost missed the monkey show outside after. The monkey show was where everyone stood in a circle around a tree, was handed a couple of bits of banana and we had to try to feed the monkeys.

The monkeys would approach with caution... keep a watchful eye on the person sticking out his/her hand, hesitate, and then grab the banana and run away as fast as possible, up the tree and sit on a branch to eat it.

Some of the other monkeys were braver though. There was one little fat git that went around to several people to collect banana pieces. He/she was very polite about it too... he/she would take it calmly then move on to the next person and then he/she would mosey off to a spot just a couple of metres away to eat before going back to get some more. It was quite remarkable that monkey hadn't developed type 2 diabetes given all the sugar that it was eating. Either that or simply burst into flames given that bananas are high in potassium (for those who don't know, potassium is extremely reactive and even contact with the air causes it to react. Put it in water and it bursts into flames).

Alcides took the banana pieces, said "fuck you" (fock yuu with the accent) to the monkeys, and ate them. I couldn't help but laugh. Exactly what I expected from this I don't give a shit about anything, flip flop wearing geezer. He said that the monkeys do the show almost every day, so they would not starve.

After the monkey show was the parrot show. They had a variety of parrots but the main one of the show was a blue one with a yellow face around the beak – a Hyacinth Macaw if you wish to look it up.

It was a nifty little show. Some guy would feed some parrots then try to entice one from a tree to give it some food. The parrot stayed where it was. Then he tried again and then again... and just when the audience started to feel a slight pang of disappointment, the parrot flew down and took the food. And he does that three times a day, 6 days a week.

We had a few photos taken with the parrot on our arms and shoulders... If I'd had an eye patch, I'd have looked like a pirate.

After the shows, we got to go out on a walk again with the guide to another pond with a zip wire, passing a smaller pool on the way where an anaconda had decided to hang out. We were given the go-ahead to go swimming/paddling (it may have been shallow, I didn't understand) by the guide but he warned us to stick to the right half of the pool because the anaconda lives somewhere over to the left... He did say that it had fed recently so it was pretty safe, but still... an effing anaconda... they are the biggest snakes on the planet that can swim up to you, grab you, crush you to death and then swallow you without even chewing – so I decided against swimming, and the same went for everyone else. The tapir Gigi appeared though and went for a swim... she didn't care about the anaconda. But it did serve as a fairly good canary in a cage test. If the snake didn't attack the tapir, it probably wouldn't have attacked any of us... but still, to us, it was the danger equivalent of trying to give a sleeping crocodile a dental examination.

The zip wire started from a ledge approximately 5 metres above the water and zoomed out over the river about 20 metres or so. At the other end, you would simply drop off and into the water. That was actually quite good fun but like so many moments in life, I reached a part where I realised I wasn't 21 anymore. I grabbed the handles on the zip wire and jumped off the ledge... my hands gave way instantly and I fell the full 5 metres or so into the water. The guide looked over the ledge to shout, "you ok?"... I looked back, "YES".

But I wasn't ok.

Well, I wasn't in any physical pain, but that was one of the moments in my life when I realised I was not as strong as I used to be – something I bet everyone else in the world goes through at some point in their life for one thing or another. I used to be able to climb a couple metres up a rope using only my arms, but just then, I couldn't even hold my own body weight up… how awful.

I had to try again. I could not let this conquer me. Up at the top, I tried once more. I clung on for dear life and I could feel the enormous weight of my body as I hung from the handles. I did it though, I managed to go all the way down without falling off but I think that scar will remain.

We left the farm to return to the monster motorhome. The drive home was very picturesque… We saw a giant anteater happily eating in a field just a few tens of metres away. We also saw a pair of scarlet macaw parrots, i.e. the very typical parrot look – when you imagine one, in cartoons, on Long John Silver's shoulder, etc… red with yellow and blue wingtips. It was amazing watching these two flying together, side by side with one slightly in front of the other… like two fighter jets flying in a pattern, mimicking each other's moves.

Macaw parrots come from central and southern America. Their natural habitat is the tops of the trees in the jungle. There are 17 species of macaw which are broken into 2 groups; large macaws and mini macaws. They also all have a distinctive-shaped head with a beak… basically, the beak is hooked and the head looks bigger than it should be.

The Hyacinth Macaw can allegedly break a coconut shell with its beak, but to be honest, I don't know how the hell it would get its mouth around enough of one to break it. I've got a bigger mouth than a parrot and I can't get a whole coconut in there so it could be complete gonads... a bit like the whole 'a swan can break a man's arm' talk. Well, one *might* be able to if the man is startled by the charging swan, falls and breaks his arm... but that's not the swan breaking his arm. Maybe they are talking about green coconuts rather than the shrivelled up brown ones we get in the UK. That I might believe. Green coconuts are much softer than the brown ones. With some robust and persistent pecking, maybe they can.

They are pretty amazing birds actually and they can live for a long time. Apparently, it's not uncommon for these birds to outlive their owners... unless their owners are particularly young, but then again, young people are not as good at looking after pets as adults... usually. I remember my pet goldfish, Joey (I have a great imagination for names). He (I assumed he was a boy) had a lovely glass bowl to swim in with a stone I'd taken from the garden for his enjoyment. Ok, it might not be the latest Nintendo but, hey, it's a fish, it has the IQ of a politician. I was so proud of little Joey – with his little stone in his bowl. I fed him, kept him company, talked to him, I'm sure I had the right food... but the little git never seemed to eat anything, or at least never ate anything in my presence... a bit like the fat people who are constantly on a diet and seem to eat nothing except a stick of extra low-fat celery for lunch. You just know that as soon as they're alone, they go straight for a McDonalds, then a KFC and then wash down the copious amounts of food by raiding the chocolate aisle of Mr Rashid's corner shop whilst cursing that these places aren't drive-through – before feeling so guilty that they promise never ever, ever, ever, ever to do it again... until 24 hours later. But no, little Joey didn't eat a flipping thing in front of me. He turned his gills up within a month, maybe even a week, I can't remember exactly. He got the usual lavatorial burial and I shed a tear, but mainly because I had half a box of fish food left and it felt like a waste to throw it away. I only managed to eat a third myself but it was pretty grim. Hardly surprising Joey didn't want to eat any. Anyway, that's a kid looking after a pet, however, unlike parrots, goldfish aren't usually known for outliving their owners.

In the evening, we hit the Bonito town... it's a lovely town. It's picturesque but hasn't exactly got the London nightlife. Although, having said that, it hasn't got London prices either. We managed to get food, drinks and a dance out here for about the same price as a thimble full of stagnant water in London. But you know what they say, it's not the location, it's the company and for the evening in Bonito, the company was perfect. Coincidentally, we even saw the group of Brazilians (with the hot Brazilian girls) in the same restaurant as us.

A few drinks into the evening, we saw a few older couples having a dance and Vesi and I were coaxed into getting up and dancing too by Alessio and Priscila. Now – I don't mean to brag... ok, I do... but I'm a salsa dancing diva. But I can't deny I felt a little strange. Brazil is the home of Samba, Forro, Lambada and probably a load of other tasty sounding dances. I kind of felt out of my depth. But what the hell... Vesi and I got up and danced anyway.

By the end of the song, we got an applause from the whole restaurant. Holy shit I thought, I've been clapped many times in the UK before but this is Brazil – home to all the fun and sexy dances I mentioned. It felt good. I even had a bunch of men in their 50s and 60s come up to me and shake my hand. I can't deny that I felt pretty cool.

I went to sleep on a high... but that may have had less to do with the dancing and more to do with the local dodgy beer we drank.

Day 17 – Bonito

Up at 7:15 in the morning, climbed down from our bed and went for the usual morning pee. This wouldn't normally be noteworthy but I think Norris McWhirter would have been crowning me with a world record – and if you don't know who that is, Norris McWhirter was the guy who founded the Guinness book of records. The book that originally started out with impressive world records such as tallest/shortest/fattest/oldest man ever, longest bridge, tallest structure, fastest man, fastest car and has descended to also include crap like: largest collection of sick bags, fastest time climbing into a suitcase and zipping it up and the most steps walked down by a dog whilst balancing a glass of water on his nose – BTW, it's 10 steps (undoubtedly records that will stand for many years to come as, frankly, nobody gives a shit about trying to beat them, and they are hardly worthy of someone's CV).

Interviewer – Here at *Complex Future* we always search for the most unique of people. Ambitious self-starters with impressive track records. I see here that you hold two world records. That is astounding. What were they in?

Interviewee bod – Ah yes, bouncing on a pogo stick underwater while wearing a stripy vest and an eye patch – Yes – I bounced 3 times. And for my second record, I found the world's longest twiglet in a fun-sized pack of twiglets.

Seriously, Norris would be turning over in his grave if he'd been alive now to shake the hand of the man who managed to insert 2009 needles into his face and head (well, he sure as hell wouldn't have given him a European style double kiss on the cheeks).

Anyway, good old Norris should have been there to witness my pee. It was so long that my legs got tired before I finished. It was the longest pee I'd ever taken in the morning, without exception. I even looked at the time about 30 seconds into it while it was still going strong.

For some unknown reason, only my brother was impressed with the story of my wee. Vesi and Priscila didn't care. Personally, I just think they were jealous. We had the breakfast I have now come to associate with living in Brazil (mainly fruit) and prepared ourselves for another adventure.

A 15-minute drive away and we reached an area of nature preservation on the Formoso River. We were going rafting. It wasn't full on white water rafting but we were going to take a ride in a dinghy, go over some small waterfalls and through some small areas of white water as well as to look at nature, birds, monkeys etc., so I was looking forward to it.

When we arrived, we were really early for the trip so we walked around a bit to see the surroundings. Alcides was chewing tobacco and I remember becoming super curious about it as a child when I saw the film Predator with Arnold Schwarzenegger, where Blain (played by Jesse Ventura) was chewing it in the helicopter near the start of the film.

I was offered some and I could not in good conscience turn it down. It wasn't like heroin or crack cocaine; it wasn't even a cigarette... it was chewing tobacco and, sure, prolonged use can have adverse effects outside of bad breath and brown teeth, mouth cancer, no friends, etc. but this was a one-off. Some people say it tastes like liquorice – I had to try it.

Alcides told me I should shove it between my gum and my cheek above my teeth. I guess that's one of the places where it can be absorbed more easily.

I put some in my mouth. Whoever said it tasted of liquorice was a lying bastard – it tasted like a snooker hall ashtray so it is fair to say that thoughts of Blain gleefully shovelling it into his mouth, chewing it like gum and making it look like it tasted great instantly became the realisation that Blain was a fucking idiot squaddy bastard who lied to me.

I'd only had a tiny bit, but a couple of minutes later, it hit me, and when I say it hit me, I mean... flipping bloody hell did it hit me. The most accurate description I can attribute to this sensation was the description given by Arnold Rimmer in the Red Dwarf sitcom series after having unwittingly eaten some hallucinogenic mushrooms. It was "what could only be described as a voyage to trip out city".

My vision changed. It was like I was seeing everything in slow motion. I could barely keep my balance. My head felt a rush going through what I could only compare to a load of fluids circulating through my brain and my eyeballs. I became acutely aware of everything in the world that was completely unimportant and nonsensical like, why do the veins on my hands track different routes? Has my head always been this far away from my feet? What if my big toes were on the outsides of my feet instead of the insides, would that make any difference? I'd still wear the same shoes except the right on the left and the left on the right. So, I'd still be spending the same money on shoes and still own the same shoes but wouldn't it make my feet look a bit weird? And what about my shoe rack? All the shoes would be the wrong way around in there. OMG, with the toes pointing out they'd take up more space. OMFG, I'd need a bigger shoe rack. Where would *that* fit in the house? Hang on a mo... could this theory be applied to my thumbs? Would the veins still look different on my hands? How would I tie my shoelaces? Damn, it's good that my big toe is where it is.

You get the idea. It's the kind of thought process that you get at the top levels of government, except my insane babbling made more sense.

In the meantime, it was really difficult to pretend to the others that I was completely ok. I didn't look ok. I didn't feel ok. We were near the river waiting for people to turn up. I had to go and sit at the edge of the water in case I was sick or fell over. Or in case I was sick and then fell over. Or I was sick and fell over into my own sick. Or I was sick, slipped in my sick, fell into the water and was sick again. I pretended I was just "looking at the beauty of the water".

"Ok," Vesi said, "he's whacked out".

It took about 15 minutes to regain any sense of normality – which meant that I managed to accept that my big toes were not on the outsides of my feet. It also meant that I could stand up without wobbling too much and looking like I'd smoked half of Jamaica's weed plantations in an afternoon. It also meant that I could re-join the others who were on the water trying out some paddleboards.

Paddleboards. With people on them, they look fantastically unnatural – like a little old lady on a unicycle. The best I can glean is that they are primarily used for water sports but are basically surfboards that people stand on in the water, moving and manoeuvring using a single oar. The notion of standing on a board or in a little boat and paddling around has been around for thousands of years. The origins are pretty much unknown, probably because it was used by many different cultures to travel/fish/wage war, etc. In fact, for about 3,000 years, Peruvian fishermen used a craft called a 'Caballitos de Totora'. A small craft where its inherent instability made it like riding a horse – hence the name Caballitos, translated 'horse rider', aka cavalier (get the link? Cool, eh? Isn't linguistics a fascinating thing?). 'Totora' is the large reed from which it was made. Legend has it that after a day's fishing, they would then ride the waves just for fun which could be one of the many origins of surfing. But basically, you probably see how it developed into a hobby/sport from there.

When you look at people on these things, they look – well – wrong. They usually stand with their feet in side by side, shoulder width apart, and push themselves along with the oar from this unnatural position.

After the virtual trip I had on tobacco – which I refused to spit out and had to sit down to avoid being sick – my head cleared up enough to have a go on one of these things. And when I say that my head had cleared up, I mean it had actually cleared up, not that I was still super woozy but thought I could possibly control this thing anyway – like those people who claim that they drive better when they are drunk. "I drive better when I'm drunk because I'm more careful," which means, I have to pay a lot more attention to the road to try to drive normally because I'm pissed. Don't believe idiots when they say that. They are usually 17-18 years old and have written off at least one car.

But that's not what I'm like and I felt pretty good, so I jumped on a paddle board. A couple of seconds later when I emerged from the water, I swam to collect the oar and clambered back on the board.

Standing up on one is not particularly difficult, but moving forwards feels about as natural as riding a pushbike, turning the pedals with your hands. I can see how it can build core strength though because it's a damn good workout on your shoulders and upper body.

The most unnatural thing about it is – at least for a number of people, including me – your legs stay parallel and square with your shoulders. When you look at someone on one of these things, you automatically think, surely it would be easier with one leg in front and one behind; that would provide more stability when trying to paddle forwards. But in actual fact, it was a lot more difficult to paddle like that. It's a freaky sensation I tell you, and more than that, I was under the impression looked like a plonker for doing it because it looks so awkward.

I tried rowing while sitting but that was hard work. I tried kneeling and that felt ok when I hummed the tune to Hawaii 5-0 but standing with my feet shoulder width apart was pretty much the most efficient way, even if it looked stupid.

I can't say it could ever become my favourite hobby/sport but it is pretty good exercise. If I did that on a regular basis, I would probably develop muscles in my upper body – or at least, down one side of my body if I kept paddling on one side.

We made it to the canoes a short while later. I say canoe but it was more of an inflatable rubber dinghy large enough to hold 10 people with life jackets.

Out on the Formoso River we went, several of us paddling with 3-foot-long oars. We pushed the dinghy into a gentle current and were swept along. We saw parrots, toucans and a whole range of other exotic birds. We also caught glimpse of a snoozing anaconda. Apparently, it had fed recently and wouldn't be feeding again for a couple of weeks. In any case, there was a big fat woman on the dinghy with us so she was more than enough security for me.

The common anaconda in Brazil is called 'Sucuri' and I know it sounds weird to say '*common* anaconda' in the same way as saying it's *common* to find a person in tracksuit trousers queuing up at a McDonalds, but that's how they are referred to.

There is the legend of the 'Sucuriju Gigante', which is a giant constrictor snake and is a subspecies of the common green anaconda. Speculated to reach 40 metres in length, 80cm in diameter and weigh 5 tons. To put the length into perspective, the average height of a two-storey house right to the top is around 8 metres. At 40m long, you're looking at 5 times the height of an ordinary two-storey house. Your average anaconda gets to around 10 metres.

HOWEVER, there is no evidence of this snake actually existing – at least – not anymore. There are tribes in the Amazon that refer to this anaconda as the controller of the area it inhabits and is the creator of the Amazon River. Clearly that's bollocks and is probably the result of some Chinese whispers handed down from generation to generation. You can bet that within a few more generations, they'll have the snake turning water into wine too.

Anyway, over the course of this trip, the people rowing changed several times but, somehow, I always ended up being one of them, mainly because I saw someone struggling so I took the oar from them. Still, it was good exercise. My only – well, one of several – regret was that I did not bring my glasses, so I couldn't see the wildlife properly. I didn't bring a cap either so I was at risk of getting heatstroke and could have hallucinated that I was the king of the jungle, and finally, I didn't put on any suntan lotion, so I could have been burnt and spent the last few days of my holiday in pain. Apart from that, it was all good.

We went down some small rapids and small waterfalls, splashed other dinghies who were on the same trip with buckets of water and had a swim (yes, the water was cold but I've given up wussing on this trip) when we reached a calm lagoon area. It was really lovely.

At one point, Alessio had the bucket we were splashing other dinghies with and the fat woman wanted it to sit on. She'd been moaning about getting wet and how she didn't like the waterfall bits and how nobody had any cake on board (ok, the last bit was made up), so Alessio asked her in Portuguese "do you want it?" "Yes," "are you sure you want it?" "Yes, give it to me." What she didn't know was that the bucket was full of water, so Alessio, being the gentleman, threw the entire bucket of water over her. She complained – we laughed – others clapped – he bowed – she moaned some more – we felt proud.

As we left to go to the car, we saw a sign telling us not to go on the paddleboards as they have to be rented. When he saw this,

Priscila's dad stuck his middle finger up at the sign and said, "fock yuu" (accent included) in his nonchalant sort of way that I'd not be able to describe but sounded hilarious coming from a guy wearing flip flops.

We were then taken to a leisure complex called the *Balneario Municipal* which is free to the locals but not to tourists (which I think is a great idea). I don't know if *we* paid. Maybe because we went with some locals, they just let us in. I love the outdoor life. In the UK, a leisure complex is a bunch of buildings with activities that surround a car park, which is fine, but it's very different. Here, it's swimming in slow-flowing water, lazing in hammocks, playing outdoor sports, and walking around outside. It's a different world.

This Balneario Municipal had the Formoso River running by it. There were some restaurants, lagoons to swim in, hammocks to lie in, volleyball courts and it was just a lovely place to be.

We had lunch and then went for a swim in the river surrounded by fish – the same piraputangas that we swam around in the farm area yesterday. We jumped into the water (yes, freezing again) from one entry gap and just floated there letting the current carry us downstream to a different exit a few tens of metres away where we climbed out. The river between these exits wasn't particularly deep but we had to float as close to the surface as we could because there were rocks and tree roots sticking up from the bottom. I found that out when I caught my big toe on a branch which was pretty painful, not to mention frightening even though the water was beautifully clear. It is amazing how something touching your foot from below the surface of the water instils a sense of panic that can only be comparable to the panic felt when you dream about turning up to school exams in your underpants and no pen. Maybe I've seen Jaws one too many times or found one too many used condoms floating in the water, but I bet it's an innate fear that most people have and if you think it's not one of yours, just have something unknown brush up against your leg or foot when you're in the water, it's really freaky.

At the other end, next to the exit gap, Fatima was throwing handfuls of food to the fish. She threw some food in my general direction and as soon as it hit the water, there was a furore of activity around me with the fish jumping out of the water and bouncing into me. From a distance, it looked like a piranha feeding frenzy but it felt like nothing more than an upper body tickle from a load of slimy fish as they jumped to grab the food.

After climbing out of the river, we went for a lie down in some hammocks that were there for a snooze and a light chat. Unlike in the UK, the hammocks aren't a novelty here. In the UK, on the few days when a hammock can come out in a public place, there are always queues of people waiting to lie in it regardless of where it is. It could be straddling a runway at Heathrow or just inches above the snapping jaws of a crocodile and there would still be a queue to lie in one. No, here, people were happy to go about their daily business without the desperate need to lie in a hammock and utter those immortal words, "it's quite comfortable actually," and "look, I can lie in it sideways."

Today, in the grand scheme of things, had not been mind-blowingly exciting, although admittedly the dinghies were good fun and the tobacco chewing took me to a higher state of consciousness, but apart from that, it hadn't had the same excitement factor as some of the other days we'd had on this holiday. Instead, it had been a plain wonderful from the word go. My record-breaking wee put me in a good mood for the day and it had just stayed that way right up to and beyond the moment we left the Balneario Municipal.

Later on that evening, we all sat outside the house and Alcides brought out a little vase, about 15 cm high with a metal straw sticking out of it. "Aaaahh, finally, true colours revealed, now we're gonna get down and do some drugs", I said to myself. "I thought he would do something like this. He is so the type. Those flip flops are just a ploy to make us believe he's something he's not."

A partially disappointing revelation was that it turned out to be some kind of tea. They call it Chimarrão – or Mate – pronounced matt-e, the e sounding like the e in mathEmatics

The little vase is filled with a tea and with hot – but not boiling – water and a metal straw is jammed inside where it tends to stick. The bottom of the straw has a filter which allows the liquid to pass but not the tea itself. It can be mixed with any herbs or additional flavours such as citrus peels, but this is sniffed at by puritan Mate drinkers.

The tea is then drunk socially and is passed around like a marijuana joint would be. One person has a couple of sips then passes it on to the next person who sips it, then passes it onto the next and so on. Then, when it's empty, the water is topped up and the process continues until either the tea loses its flavour, people get a bit bored or too long of a queue forms outside the toilet with people needing to pee.

It was actually really nice sitting in a circle passing this thing around. It felt really social but OMFG would it look dodgy in the UK. It would look like some new kind of drug, leading the government – who didn't actually understand what it was – to ban it under the orders from Twinings or some large tea company for fear of losing sales – "WE CAN'T HAVE PEOPLE USING TEABAGS MORE THAN ONCE, OUR PROFITS MIGHT BE REDUCED"

It also made us understand what on earth some people were doing sitting on benches with these little vases and looking dodgy. We'd barely picked up on it before even though we saw a few people last night sitting on benches or on the curb, vase in hand. At the time, naturally I thought they were smoking a bong and my only thought was 'progressive town'. But, now I realise that they were just drinking this tea. It seems to be a proper national hobby here.

I found out that the drinking of this tea dates back to the indigenous Guaraní people and also spread around by the Tupí people who lived in Southern Brazil and Northern Argentina, so it does have serious history behind it.

Today, it has become part of the Brazilian culture with its own particular etiquette.

Primarily, it is drunk from the same little vase/cup, meaning if one of the people has a cold, then everyone runs the risk of getting a cold OR if one person has mouth herpes (cold sores), you might one day find yourself being accused of having given oral sex to an unclean partner – and even though it might not be true, try convincing people you caught herpes from drinking a cup of tea. It's like being caught masturbating by your mum and then trying to convince her you just had a really itchy willy.

One person prepares it, aptly named (in Portuguese) the *"preparador"*. Then that person would fill the vase/cup with water and drink the whole lot to ensure it's free from loose particulates, debris, dead rats and the like and to make sure it's good quality all around. They wouldn't think of giving the first sip to someone else, that's bad etiquette. Besides, if it's poisonous, it wouldn't bode well with the others.

Then the preparador refills the vase/cup and passes it to the next person. This is where traditions split. One is that they drink it all and pass it back to the preparador to refill it with water and then pass it on to the third person who drinks it all and then passes it back to the preparador to refill, and so on until the tea becomes *'lavado'* or washed and effectively loses its flavour.

The way we did it though was that Fatima acted as the preparador who started passing it around the circle. We all took a couple of sips and continued to pass it around until one of us was making gurgling noises sucking on an empty vase/cup and then it was passed back to her for refilling. Again, quite similar to a joint where it gets passed around and, occasionally, it goes out and there's the little ritual of sucking a bit before saying, "yo, it's dead, dude, pass the lighter".

It's such a funky little ritual that we couldn't help but love it. What did it taste of? Well, it tasted of some kind of herbal tea. It was pleasant, slightly bitter but altogether very drinkable.

Mate/Chimarrão. If you ever visit Brazil and you happen to be in an appropriate setting, I recommend partaking in the sharing of one of these.

So, after an evening of drinking tea – which has diuretic properties – I was pretty sure I'd be playing bed yo-yo all night and getting up every 5 minutes to take a pee.

Under these circumstances, I make peeing a priority and try to make it the last thing I do before going to sleep. So, I had a shower, peed in the shower, brushed my teeth, took another pee and as I was about to climb into bed, I remembered I needed to take something out of my bag, so I went to my bag, rummaged around, then squeezed another pee out before climbing into bed. Then I wrote my journal for the day. Now, before sleeping, I think I'll take another pee.

Day 18 – Bonito

Today was our last full day in Bonito and when looking at how cool and nifty the last couple of days had been, today was up against some stiff competition.

In the morning, we wasted no time, straight out to the Gruta do Lago Azul (Blue lake cave, although it somehow sounds cooler in Portuguese than in English).

This was the compulsory cave visiting part of the holiday. So, often when you go on holiday, someone, somewhere recommends a cave or takes you to see a cave and, in all honesty, if I had the chance, in the UK, I'd probably take someone to see some caves too, although with the prohibitively expensive caves at Cheddar Gorge near where we live, I'd rather tell them that they are quite nice but say, "actually, you're better off seeing some photos on the internet and then going to a coffee shop near them and maybe buying some really expensive but beautifully wrapped cheese."

Caves are such an easy tourist thing to do. They are almost always amazingly beautiful even though there is the whiff of – if you've seen one, you've pretty much seen 99% of them. Still, let's be honest, there is always something about stalagmites and stalactites that makes me put my hands on my hips and nod my head in approval and mutter smugly, "ok, creationists, how did they come about then… explain that," – to which I get the smug response, "God did it."

Ok, that shut me up. How can you argue against the infallible logic where everything and anything you don't know can be explained away with those 3 little words?

So, we listened to the blurb by the guide at the entrance – which I understood little of – Vesi understood a lot more than I did but, still, she didn't get an awful lot.

The Gruta do Lago Azul is one of the world's biggest *flooded* caves and gets its name from the exceptionally clear and blue water at the bottom. It is so clean and clear that nobody is allowed to touch it – NOBODY – which actually makes you want to touch it. It's an, "ooh, what does this button do?" moment.

The cave was discovered in 1924 by a local Indian – and by Indian, I mean native, not some bloke from Bombay who phones you up every day trying to sell you some crap or tell you that you are about to be taken to court for some massive fraud you had no idea you committed – and it has been protected since 1978. But this does make me question whether back in the day this local Indian changed the entire ecosystem of the cave by washing his feet in the water.

I think the guide told us that there were some albino fish or crustaceans in the water but we didn't actually get close enough to see any.

Overall, the cave is lovely. The lake is a good 50 metres below the entrance. The water, between September and February, takes on a beautiful blue colour which, of course, begs for the compulsory 500 crap photos – like at the statue of Christ the Redeemer, "oh no, I shouldn't use the flash, it reflects off the water and your faces are too white," – "ok, don't move a muscle for 14 seconds or it'll be blurry" – "whose fucking hand is that looking like they've punched you through the head?"

Lunch was at the Nascente Azul which is an ecotourism complex, or at least, that's how it is advertised. What is it in my terms? Well, it's a place with lots of water and open spaces, a bit like the Balneario Municipal except with fewer people. This place looks like it's more geared up for tourists, although we were the only people there.

We were there to do some floating. No it's not some new funky drug. We were there to float down a gentle river with wetsuits and snorkels and watch fish swimming around.

We walked up a hill to where we were to be picked up by someone in a jeep – please note, it was now about 2pm and it was 35 degrees so we were all hot, sweaty and sticky by the time we reached the top.

This was followed by the less than desirable instruction to 'put on a wetsuit, a lifejacket and some crocs (those plastic shoes with massive holes in them), then pick a snorkel and a mask and wait outside.'

When people talk to me about wetsuits, it's because they like to go surfing in January somewhere near the arctic circle where temperatures are just a couple of degrees above absolute zero (-273.15 degrees centigrade), but there we were, the four of us, standing outside in the sun, waiting for a lift in 35-degree heat dressed in tight insulated rubber. I can't deny that it felt somewhat strange and insane at the same time.

Finally, some guy arrived and the four of us squashed into the back of his jeep, the inside of which was about 45 degrees even with the windows open. By this point, I had come to terms with the fact that I was going to die so I told Vesi that, if she survived, she could take full ownership of the car, my collection of Red Dwarf DVDs that she'd bought me a couple of years earlier for Christmas, and I apologised to her for any times when I had been a shit. I was surprisingly calm about it actually.

In return, she graciously accepted and told me to shut up.

When the jeep came to a stop, we all rushed out and went straight for the water. Instructions were – don't touch the bottom as it would disturb the silt and the water would get murky for a long time, so avoid it.

I welcomed the freezing water – well, freezing to me. It was no colder than the river water at the farm 2 days ago.

I tried to swim but with the lifejacket, wetsuit and the crocs, I had so much buoyancy that I could have almost done a Jesus and walked on the surface. I have never felt so out of control whilst swimming in my life. Most of the river was no more than a metre deep but in the few deeper parts where I could position myself vertically, I could feel the buoyancy from the wetsuit and the crocs pushing me up to try to make me lie flat on the surface.

So with minimal hand flippering we floated face down along the top looking at the fish in the crystal-clear water. Swimming under water was almost impossible except for at the very deepest part of the river where there is a taut rope from the surface right down to the bottom and were able to pull ourselves down to look around from a couple of metres below.

Many of the fish were nothing more than piraputangas but there were lots of other fish too. It was like being in one of those documentaries with David Attenborough. It was a totally different world. In this setting of super clear water, fish look like they are actually flying or at least swimming in the air. It's quite amazing.

I even felt partially guilty when I needed to pee. I didn't want to do it in the water, but then I thought, hey, fish don't get out, unzip their flies and pee in a bush, so I relaxed about the whole thing and let rip.

THE ONLY PROBLEM WAS....

The water was actually so cold that my foreskin had puckered to the extent that it had sealed shut over the tip of my willy. However, that was the first time it had ever happened to me and I didn't instantly recognise what had happened, so I panicked as a little balloon of wee inflated at the end of my willy – so, I stopped peeing. Instantly, I got scared and wondered whether I'd ever be ok again. Will my wee go back inside my body and give me an infection? Will my willy burst? Will I ever get the chance to play the banjo? (Why the banjo popped into my head I'll never know. I think I'll need some regressive hypnotherapy to get to the root cause of that one).

All this happened in the space of about 4 seconds, a lot less time than it took you to read. In the end, when I realised what it actually was, I calmed down and gave the balloon a little squeeze and felt a satisfying pop – well, not exactly a pop but that's the best description I can give it. Sorry, but I've got a fairly limited vocabulary and some of my favourites are swearwords – why be articulate when you can *eff* through most things?

The floating experience on the whole was wonderful. The current was so gentle that we could easily swim against it if we wanted. I would have liked the floating experience to have been longer. The only things I wasn't overly content with were the mask and snorkel I had on. Snorkels are a pain at the best of times if you're not used to them. If you lean your head back too much, the open end dips in the water and you suddenly breathe in a mouthful, causing you to cough and splutter. Then there is the mask. Sure, it keeps the water out most of the time but once it is on, it's like a suction pad has been stuck onto your face. When you do finally take it off, you're left with a bright red ring around your eyes that makes it look like you've been whacked in the face with an Oompa Loompa's toilet seat.

Also, the mask isn't perfect. It does let water in occasionally so you have to keep pushing it against your face to create more suction to seal any gaps. However, that can lead to the suction increasing to such an extent that it makes the veins around the eyes start throbbing and feel like your eyes are going to explode outwards.

Apart from that, it was a wonderful experience and I can see why they get people to wear the wetsuits. The water is a bit too cold to not be moving, but I don't understand why they have us put it on in hot weather before driving us to the starting point in an even hotter vehicle.

The drive back to the camper we were staying in was beautiful. We drove past a bunch of wide open spaces where the earth looked much redder than ordinary soil – like on postcards airbrushed to make the scenery look better. And this in conjunction with orange beaked toucans flying around, I couldn't help thinking this was a tiny slice of heaven. For a fleeting moment, I forgot about the world's problems; climate change, resource mining, oil drilling, the annihilation of entire ecosystems and the other things that politicians and corporate vampires champion in order to make a few quick pennies. For that briefest of brief moments, all that disappeared and it felt like the rest of the world couldn't be anything other than equally perfect.

Back at the house, we sat in a circle and had some Mate tea before going out for dinner. It was a lovely little send-off, although, whilst we were drinking the tea, Alessio and Priscila buggered off to get changed for dinner, leaving Vesi and me to talk to Alcides and Fatima. These are the moments in life that make you realise that no matter how awkward farting in a lift may feel, it's more short-lived than the, awkward, non-conversation borne out of pure politeness.

The silences, the forced 3 words that we can say and understand, the fake laughs and fake understanding at what's being said, the hope that you're not being asked a question and you can get away with staring blankly and nodding. These are the small tests of life. In all honesty, it's exactly what I have to do when I go to Bulgaria with Vesi. I spend however many days not having a clue what's going on, smiling sweetly and coming up with ideas in my head for future personal projects. It's over there I managed to perfect the art of pretending I have the slightest clue what someone is saying when, in actual fact, I haven't the faintest idea and I'm just studying body language to understand what reaction they expect of me. Too many times have I done this where they expect me to answer a question and I just give a nod or appreciative laugh to the bemused look of the other person – whereupon I try to wriggle out of it by saying, "oh, I didn't understand the last part of what you said, can you repeat it please?"

We were saved after about 15 minutes of clueless chat which contained lots of nodding, pointing and smiling by Priscila (who thought we were having a deep conversation) and we all went out for dinner. By a happy coincidence, we saw the group of Brazilians we'd seen several times over the past couple of days there too.

Dinner was, in very Brazilian style, full of meat and there were 6 of us there. The little Chilean guy who claimed that every Brazilian dish should contain rice and beans may well have been right, but from our point of view, a real Brazilian meal should contain oodles of meat.

Fillet steaks; £15 for a plate for 2 (53 reals) and with drinks and all the other gubbins that go with eating out, the whole meal for all of us came to around 320 reals which was less than £100 for 6 of us. Pretty astonishing really. Vesi and I had set out to pay for it as a thank you to everyone for hosting us and taking us around Bonito which is a lovely place.

Bonito itself, for its size, has a lot to do and feels extremely safe. It's growing as a city – probably from tourism which is also bringing work, but in some ways, I think it's almost a shame that it is.

If Bonito grows too much then it would lose its *'Bonito'ness* and become just another tourist town that would collapse under its own weight if foreign tourists left overnight. It has lots of farmland, which is the very foundation of an economy. Personally, I think it would be a shame for Bonito to expand much more. It would go from being a quaint little town with a lot of lovely places close by to visit, to a town that is utterly rammed with tourists, and before you say that tourists wouldn't leave overnight, they can do for a number of reasons – prepare for a feeble example below.

I grew up in an English town called Basingstoke. Somehow, a lot of people have heard about it but they only really know it as a bit of a shit hole – which it may well be, but still, I called (and still do partially) it home and there are a number of little areas which are pure havens for me that I try to visit when I go there to see my parents. Going out on Friday and Saturday nights there, I remember how the town centre used to fill up so much that bars were charging entry fees and even that was to enter a place that had standing room only.

The town centre was given a facelift. They got rid of the old bus station and the permanent fixtures of old women who sat there – doing nothing, just sitting there. Were they alive? Nobody knew. This was replaced with a much more modern bus station, i.e. one without old ladies. They then slammed a roof on top and filled the rest of the town with the standard homogeneous chain shops you find in virtually every other town and city in the UK. They basically built a mall there.

One of the new parts has several bars and restaurants (all chain of course) and, in doing that, the rest of the town that used to be teeming with life has virtually become a ghost town. Pubs that used to have a one-in-one-out policy by about 10pm are now half empty at 11pm with lots of seating available. Effectively, the area I used to hang out in has now lost most of its custom.

The point I'm trying to make is that Bonito is not immune from a potentially similar fate. I'm not saying it will definitely happen but if it becomes too touristy, it could end up relying so much more heavily on tourists and become like that undercover market in Salvador which is purely for tourists and where you can buy exceptional amounts of exceptional crap for exceptional prices that would only be worthy as gifts for unexceptional acquaintances.

If you want a case in point, look at Manaus. Thriving booming city until the rubber tree idea was nicked after which it collapsed, never to regain its former glory. The lesson to learn is sustainability and resilience. Relying too much on rubber or tourism can only be sustained for as long as there is need/want for your product/services, and although it can be sustained for a long time, it's not a particularly resilient way of living. I mentioned this earlier when talking about Rio de Janeiro's beaches too. It's massively touristy, but it's still its own city so it has resilience too.

It's probably a fairly personal thing but I don't think that most places should try to expand/grow ad infinitum. This *will* be an extremely painful lesson our species will learn one day with an expanding population, limited and diminishing resources and a desperate need to 'grow' the economy. Unless you're insane or an economist, or both, (the two are not mutually exclusive) you should understand or know already that this cannot be done.

<u>What I learned in Bonito:</u>

1 There are some places in Brazil that feel less dangerous than Rio, Manaus and Salvador. Maybe an

obvious statement, but given the media coverage from the UK, – well, you know.

2 People here seemed much more relaxed than in most other places I've ever been to in the world.

3 Bonito feels like it could be fairly self-sustaining on the food front with all the farmland it has.

4 I think it's the kind of place which, although perhaps a little quiet, I'd be happy to raise children. Outdoor life, activities in the vicinity, e.g. Balneario Municipal.

Santos

Manaus
Salvador
Bonito
São Paulo
Rio De Janeiro
Foz Do Iguaçu
Santos

Day 19 - Santos

We had our last few hours of sleep in the luxury camper and woke up at 2am for our final fruity breakfast in Bonito before leaving at about 3am. Some might say that's in the early hours of the morning but I'd say it's *before* the early hours of the morning. We were driving back to Campo Grande airport for our early flight back to São Paulo.

We diligently followed Alcides for the first few miles and then peeled off into the night ourselves driving, not via the same potholed/serial killer route we came in by, but by following the road signs until we reached a particular roundabout. From then on, the road signs – in technical terms – turned to shit as they suddenly started pointing to places we didn't actually want to go.

A good deal more driving later and we were, for want of a better word, lost. We panicked again, as we did on the way *to* Bonito but for a different reason. It was 4am so there was nobody to ask and running out into the middle of the road to stop an oncoming car didn't feel like the safest thing to do when there were virtually no streetlights and cars were travelling at around 60mph – besides, they could have been serial killers themselves.

We started getting pretty worried we were going to miss our flight and we were running out of ideas. I made the genius suggestion of using the stars to navigate, but unfortunately, that was a bit of a non-starter since, 1 – the constellations in the southern hemisphere are different to the northern hemisphere and 2 – I don't actually know how to navigate using the stars in the first place.

Had there been just a tiny bit of sunlight, at least we would have known the rough direction we were facing. But without knowing where we were on some crappy map and after having driven around in circles several times, we didn't even know which way was north.

Then I remembered from watching a film how to find north using the stars. According to the Muppets Treasure Island, the star Polaris always points north. We were saved.

But no, we weren't. My exuberance made me temporarily overlook two tiny details. 1 – I don't know how to find Polaris and 2 – it probably not bloody visible in the southern hemisphere.

What a nearly heroic plonker I felt.

Up to this point – I should add – Vesi had been sleeping. She had no idea we were lost but woke up naturally to the sound of three blubbing poofers driving around in circles.

She took the map, identified a couple of bits on the roads, had us go back to the bastard roundabout where all this started, pointed us in a particular direction, and within 5 minutes, she had us back on the right road.

I swear, in the olden days, Vesi would have been accused of being a witch and using dark magic. How she does what she does is something that only she knows. Maybe part of it comes from her having driven in the city of Plovdiv in Bulgaria. I've driven there too and the roads seem to loop back on themselves. It's like something out of the Blair Witch Project. Whichever way you go, you always end up back where you started. It's worse than Ikea. You need some special ability to get out. Maybe that's where Vesi developed her mysterious sixth sense.

As the sun started to come up, I was then able to contribute feebly to the navigation efforts by identifying the general compass directions north, south, east and west (which would have been more useful 3 hours earlier), and as we closed in on the airport, we followed the aeroplanes in. Some might say I didn't contribute at all but I still felt smug about it, even though everyone else made fun of me for it.

We even managed to stop for a coffee and a pastry and made it for our 08:05 flight with time to spare. There was also time for Priscila to complain about the broken satnav charger – remember? The one we repeatedly smashed with the door. She even got a partial refund. You see, in some places… the system works ☺.

After the whole flight rigmarole where I threatened to slaughter the woman in front for reclining her seat and eat her husband's beating heart, we landed happily in São Paulo. Ok, so I didn't do any actual threatening. I just thought it and performed the actions several times on a pair of imaginary people afterwards while walking to customs to the horrified look of some security guards who tightened their grips on their machine guns. Catharsis may not be good for the soul but it sure as hell makes you feel better.

We picked up another hire car to drive to Santos where Priscila's mother has a house. It was a fairly large car but it only had a 1000cc engine so it didn't go very fast. As Vesi and I were paying for the petrol, it didn't stop me from hassling Priscila for being in the wrong gear half the time. "YOU HAVE FIFTH GEAR. WHEN THE TACHOMETER REACHES 8,000 REVS – BUT PREFERABLY BEFOOORE – CHANGE GEAR, LOVE".

São Paulo is pretty big. In fact, it's one of the biggest cities in the world and has more than 6 times the population of Wales at around 21 million people and has an organically developed road system, i.e. it makes absolutely no sense. There are roads that loop into themselves, some that lead straight into brick walls, pointless bridges that go over nothing, etc. It really looks like it was designed by a hippie called Pedro on his return from a 5-day open air festival.

I really should have cut Priscila some slack – particularly given that she'd only had about 3 hours sleep and we were crawling along at the end of the rush hour in a place where people would drive to their neighbours' houses. I've actually seen that happen in Florida – it's surreal. But no, Priscila was unfailingly kind. She didn't kill me even though she had every right to.

We made it out of São Paulo within 2 hours or so, which is not bad considering it's similar in size to London and is absolutely stuffed full of cars. It is actually incredible to drive through; the sheer volume of traffic, the endless grey high-rise buildings that all look the same. Mile after mile, they just kept appearing one behind the other behind the other behind the other. I was in absolute awe of how much concrete and glass had actually been used. It felt like all the concrete in the world had been used right here. It was a pure urban jungle. The buildings were nearly all identical. I couldn't help but wonder how people knew which concrete building they needed to enter for whatever reason. It was like looking out at the sea of tents at Glastonbury festival and wondering how people were able to find theirs in the mishmash of multi-coloured waterproof nylon.

Eventually, the buildings did stop and we managed to escape the city and arrived in Santos at around lunchtime. We grabbed some bits of food out along with a Vitamina and some ice creams at a place Priscila recommended.

Santos is a fairly typical city. It's not especially pretty but it's close to the sea. As far as I can see, it's Brazil's equivalent to Bournemouth – except bigger.

Santos is famous for having been Pele's football club and there is a memorial (i.e. a shrine) for him.

Weather-wise, it suffers on average about 2 metres of rain per year (yes you read that right, 2 metres) – which would be a pain if it all came down in one go but, fortunately, it doesn't and has a tropical climate even though it's located outside the tropics.

We arrived at Priscila's mother's house a little later on in the afternoon. She was away so there were no unnecessary pleasantries which was quite nice because we were all absolutely shattered. We were due to go out to meet Priscila's brother and then go to his house for his wife's birthday at about 9pm, so an afternoon snooze was essential if we were hoping to be fresh.

Alessio was about to step into the bedroom when Priscila saw an unrecognised mole on his neck and drew in to examine it. It turned out to be a tick – a small bloodsucking parasite that actually looks a lot like a mole. Priscila got really excited about this. Why the excitement? I don't know, but she was and she pointed it out for the rest of us to have a look. Good thing she's not a GP really, as a patient I'd feel pretty self-conscious if, after an examination, she called her mates in to show them some wicked looking haemorrhoids.

Removing it was a bit of a mean feat in itself. "It has to be burnt off". Six words that you never hope to hear regarding an ailment that you might have. She picked up a lighter, went up to Alessio's neck and like a proper professional, waved the flame close to the tick until it heated up and let go. Basically, it's meant to be cleaner than simply pulling it off while it's still clamping itself on. Three seconds of work, Alessio screamed like a girl, Priscila pulled it off and threw it in the toilet. What a bizarre experience. I was impressed we hadn't picked any up in the jungle – or had we? I got a bit panicky and started checking myself over as much as I could. Luckily nothing but it was still a freaky moment.

Midnight.

We woke up in a panic. We had missed the appointment with Priscila's brother and his wife. Priscila checked her phone and there were some missed calls. They had tried to call but nobody heard the phone ring.

Unable to get in contact with them, we promised to ourselves to make it up the next day, but before that, we had an appointment at the motel named Anonimato.

Day 20 - Santos

Anonimato

What is it?

Well, you remember the Panda motel I mentioned in Rio?

This was something very similar. In fact, it was the same thing. A place where people can rent out a room for sex in a clean location (i.e. not in a club toilet or on top of a bin behind Nando's), anonymously, hence the name Anonimato.

I said before how I would love to see inside one of these, well, we were about to find out courtesy of my brother and sister-in-law who treated us to this as an engagement gift.

There was no 'front door'. We drove down a series of small, seemingly random roads to appear in front of a darkened gate.

The receptionist was behind a big darkened window and there was a small gap through which to talk. So far, the only one who had remained anonymous was the receptionist woman behind the glass. Just the driving down these small secret roads is an announcement more than something clandestine and anonymous.

"Passports please," (in Portuguese, of course)

WTF?

They'll be asking for a fingerprint scan and a sperm sample next. This is sounding about as anonymous as something in the UK which is slowly but surely turning into a dystopian quasi stasi surveillance state – all in the name of fighting terrorism (which was enhanced by us), but that's another story.

So, we drove in and parked the car in an allotted garage, but this was after having given them our most intimate details which, by the time we stopped, was probably on the internet and in the hands of some random hackers, ready to be published to the world at the click of a button.

From the back of the garage itself, there was a door that led up some stairs and straight into the bedroom. Now, don't sit there thinking we had a menage a quatre. Vesi and I had a separate room to Alessio and Priscila. I can't imagine I'd have been particularly comfortable with them watching us consummate our engagement, or worse, join in. #Shudder.

Admittedly though, the door at the back of the garage had started to make this place feel a little more anonymous. In the UK, there would be CCTV everywhere, hidden of course, so this was quite refreshing.

The types of rooms available are basic rooms with a double bed, a TV and nothing else. Then there are double rooms with two double beds, a TV and a Jacuzzi and then there are the deluxe double rooms with two double beds, a TV, Jacuzzi and a steam room.

We had a double bedroom deluxe for the whole night. This is basically the most expensive room type in the hotel; 135 reals for the night with breakfast included. Basically, it was a little under £40. I have to say that again. Less than £40 for a large room and food in the morning.

£40 is about what we'd expect to pay for a 2-course meal for 2 people with no wine in a reasonably good UK eatery. It's about the cost of 3 people going to the cinema to see a film with only 1 person having popcorn. This was incredibly cheap. In the UK, you could hardly get a single room in a condemned building where you're likely to be robbed for that price. And here we were getting breakfast too… how cool was that?

Anyway, the walk up the stairs from the back of the garage felt a bit lonely and freaky. It reminded me of one of those horror films where people are caught in a house with a vampire or a madman with nowhere to escape. There were no windows, obviously. In the event of a power cut, our dehydrated corpses would have been found a week later halfway up them.

At the top of the stairs just as we were about to enter our room, in the dimly lit space not much bigger than a downstairs toilet, there were 2 doors, 1 of which was locked and the other was the entrance to our room. There was also a table, and in the wall was a shelf on a vertical roller, I guess for posting breakfast through in the morning. This part was definitely anonymous. We didn't have to see anyone anymore. It wasn't like in the morning we were going to go downstairs to a dining hall, give our room number and sit down with a bunch of other guests for breakfast. No, it was all hush-hush now with no outside human contact.

Shame really, I'd love to have seen the other guests at breakfast. "Hey, Pedro, how was your night? Wow, 3 women with you all called Pedro? And what babes they are but I'm starting to think that the one with the huge Adam's apple was more of a handful – if you know what I mean."

On entering the room, we were confronted with a pretty big Jacuzzi and next to it, a double bed. Walking over to the double bed, it had no sheets but the mattress was covered in plastic, clearly for some post Jacuzzi fun. My first thought was, 'I bloody hope they cleaned this place properly' and that was closely followed by, 'that's a big Jacuzzi, I wonder how much water is wasted by running one of those every day? And I wonder how long it takes to fill? We've got an – included in the price – breakfast here.'

There were only 2 windows in the room. One was in the bathroom and had the usual obscured glass and the other one in the main bedroom part was completely blacked out. With such an emphasis on privacy, I wondered why they could be opened.

Although the room was geared up for private sex, it reminded me of a scene in a film where people made snuff movies. I almost kept waiting for the surprise appearance of a nutter with a machete or, more likely, in a place like this, some insane gimp with a pair of electrified testicle clips.

Imagine conceiving children in somewhere like this, "mummy, daddy, where were you when I was made?"

"Oh, darling, you were conceived on the bed of an anonymous sex motel, like most accidental pregnancies here in Brazil. I think it was on the plastic bed after the Jacuzzi straight after the film Suzie slaps Fifi's flaps."

In all honesty, after a few days of running around, swimming, driving, flying, drinking tea, missing an evening with Priscila's now pissed off brother and the prospect of a free breakfast as long as we got up on time... I wasn't massively in the mood for – rocking the casbah. But there were some dirty channels on TV so it wasn't a hopeless case, even though it felt a bit forced. 'You are here and you will have sex under the watchful eyes of the erotic ornaments dotted around the room.'

Still, it's hard for women to appreciate how sex for a man can't be faked. We can't fake being turned on. If the man falls asleep during... it's over. The woman can't carry on as if nothing had happened, we can't fake our orgasms. For men, it's all real. Any of those things I've just mentioned can be faked by women without massive detriment to the love-making process. A bit of lube and she doesn't need to be turned on, orgasms can be faked with just some heavy breathing, falling asleep can be mistaken for her keeping her eyes closed from the sheer pleasure – unless she starts snoring. So, ladies, please appreciate that it's not the only thing we ever think about.

Next to the plastic covered bed was the bathroom which also led to the steam room. Pretty nifty. We turned it on with a, "we'll go in there in a moment".

Then there was a whole other little area with another double bed – this time with ordinary white sheets, some erotic glass sculptures, a long table with chairs that could easily support our weight and some mood lighting.

There were also 2 televisions which, when flicked on, went straight to the porno channels.

In short, this was not the place you would bring your children. Although Alessio and Priscila did a couple of years ago. It was just for a night in a hotel. Still to this day they've never been able to tell us how they explained to a 7 and 9-year-old what the 12-inch glass sculpture of a cock was.

We filled up the Jacuzzi, a large part of it being from my tears at the incredible waste of water. We were in a sex motel. Energy and water conservation were not their concerns. I had to bite my wobbling lip and simply go with it. You know the old saying – when in Rome...

We whipped our clothes off and dived into the water together.

INTERMISSION

CUE SCENES OF A FLOWER OPENING UP, A TRAIN GOING INTO A TUNNEL, NODDING DONKEYS, THE TIDE GOING IN AND OUT, A SPOUT OF CRUDE OIL TO THE SOUND OF A TRUMPET.

INTERMISSION ENDS

We awoke in the cloth bed which, I should add, had mirrors on the ceiling – a bit like the Hotel California. We had woken up in time for breakfast *yippee*. Late hotel sex AND breakfast. Life just does not get any better than this.

The phone was on Vesi's side so she picked it up and had been instructed what to say in Portuguese to order breakfast, which Vesi did flawlessly. However, her face turned to shock horror when she was asked a question, which she didn't understand, so she just asked for breakfast again a couple of times and apparently the guy on the other end simply chuckled and said, "ok".

Now, it's all fine and dandy pretending you know what you're talking about when you are the one saying something in a different language, but when you have to *respond* to something being said, it's different and it's not difficult to feel like you're standing out like a boil on the buttock of a buttocks model.

Simple example from my German GCSE oral exam – translated into English:

"What have you got for lunch today?"

"Ahhhh, yes, I go by car."

Enough said.

I got my long-awaited breakfast. It was good, satisfying, they used margarine instead of butter but that can be forgiven and while I was munching on my croissant, I did something that probably no other guest has ever done in the history of this motel. I opened a window and looked outside. Ooh, it felt so naughty. It had the same taboo value as sniffing a bike seat outside a women-only gym.

The view looked towards the centre of the motel and down into the car park where the cars drove to get to their assigned garage. The motel was like a square ring with rooms facing both the outside of the ring and inside towards the centre. Looking around, I could see a bunch of other blacked out windows – needless to say that I was the only person with the window open.

Then I did the next most taboo thing. I opened the front door to the room. This looked into a badly lit corridor with doors to other rooms, all closed. God this place was freaky. They give promiscuity and adultery a bad image.

A short phone call with Priscila later, we were outside and driving out of the tightest exits possible. I think the irony of a *tight exit* at a sex motel is probably lost on most of the patrons normally, but I had to chuckle.

Next stop was the wife of Priscila's pissed off brother. She's called Fabiana and Priscila's pissed off brother is called Rodrigo (I've asked why he's not called Pedro and we think it's because there is an element of native American to the family). We wanted to apologise to her for not making it to her birthday but saying something like, “we had to sleep because we were tired and we were planning on going to a sex motel” didn’t sound like something that would make her roll out the welcome mat. Maybe a flat tyre? Nah, we were shattered and fell asleep. We tried to contact them when we woke up but they didn’t pick up. Simple.

We were all pretty nervous because by not answering the phone, it indicated to us that she was probably pretty pissed off at us. From their point of view, we fly thousands of miles, they’re excited to see us and we don’t turn up because – maybe we think we’re too good, maybe we just don’t care or maybe we’re just a bit shit. So, yes, we were pretty nervous about meeting up with her.

However, we turned up to her workplace unannounced and as she came downstairs, she smiled which stopped all of us from dropping nervous farts. It turned out in the end that she was actually ok with it. Admittedly, that was after we’d brought her a bunch of flowers and a couple of posh looking presents. In that part of Santos, image is a big thing and she’s into image. It’s a bit like Korea’s Gangnam area – the zone for young, hip and trendy people who are too good to wear pants six days in a row, except without the silly oopa Gangnam style dance that makes you look like you’ve got chilli peppers in your arse.

We went to a restaurant to meet up with Pedro – no, sorry, Rodrigo – too. We wanted to catch him by surprise and buy him lunch to smooth over any animosity he might be feeling.

Lunch went smoothly too. It was quite touching actually. He'd only ever met me once before, 12 years earlier at Alessio and Priscila's wedding when I was in a wheelchair after a particularly brutal accident where I broke 3 of my limbs, so he'd only ever seen me sitting down. So, when he walked in, it was like he was in a daze and the first thing he said was, "Sergio", in a low and dazed voice. I found that quite touching. And I was impressed too. He'd never seen me standing up so he didn't know that I towered about 2 feet above him. We were similar heights when I was in the wheelchair, so technically, he could have probably guessed.

We were invited that evening to their house for an 'eat all the food you bastards didn't get through last night, you bastards' party.

How could we refuse?

Their house is lovely. It's in a high-rise building with a lovely view. It's clear they have high-paying jobs. Fabiana works in some kind of financial institution doing… I don't know what but it pays well and Rodrigo is a professional bullshitter. Basically, he works for an insurance company assuaging clients who might have problems. Probably something like this:

"Jiu 'ave no peyd me mai mony for some bastard crashing into my ecar why enot?"

"Well, Meester Pedro, iis no problem. Jiu see, de peepols in de payment department 'ave cleerly maid an error, ees someting dat can be sort out een jost 1 day"

"Jou say dat 6 monts ago"

"Ah well, dat ees beecoz we need to fill in de paperwork an it need to go tru de 64 level of cheks and complaianses..."

"Jess, well, 'ow long dos dat teyk den?"

"Ah, Mister Pedro, not moch for a client we love so mach as we love jiu. For soch a 'andsome man and peitient man no moch mor dan jos 'alf a yeer.

"Oh deeer got"

Anyone who bullshits clients is bound to be paid well.

Rodrigo himself is proud to be properly obsessive (OCD obsessive) about cleanliness. In fact, the house is utterly spotless and when I mean spotless, it is clean enough to let your child lick soup off the floor from behind the fridge. THAT'S how clean it is.

Rodrigo himself is spotless too. Pristine hair, clean, ironed and fresh clothes, it's miraculous. I mean, I wash regularly but I'll only have a full shower every few days.

He did get slightly panicked at one point when he thought Vesi had gone for a poo in their clean toilet. Ok, I think we can draw a line under that. OCD and proud.

Vesi is remarkable though, she is so lovely that everyone seems to take an instant shine to her. I did, so it doesn't stand out as a surprise that other people do too. Just by standing there, smiling sweetly and saying *"lindo"* to mean *"cool"* at things occasionally, Fabiana took a real shine to her. We were 2 days away from leaving Brazil and she gave us (well, Vesi mainly) a bottle of Cachaça (pronounced kashassa – the main alcoholic spirit in the cocktail caipirinha) made by some friends of theirs to take away with us.

We only stayed for a couple of hours because we had to go to a different gathering of people. It was more of a barbecue with a bunch of Priscila's old school friends. And they were very friendly. The whole atmosphere was a lot more relaxed.

The food was nice and the drinks were free-flowing. Not much to be said about that except for the fact that by the end of the evening, Vesi had disappeared only to be found sleeping on the couch and I got into a deep philosophical discussion with one of the guys about the differences between art and engineering, which somehow ended up with everyone listening with incredible interest to us talking about how beautiful is a chair leg that has been designed to support the weight of a person.

Needless to say, we don't remember much about how we got back to where we were staying. But somehow, we did. It's the miracle of the 'beer legs' if you have ever read it. These are legs that can get you back to your house without you remembering it. It's your body's inbuilt satnav. They know the way home even if you don't.

Late night tonight.

Sadly, tomorrow, Alessio and Priscila leave to go to the wedding we were also invited to and we'll be spending the rest of the holiday without them in Priscila's mum's flat.

We go home in 2 days. It's a time we knew would come but a time we have most definitely not been looking forward to.

Day 21 – Santos

Ring the bells of mourning, today was our last full day in Brazil.

Temperature was probably in the mid-twenties but the sky was very grey and it was raining. We did not want this.

We barely moved before 12pm because of the rain, and when we did, luckily, the continuing blanket of rain had stopped but short-lived showers had started. You know – the ones that wait for you to go outside before they begin. Then as soon as you step back into a building, they stop and wait for you to go out again.

We managed to get outside around lunchtime and ended up in a mall to take cover from the rain. In all honesty, malls aren't the most thrilling of places. I've said that before. People like me don't go on holiday to encounter things that we see every day at home. Although, this mall had something I never expected to see: lift attendants, and when I say attendants, I mean some bod who stands in the lift from the start of his shift and presses the buttons to go up and down a whopping 3 floors for people who get in. Probably not the most rewarding job in the world; scenery maybe not quite as inspirational as that of – say – a gynaecologist, but hey, neither is that of an office employee who stares at some computer screen all day.

But you know what? In the end, it's a job and someone does it. Necessary or not, it is done and it keeps someone out of the dole office equivalent.

It's not like the English haven't had their fair share of shitty jobs that seem pointless – when in fact, they are not. For a number of years, there were attendants in nightclub toilets all dressed up and looking clean who would chase you around trying to help you wash your hands, dry your hands and squirt you with aftershave. I used to think it was just another ploy from the nightclubs to squeeze more money out of you because it felt like you had to tip these bastards for any help they gave you.

I always wondered this though, what do people like this put on their CV? Is it along the lines of:

Job title – 'Nightclub toilet attendant'

Job description – 'chasing men around the toilet to try to help them wash their hands before dousing them in aftershave,'

Wages – '£1 per soap squirt and hand towel accepted from a drunk.'

As it turns out though, the toilets by the end of the night were actually a lot cleaner with these attendants standing in them. Without them, they were horrendous from drunks peeing on any surface and occasionally the urinal, toilet paper soaked and thrown around, and soap emptied from the containers into gloopy puddles on the floor. It was a mess. I know because, at some point in my past, I was one of those drunks. With the attendants in there, the damage was massively reduced and confined to the toilet cubicles, therefore, it made sense to have them.

What does this have to do with the lift attendants? Good question. Well, one possibility is maybe people leave a mess in the lift and the attendants' presence stops that from happening – yeah, yeah, it's far-fetched, I know. I remember when I was a child, I peed in a lift – on purpose (yes ok, I was a punk kid), so I totally understand the need for someone in the lift to prevent another version of a young and stupid me from doing something equally stupid.

Also – however dull the job is, it's good for the Brazilian economy. Better someone standing in a lift pressing buttons than out on the street stealing from people.

Truth is, I don't know. Maybe they wanted to make the place look more poncy than it is, maybe many Brazilians are too short to reach the buttons or maybe he's not actually employed but is just someone who *really* can't decide which floor to get off at. Whatever the reason, he was there going up and down in the lift.

It was a sad occasion, but with pizza and wine, we had our last supper as a group. It was quite moving even though none of us was destined to be crucified. It was just the end of the holiday as a group.

Alessio and Priscila left for their friend's wedding at around 5pm and Vesi and I were left with a set of keys.

Without Alessio and Priscila, Vesi and I just ended up walking around the neighbourhood under the grey sky and the occasional bouts of spitting rain. We were a fairly short walk from the beach actually but, somehow, it would seem a tiny bit too British to go to the beach at half 5 in the afternoon on a rainy day to sit down or paddle in the water. The only thing that could have made it any more British would have been to go wearing socks and sandals.

We stayed outside, walking around more out of determination to make the most of being outside whilst on holiday before admitting defeat and going back to the flat. But also, there is a strange feeling attached to being in someone else's flat when they are not there. Especially when the evening starts drawing in and the light starts to fade. We weren't overly comfortable with it admittedly.

Later, we found one of those self-service *joints* – I wouldn't call them actual restaurants – and stopped to get some food. Can't say the food was overly fantastic in this *joint* but it was edible. We ended up playing it quite safe and eating some vegetables with some bits of very cooked stew. It didn't feel like Salvador where, as it turns out, it's as easy to get food poisoning as it is in Mumbai, but given we were meant to be travelling home the next day, we wanted to make sure that we were not going to have to make a toilet stop every 2 minutes.

After some food, we walked back up to the flat to relax and watch some DVDs.

I'd say it was a pretty ideal ending to the holiday really. We've been rushing around like blue-arsed flies for the past 3 weeks, barely stopping. We've seen some of the most wonderful things and had some of the most amazing experiences from hang gliding over a beach in Rio de Janeiro to swimming in piranha-infested waters in the Amazon.

I can't deny, Santos would have a lot to live up to if it wanted to measure up to most of the places we visited in the past 21 days, so stopping here – somewhere I would consider to be *normal*, yet still on holiday – before flying home was a great way of gently bringing us down from cloud 9 prior to returning home and getting back to normality.

Usually, when coming home from a holiday, it is a slam dunk back to normality. It's often a pretty big shock to the system which is why people get the post-holiday blues.

I remember when I was about 27, I went to Ibiza with a couple of friends. It wasn't a proper clubbing holiday – I'd done that in Ibiza several years earlier. This was more a holiday to hang out with a couple of friends, chat, drink a few beers, ogle at women we couldn't have because we were crap at pulling (maybe the stupid nodding pigeon walk would have worked in hindsight), sit at Coastline Café or Café del Mar to watch the sunset, cocktail in hand and applaud as the sun disappeared behind the horizon.

ANYWAY, I digress. I was talking about returning from holiday with a bump. I remember the evening before returning to the UK, we were sat at Coastline Café, a chill-out bar, sipping cocktails watching the world glide by. We saw beautiful people with tanned bodies sashaying by with nonchalant demeanours and an easy smiles in the warm orange hue from the sunset. Things were, to say the least, perfect.

We boarded the plane at around 02:30am to land in the UK for about 5am and went by train to Clapham Junction. Now, if you've not seen it, Clapham Junction is a major train junction near London. We sat there waiting for a train to take us back to Basingstoke which is where I was living.

Never have I felt more depressed than I did at that moment.

We had left our comfy chairs and an ambient temperature of 28 degrees under a cloudless sky and were now sitting on a narrow bench on a windy platform at a temperature of 15-degrees with a blanket of grey cloud above us.

I took out several long-sleeved tops and threw them on.

Instead of tanned people walking past with easy smiles, some fat bloke was sleeping on another bench after a night out next to a pile of his own vomit. An obese couple walked past in long trousers and flip flops with miserable looks on their faces.

Instead of the orange hue from the sunset reflecting off the water in a million sparkles and giving the sand that eternally warm look, we were sat on a train platform in front of some brown and grey buildings and some filthy sludge-ridden railway lines.

And instead of chillout music filling the air with the intermittent sound of waves lapping on a nearby beach, we were privy to the sound of low flying jets as they took off from Gatwick airport and the occasional announcement telling us that a train had been delayed.

It was a difficult moment, I cannot lie.

The return from Brazil could very easily be similar without the comedown day in Santos.

We made sure our bags were packed for the return trip home and in a hugging position, went to bed early as we were getting up at 5am for a taxi ride.

Lying there with the snoozing Vesi in my arms (she could fall asleep on a rollercoaster if she wanted to), I could not help but feel an extreme sense of gratitude towards her. This holiday had been her idea. She had planned it all from day one. She knew exactly where to go and who to contact at various stages. She knew where to eat and what to visit. She had planned it all out meticulously. I had done none of it. Admittedly, I am not very good at it, whereas Vesi is both very good at it and she enjoys it – and she had done a great job, so for that, I will always be grateful.

Goodnight, Brazil. Until the next time.

Day 22 – Santos to the UK

5am. Temperature outside: 20 degrees

Weather: cloudy with intermittent rain.

We took a taxi to get to the coach station and then a coach to get to Guarulhos, the airport in São Paulo. The coach we took had some woman on there like a stewardess – ahem, flight attendant to new-age pedants. She just sat there, occasionally walking up and down (not the easiest thing to do on a moving coach) giving people drinks of water. She was very friendly which was nice. She even told us which check-in desk to go to when we reached the airport. It was actually quite a nice touch – and adding to Brazil's economy.

There were toilets on this coach too and they were a bit like aeroplane toilets, except, you know how hard it is to pee in an aeroplane toilet? (Women might not, unless they stand up.) Well, take that and multiply it by 10 for the coach and then you might understand why various areas of the toilet were wet.

Aeroplanes jiggle a bit and quite a bit more when they encounter turbulence. Coaches are like aeroplanes with spasmodic mood swings. They go in and out of lanes, turn left and right, brake and accelerate, etc. Frankly, turbulence is an absolute picnic compared to this. Aiming accurately would be like trying to pee on a 2p coin whilst standing on a rollercoaster – I say 'would be' because on opening the door, I realised it wasn't the kind of place I was comfortable whipping my willy out and trying to balance. Besides, the toilets are not built for comfort. You wouldn't want to sit down and take out the extended version of War and Peace. In all honesty, it would be difficult for anyone even slightly overweight to stand in it without leaning on one of the mysteriously moist walls.

The journey was a good couple of hours long; up a mountain, through some low-level clouds, around and about and then through some rather grim looking favelas and really run-down houses, many with satellite dishes and beaten up cars outside. It looked a bit like some areas of Liverpool.

During one part of the journey, to our left we were looking at high-rise office buildings and saw a helicopter coming in to land on top of one. Something we read – São Paulo has more helicopter landing pads on the tops of buildings than anywhere else in Brazil. But considering it's a gigantic city and a large portion of Brazil is covered by Jungle, then realistically, it's not that much of an amazing feat. It's a bit like saying London has the most office blocks in Britain. Bit obvious really.

The point of this was the contrast. On one side, there were plush yet homogeneous office blocks, and on the other, there were grim looking favelas. It was a sight to behold. The absolute divide between rich and poor – it's shameful really. Brazil is a place of huge and obvious differences. There are few places where the differences between the haves and have-nots are so vast. India is similar from images I've seen, but I've never been so I can't really comment with any certainty. But it is sad to see areas of plenty right next to areas of abject poverty and it's really sad when you can see a dividing line between the two, i.e. in this case, the dividing line was a large road. I would love to know whether the homes are cheaper where the verandas face the favelas. I can imagine it to be pretty disheartening watching some of the poorest people around you scrubbing and washing their clothes in a bucket of water while you're sitting with a few friends on a balcony sipping champagne and eating hors d'oeuvres and canapés and other foods with flashy sounding names that are not always much more than cheese and pineapple on a toothpick.

We didn't really see enough of Santos as a city to make any kind of real judgement about it – to be honest, we didn't see enough of anywhere to be truly critical, but we visited Santos as tagalongs more than tourists so we didn't actually get any kind of flavour of the place. However, what I would say I learnt from Santos is that it is just like any random town or city in Europe. There is a mall which has echoes of standard town/city builds. It's nice, it has lots going on it seems, and it has a beach, but apart from that, I would say it's hardly touristy or a *must-see* place. I'd say it's more like being in the UK and planning to go and see Reading.

We reached the airport around 5 hours before our flight was due to leave. The duty-free shop accepted dollars and if we wanted to use reals, they gave us a really shitty exchange rate, so screw you bottles of water, we'll wait.

However, as most men will understand, you can't argue with a woman sometimes, so we walked out with 2 bottles of water and some bits of food. I felt pretty cheated, but then again, I always feel cheated at airports.

There is always a moment of sadness before boarding an aeroplane to return home after having spent the last few weeks in a state of constant wonder and awe. The memories of the last 3 weeks flashed through my mind, I guess, the same way humans see their lives flashing before them moments before they die. I've often thought about trying to find a way to replicate that sensation but without the actual dying bit at the end so that as my life flashed before my eyes, I might suddenly remember where I put that car key I lost. So far though, a horrible coughing fit is as close as I can get.

We boarded our flight – another A330 as we did on the way here. We were lumbered with 2 seats in the middle section. The 4-foot-tall slag in front managed to wait all of 10 seconds after she sat down before *doing the dirty*. The flight crew on Air Europa didn't really care much about the usual safety protocols so they didn't get her to straighten her seat for take-off. I kneed her in the back several times and I'm pleased to say she wasn't very happy with me doing that, so when she told me that she could feel my knees, I looked at her and replied, "I know" and carried on reading.

I know I shouldn't complain about this, it's the fault of the manufacturers – Airbus in this case – so it's their wrongdoing, not the short, fat, ugly, dozy, thoughtless, probably badly dressed arses sitting in front, and I should be annoyed at

Airbus rather than wishing for her to be crucified upside down with her head dipped up to her eyeballs in pig vomit.

The flight on the way back to Madrid was shit. It was dark, I was cramped, my TV wasn't working, which I could have accepted if it wasn't for the fact that my light wasn't working either. So there wasn't even the slightest form of entertainment besides dreaming up ways of torturing the dumpy cow in front of me.

Maybe I've had this all wrong.

Maybe this is actually a deliberate plot to make us look forward to getting off the plane after having had an outstanding holiday and helping us to avoid the post-holiday blues. By the time we've managed to recover from sitting in seats that are less comfortable than spending 11 hours in an iron maiden and boredom exceeding that of an accounting seminar discussing whether it's better to use the word *shall* or *will* in accounting standard FU52148-56LK1, we'll have been at home 2 weeks already and so back into our usual routine. Seamless.

We landed in Madrid, but unlike the normal transfers where you walk through from one aeroplane to the next, we had to queue up and go through security all over again. We'd not even had to show our passports and, suddenly, we had to go through the whole rigmarole of giving up our water again. So, instead of the usual 15 minutes, it took a healthy 2 hours.

They say that travelling is quite stressful and I can see what *they* mean, whoever *'they'* are. Usually, *they* are some newspaper dubbed *'experts'*, but experts in what? God only knows – probably something like photocopying, YouTube commenting or economics. However, *they* nailed this one. This travelling experience was so stressful it felt like the next stop was going to be Auschwitz.

We made it to the aeroplane in the end – obviously.

I sat in my seat on the dark runway thinking about all the times Vesi and I have sat in aeroplane seats in the past 3 weeks – crying about the carbon footprint but waiting to go somewhere new, somewhere exciting, somewhere we could talk about for years to come. This time though, we were going somewhere familiar. We were going home.

As the aeroplane lifted off into the darkness, headed towards Gawitck airport and as the city lights faded into nothingness, I took hold of Vesi's hand, squeezed it gently, looked her in the eyes and said, "thank you".

Epilogue

Day 23 – UK

Arrival in the UK was at around midnight. Our body clocks mistook it for around 3am. We were at Gatwick airport and were fully committed to picking up the car and driving the 132 miles back home to Bristol.

I was surprisingly chirpy for someone who had woken up at 5am and travelled for around 18 hours, of which I had managed to get around 2 hours sleep, so I guess it was fair to say I should have been tired. Vesi had managed several hours of sleep on the plane somehow. I don't understand people who sleep on planes. Ok, I'm jealous of them.

In the past, I've driven back from Alessio and Priscila's house at around 11pm to get back in time for work the next day. Alessio and Priscila live close to Gatwick. I had attended a seminar which turned out to be some bollocks sales pitch. Still, it was good fun, full of music and dancing and I ended the evening feeling really pumped. Having said that though, it was 11pm and I still had to drive around 130 miles to get back and I'd woken up that morning at around 6am. I had a full cafetiere of espresso which is about 4-5 cups worth and a can of coke before leaving. I managed about 100 miles before I recognised the feeling of being tired while driving, so I put on my CD of the band *Cradle of Filth* which is horrific thrash metal 'music' that I originally bought because the CD box was in the shape of a coffin and I thought it looked cool – bye bye £16. The music itself hurts my head and gives me a sickly feeling in my throat, so for this purpose it was ideal.

It helped but you can't battle the forces of nature forever and I became more and more tired. After a while and not too far away from home, along with that pelting out at full blast from my stereo on the empty motorway (it was now almost 1am on a Monday), I was weaving across the lanes (on purpose) with my head out of the window screaming at the top of my voice. I looked like one of those dodgy mutant rebel guys on motorbikes from the Mad Max film (the original). Had anyone seen me, they would have thought I'd been sniffing cocaine. And if the police had seen me, after calling the armed response unit, I'd have had my licence revoked and spent the night in a padded cell.

And that's what it's like driving back from Alessio and Priscila's house late in the evening.

But back to our journey.

We managed to leave the car park at around 1am with me driving the first stint as I was wide awake but I knew I would get tired before Vesi since she had slept and I hadn't. We'd said we would stop several times, especially on the M4 where there are no lights.

We did quite well. I managed to drive around the M25 which was mostly lit up. I scoffed at the traffic as we flew past Heathrow which normally turns the M25 into a car park and turned onto the M4, after which, the lights went out and we were plunged into darkness.

That's when I started to get tired but I would love to know why we can never admit to ourselves that we're tired when driving. If I'm tired, I can normally admit it. I'll even say, "ooh, I'm a bit tired".

BUT

When driving, it's like the child whose eyes are closing and when they are ushered off to bed, they complain, "I'm not tired" – "please" – "5 more minutes… 3 more minutes… 1 more minute… please… just 1 more minute."

Whilst driving, our brains (probably not everyone… but I bet a lot of people do this) refuse to admit we're tired. On the first slow blink, you seem to say to yourself… 'ooh… that was dodgy… I don't want to get tired'. TOO LATE, MATE, you're already tired. So, a good deal of shuffling – besides making you look like you have a chicken pecking at your crotch – usually gives you a few more minutes of driving alertness.

After a few shuffles, you give up because, frankly, you get to the point where you have to jiggle constantly and stopping would make you tired instantly. And besides making you look, to the casual observer, like you are driving while being electrocuted, the person next to you will ask, "are you tired?", "who, me? Noooo, I am just trying to get comfortable", "you've been trying to get comfortable for 10 minutes".

In the end, unless you take the thrash metal at full blast whilst screaming with your head out of the window approach, you have 3 options:

1 Stop for a coffee and/or a rest.
2 Use the rumble strips on either side of the motorway to keep you driving within the 3 lanes as you weave from one side to the other – although you need a fairly empty motorway for this.
3 Crash and miss out on the rest of your life

Fortunately, I had a Vesi. That's option 4. She talked to me a lot to keep me awake. And it worked really well until I was actually so tired that I said, "hang on, can I just concentrate on this part of the road?" On a fairly empty motorway, the only things you have to concentrate on are keeping to the lane and staying awake.

"Pull over."

We had to stop by about 02:30 when I had my face over of the steering wheel, staring so hard at the road that I could barely see it and I was weaving involuntarily. It wasn't until Vesi told me to pull into the services that I realised how tired I was. I couldn't even read the sign for the car park. My brain was working so hard to distinguish between the arrow to the left that pointed to the car park and the arrow to the right that pointed to the parking for articulated lorries. I had virtually stopped the car to work out the sign when Vesi pointed me in a certain direction and said, "go that way".

A coffee and a walk later, I said, "I'm ok. I'm good, I'll drive the rest".

Clearly, Vesi didn't let me.

When other people are driving, I try to remain awake to try to talk to them to keep them awake and warn them if they are falling asleep – which I did admirably for a while until I said to Vesi... "hang on, I just need to concentrate on this bit" – even though I wasn't driving.

My eyes were open and I was looking at the road and I must have been hallucinating or something because I thought we were driving over a mountain while it was snowing, which it wasn't. It is September.

I lifted my head off the dashboard just before 4am as we were reversing into our drive. I looked at my eyes in the little mirror on the sun blind to see my deeply red eyes and a red pattern on my forehead carved out by the dashboard that made me look like a Maori warrior.

Vesi looked at me with deeply tired eyes and laughed at the print on my head and the trace of drool down the side of my mouth.

"We can unload tomorrow. Let's go to bed. Tomorrow, I start planning for our trip to Thailand."

About the author (that's me)

www.sergioromagnoli.co.uk

Sergio Romagnoli was born in Italy when he was very very young.

He moved to England when he was 2 years old around the same time as his parents took him there and he spent a few years trying to grow up.

Sergio always loved to write. As a child he had an exercise book where he would write his little made up stories. Whilst at school though, his teachers never really liked his creative stories because regardless of the subject matter, the story always ended up being about monsters or horrible gruesome bloody murders... except this one time when it was about a computer that accidentally kills everyone in the world.

This disturbed imagination and obvious disappointment from his teachers led him to believe he should pursue something technical as a career and so studied to be an engineer before applying to be a pilot. A car crash when he was 25 damaged one of his eyes and stopped his flying ambitions on the spot. He wasn't enjoying his job as an engineer so feeling lost he decided to qualify as an accountant which he has been bluffing ever since.

As he has discovered though, pretending to be something is only possible until life forces you (whether you like it or not) to finally admit to yourself that maybe you should be more true to yourself. So after lots of soul searching, a lot of reaching deep within and some badly done meditation, he woke up to the fact that he was actually creative, artistic (not in a drawing sense) and imaginative and that he should be spending more time with this side of himself.

Sergio's first published book was a horror novella for teenagers called "Night in a haunted house". He originally wrote it as a personal project mainly to see if he was able to finish something he started. He broke all the rules of writing a book. He started with nothing more than an idea and began tapping away at his keyboard allowing the story to unfold in front of him.

Whilst planning to write a sequel (because book series are all the rage these days it seems) he went on holiday to Brazil with his then girlfriend Vesela and kept a diary of the whole thing.

Having keen interests in comedy and people watching, Sergio kept meticulous notes noting what people were like, the amazing things they did and the ridiculousness of certain situations – especially when compared with those at home.

Upon his return he started tapping away on his laptop eventually producing a full length travel memoir written in his very own unique style. He keeps it interesting for the reader by drawing comparisons to home, giving some interesting historical facts, mixing in some cultural references and throwing in the odd political blade.

Sergio has also been writing poems based around nursery rhymes in a style similar to Roald Dahl's Revolting Rhymes which he intends to complete and publish when satisfactorily completed.

Sergio is also part of an amateur dramatics group which allows him to be himself (with his clothes on). He has written parts of several short plays for them. It is his ambition to have a full length play performed as one of their main productions.

Sergio is now married to 'the girlfriend' – called Vesi – and has a little boy who takes up a lot of his time – as those of you with children can attest to.

He had intended on writing a humorous book about the trials and tribulations of having a baby but that has already been done – thank you Matt Coyne for stealing my thunder.

One of his goals is to write a funny horror book or perhaps a funny book about monsters… another goal is to retire before he's 50 but given his salary, he's probably going to have to work for about 30 years after he's dead just to pay his £8 per month mobile phone bill.

Original cover idea

On the next page is my original idea for a front cover.

The idea was to have a set of books called the 'Travel Ponder' series– idea taken from the book 'eat pray love'. Vesi suggested this and I was up for it until my notes from Thailand disappeared. Then I got a bit demoralised about it. (It really would have been very good)

I thought that the original idea – properly done – would have made a nifty cover. But *'people'* say, you shouldn't design your own cover.

I had even added a couple of really shitty made up endorsements the same way you see really shitty ones on books from mainstream newspapers like *"very very entertaining" – Bod McNobody –The Guardian* who are prepared to wax lyrical about it – just as soon as the cheque paid to them clears.

I swear, if they work to sell more books, I'll be utterly amazed. I think it's insulting to readers' intelligence to think that because some random arse from a corporate newspaper has said something positive about a book they pick up it will make them want to buy it more. "Oh look, Roger Tonkbury from The Daily Bollards has said it's *'a nice little book'*. It **must** be true."

The book cover designer (Rachel Lawston) didn't think it was a good idea. I wonder though. I'm quite an in your face type of person who doesn't like fake bullshit – maybe why I hate politicians so much – and I love to try to pick out funny moments or make moments funny... (does not go down well in hospitals) hmmm......... maybe she was right after all.

TRAVEL
PONDER
SAMBA
SERGIO ROMAGNOLI
"[SPEECHLESS]"
a TELEGRAPH (pole)
"So very very funny"
a GUARDIAN (my mum)

Printed in Poland
by Amazon Fulfillment
Poland Sp. z o.o., Wrocław

53264630R00195